Suki, Me, and World War Three

1960 And Afterwards – An Odyssey

By

Tony 'Dobz' Dobbie

Suki, Me, and World War Three
Copyright © 2021 Tony Dobbie

ISBN 9798427273077

All Scripture quotations, unless otherwise indicated, are taken from the King James Version of the Holy Bible.

Some names and identifying details have been changed to protect the privacy of individuals.

Preface

The dictionary defines 'Odyssey' as 'an epic poem attributed to Homer, describing the 10 years of the wanderings of Ulysses after the fall of Troy; more generally, an odyssey is a series of adventures and vicissitudes.' In case your English, like mine, is a bit hazy as to the meaning of vicissitude, we also find in the dictionary that 'A vicissitude' is defined as 'a change of condition or circumstances'.

Shakespeare intimated that the stars above control our fate; and yet and yet and yet, this would imply that we do not have any control over our own destiny. On the other hand, if the only arbiters of our lives and fate are the Circumstances we encounter and the Choices we make, we are totally subject to pure Chance, and the outcome of our mortal span can be determined on mere whims. Thus, in reality, our earthly progress seems to be pitched somewhere between divine foreknowledge and our own preferences. Consequently, just as Hamlet reflected on the 'slings and arrows of outrageous fortune' so we may be given to musing, "If only I hadn't been there, or said that, or done that, or if I had been there in time, stopped the... gone into the...explained my...?" as we consider what possibilities alternative decisions might have resulted in and what the outcome would have been for us.

What follows is an expansion of the above thesis, divided like a play into a number of Acts. The first Act/Prelude, in a series of vignettes, charts my transition from an ignorant and innocent youth to a willing adult participant. The following Acts involve shorter periods of time, but have much more the flavour of an odyssey, and therefore the scenes describe many incidents on the voyage seen from a more sceptical point of view. This part of the Odyssey ends with a great change of circumstances, literally through the modern equivalent of a shipwreck – two aircraft crashes, which although caused by means entirely outside my control, were instrumental in causing me to make a choice as to how my voyage would continue thereafter. The last Act, just like Ulysses, ends with a homecoming, and attempts to explain my life from a new philosophical perspective.

However, Ulysses got off lightly with 10 years, my odyssey lasted a lot longer. Moreover, an odyssey usually has a background moral message associated with it, therefore I have tried to speak as plainly as possible about myself, so that I may convey to those who read it the warning of one who wandered for a long time like Ulysses before coming into a safe haven. As such I have tried as far as possible to convey my feelings and emotions of that time, albeit with some benefit of many years of twenty-twenty hindsight.

With some 45 years involvement with the Royal Air Force, this book contains a fair number of Service abbreviations and slang. For civilian readers I have attempted to explain in the text what each of these abbreviations/slang words mean on its first occurrence; and additionally, there are a few expanded explanations of a technical nature for readers unfamiliar with the mysteries of flying.

This book is sub-entitled '1960 and Afterwards' since it deals mainly with the events of The Odyssey that occurred after that year, but it is only fair to mention that by 1960 the author was some 22 years of age, so a chapter on the circumstances that went before will not go amiss.

Act One

Origins

My father's parents were Scottish; they lived in the village of Aberargie, some 6 miles south of Perth. My father, Andrew, volunteered as a soldier on 17th August 1914 aged just 17½ years old. He joined the 6th/7th Black Watch and was sent to France where lost an eye on 16th October during the Battle of the Somme, but survived the war. After the war he worked in my grandfather's stone quarry at Abernethy until my granddad, reaching his 70th birthday, sold it in 1935; thereafter in those straitened times as a one-eyed ex-soldier, my Dad's employment opportunities were somewhat limited.

My mother, Winifred, had rather more success in her early life. She hailed from the West Midlands – from the village of Twogates on the A5 near the town of Tamworth in Staffordshire; however, her maiden name was Owen, so there may be a Welsh connection as well! In 1920 at the age of 18 she took employment not too many miles away from Tamworth with the Percy family, who owned a large house at Higham Grange, near Nuneaton. She stayed and prospered with this family until she married my father in 1932.

A Nanny Abroad

In an age when travel was generally limited to those fortunate enough to have the means, my mother did exceedingly well. A few years after she had joined the Percy family as a domestic servant, she had become the children's nurse and then nanny to the two daughters, Pamela and Carol and eventually the sons, Tony and Deryk. As such she travelled widely. Initially, although her travels were confined to journeys between England and Scotland, they were frequent. Thus in 1921, starting out from Nuneaton, a few weeks were spent at Rhyl in north Wales, immediately followed by similar periods at Carstairs near Lanark and Kirkliston just west of Edinburgh, before returning to Carstairs, thence back to Nuneaton.

In March 1922 they returned to Kirkliston for some months,

before driving up to Ayton House, a large mansion in its own ground, which was about ½ mile from Aberargie in Perthshire, where they stayed until December. During this period, she first met Andrew Dobbie, the one-eyed ex-soldier, who took her out for a spin on his motorbike! She kept a brief diary of her time as a nanny and her notes mention that she and he came off the bike on more than one occasion, which is perhaps not surprising with a driver who lacked binocular vision! In mid-December 1922, the family travelled by train to Southampton, then to Shepperton on Thames, returning to Rhyl briefly in March 1923, before coming back to Ayton in April 1923. In September 1923, the family travelled to Glasgow to take up their berths on the SS Tuscania (below) en-route to the USA, calling at Boston before docking at New York.

ANCHOR LINE T.S.S. "TUSCANIA."

From New York's Grand Central Station, they undertook a transcontinental train journey via Chicago, the Prairies, and the Rockies to Pasadena California, thereafter by car to a grand house in Laurel Canyon, Hollywood where Mr Percy had notions of getting into the movie business. He was, it was reputed, a friend of Rudolph Valentino!

One year later, in September 1924, Mum's diary notes that she and the two girls sailed from California in the SS Lochnagar, via the Panama Canal to dock at Liverpool, then by train to Perth. Her diary later recorded that Mr & Mrs Percy did not return from Hollywood until the following December (1925); this implies that she was entrusted with the care of the children while travelling half way round the world.

She spent the whole of 1925 at Ayton House and on 4th March 1926 she and Andy Dobbie got engaged, which was just as well, for on the 19th the family took the train to London, and then to Folkstone followed by a cross Channel ferry to Boulogne. The whole of the next day was spent on a train travelling to Italy, calling at Pisa and then on to Florence where they stayed in "The Villa Braggiotte" just outside the city. Between March and the beginning of November 1926, their travels included many stops in coastal towns on the Adriatic. Her diary briefly records that in November the family returned *"to Perth in a hurry"* but has no further comment. She went to visit her own father for a holiday in December 1926, returned to Perth at the beginning of Jan 1927, before taking the train back to Folkstone and thence by ferry to Boulogne.

This time the journey, in a party of 12 to the same "Villa Braggiotte" was in three grand automobiles travelling via the French Riviera. In July they motored back to England, crossing via Dieppe to Newhaven, then 460 miles to Ayton. By now my mother was quite the accomplished traveller, so it is perhaps not very surprising that after all these epic adventures, Mum's diary records in January 1928 *"life very dull and quiet."* In March 1928, the Percy's third child John Anthony Percy was born. Most of 1928 was spent in Scotland, but on 19th November the family sailed from Glasgow for New York on the SS Transylvania *"A journey to remember; very rough and very sick,"* as she recorded in her diary, *"SOS received from German cargo boat (21Nov) –The Herrenwyk. Boat sighted at 5.30pm; too rough to rescue. Funnel blown off and bridge fallen. Danish boat saves 13 men but 13 men lost."* During December Mum and Jenny Watson, the new under nurse took in all the tourist sites in New York, including Broadway where they visited many cinemas and theatres. This good life lasted until 28th September 1929, when they sailed in the SS California for Glasgow.

From October 1929 until May 1930, they stayed at Ayton until leaving for Liverpool and sailing to La Pallice on the west coast of France before driving 100 miles further south to a house by the sea, where they remained until July. On 15th July the family then motored to St Malo to take the ferry to Southampton and then the train up to

London, and thence back to Ayton. The last entry in Mum's 'diary' reads (1930) *'Nov – Home for holidays.'* Her diary for 1931 is blank, but in early 1932 she and my Dad were married in her local church in Twogates, in Warwickshire. At this point she exchanged her rather glamorous lifestyle of the past twelve years for something completely different.

Broadwell Cottage

The house that I grew up in was a farm cottage. It was quite isolated; the small village of Aberargie was a mile to the west of it and Abernethy – a somewhat larger village, was a similar distance to the east, with only scattered houses in between. Not only was the cottage fairly solitary, but also it was very basic even for those days. Many rural houses had no electricity at that time, thus requiring the use of paraffin lamps and candles for light and a Primus stove to cook on. However, Broadwell Cottage in addition to the lack of electricity, had a water supply that came from an outside cold water tap with a 'soak away' for waste water, whilst an outside dry toilet was a 'short walk away up the garden' at the back of the house. We were finally connected to the National Grid in 1953, and at about the same time the cold water was plumbed inside, and a small electrically heated hot water cylinder added to our modern comforts. But the outside loo still existed when I left home for university aged almost 19 late in 1957. Obviously, being very much in love, my Dad somehow persuaded my Mum to exchange her upper-class lifestyle for this rather humble dwelling and lifestyle.

The cottage living space (about 20 feet by 20 feet square) had a linoleum covered concrete floor, the rooms being partitioned by wooden frames clad with a single layer of tongue and groove boarding. This accommodation consisted of one main living room 13 feet x 12 feet, a main bedroom 15feet x 8 feet, and two small rooms (each 7 feet x 7 feet) with skylights – one of which was my bedroom, and the other one served as a kitchenette/diner. There was also an alcove (about 5 feet by 8 feet) by the entrance door that doubled up as a small auxiliary kitchen with a cast iron sink in which sat an enamel basin for washing. For larger ablutions we had a zinc enamel bath, which could be filled to a depth of about a foot with hot/warm water permitting a stand-up bath with flannel and sponge. At the back of the cottage my father had built a brick washroom complete with cauldron, fireplace and wringer for laundry, and a coal shed made from corrugated iron attached to this washroom.

The cottage was situated on the Perth to Newburgh main road at the foot of the Ochil hills which lie on the border of south-eastern Perthshire. But being on the north side of the hills, which are some 800 feet high at this point, between November and February, the winter sun never rose high enough to shine on the house. Consequently, it got very cold. I can remember regularly seeing the thick white hoar frost crystals on the *inside* of the windows on getting up on a winter's morning. The living room had large old-fashioned fireplace with a kitchen range, but above the fireplace was a wide chimney, which let out most of any hot air. The only portable heating we had in my childhood was a little paraffin heater generally used in the main bedroom, which I shared with my Mum when I was a toddler.

Dad's Death
As far as I am aware, after my Grandfather's quarry was sold in the mid-1930s, the only job that my Dad could obtain was as a postman, but he had to move about 30 miles away down to the town of Alloa near Stirling to take up this employment. Thus, in order to send some money home for my Mum, he was forced to take very cheap lodgings and couldn't afford much in the way of proper food

or heating. After I was born on 30th November 1938, these difficulties increased. My Mum later told me that my Dad would come in to his lodgings from his post round soaking wet and would be unable to afford the cost of heating to dry out his clothes. Tragically on 24th January 1940 my Dad died of bronchial pneumonia at the age of 43. My mother told me later that she woke up during the night and discovered that my Dad had died in his sleep. She tried to wake up a next-door neighbour, but she was very old and deaf, so my Mum then ran about quarter of a mile to a farmhouse where she managed to rouse the occupants. She later told me that her distress had wakened me, and I was probably subconsciously aware that all was not well, for when she returned after some time with Mrs Donaldson the farmer's wife, she said that I was howling my head off. This event must have affected me subconsciously, for I still find when I have arranged a time to meet my wife, if for any reason she is late, I go into worry overdrive!

After my father's death our finances were very, *very* tight, for all my Mother's worldly goods at this point were some very small savings and no income other than a miniscule widow's pension.

However, Mr Wilson, the farmer who owned a number of farms round about, including our cottage, did not require it for any farm labourers, and so let us rent it for just £1 per year! But with a small child to look after, in order to survive, my Mum seeking to augment our fuel supply, would take me with her when she went foraging for firewood. From the rear of the house, we walked up the field that backed onto the woods on the hillside to collect dead branches of hawthorn, ash, elder, and fir; tie them up with rope and drag them back down the field to a wood-shed that my Dad had built onto the outside loo in an attempt to disguise its rather obvious function at the far end of the garden. However, although the wide fireplace and chimney let out hot air, it had the advantage in that it enabled my mother to dispense with chopping or sawing up the lengths of dead wood and stick them straight up the chimney with one end in among the coal in the fireplace. This gave a good blaze, which was quite pleasant when I was bathed in front of the fire in the small zinc bath as a child! Unfortunately, when I got older, my bath time was consigned to a bigger bath in the alcove by the front door. In wintertime, enduring the cold while washing became one of the initiation rites into manhood. I subsequently became quite immune to low temperatures; I could sleep au natural in my bedroom with just one blanket for covering during wintertime with the skylight window open!

Survival and Holidays
Fortunately, for me, my Mum was not one who gave up easily. She was invited by both the Percy girls to go and stay permanently with them in Edinburgh, where they had settled while their husbands were serving in the Army during the War. However, my Mum had quite an independent facet to her character, and she declined this very kind offer and was determined to raise her son by herself. She later told me that she had been tempted to accept the offer, but felt that I would have grown up in their image and would have been over reliant upon my hosts. She passed on her well-developed sense of independence to me, often reminding me that although our circumstances were not auspicious, she had seen enough of society from the very wealthy to the poverty stricken to say to me that *"Remember, you are as good as any one. Stand up for yourself."* She was also conscious that as I did not have a father figure to look up to, it would be too easy for her to make me into a 'Mummy's

boy'; for this reason, although she was very loving, she was quite sparing in any overt affection.

However, in the meantime we did receive some occasional financial help from her ex-charges, and they, knowing our family circumstances, frequently invited us to stay with them. These mini holidays I greatly looked forward to, since the journey involved taking a bus trip to Abernethy, catching a train to Ladybank in Fife, before changing to another train, going over the Firth of Forth Railway Bridge and arriving at Waverley Station in Edinburgh, and staying in Morningside Crescent – a very gentile part of Edinburgh. While we were there, we often visited the Castle and the Zoo, and later the Museum. Just after the end of the War, the Percy girls moved from Edinburgh to Brig House, a large imposing mansion near Bathgate, some 15 miles from the centre of Edinburgh; and then secondly to Glenapp Castle (below) near Ballantrae on the Firth of Clyde. When the only holidays up to this point had been day visits to the seaside at St Andrews or interminable journeys in the blackout on trains crammed with soldiers, to visit one of my Aunts in Staffordshire, staying in such grand accommodation was a luxury to be savoured.

As an additional income, once I was just old enough to walk, my Mum worked on farms picking fruit, gathering potatoes, helping in the harvest, and weeding, sowing, and gathering vegetables on a market garden as a sort of Land Army Girl. She also became proficient at dress making and cooking, and eventually by the time that I started school, she worked on the market garden in the morning, came home changed out of her agricultural clothes into something more in keeping with her other job as dress maker and seamstress at a children's nursery in Abernethy. Finally, she took on full time employment at the nursery, doing the cooking in the morning and sewing in the afternoon. She finally retired from this job shortly after I joined the RAF.

I was very fortunate to have a mother who not only had this tenacity, but who also impressed the truth and benefits of hard work upon me.

Earliest Recollections

Recently it has been said that we cannot be sure that our earliest recollections are quite as early as we would like to believe. I have tried to recall my earliest memories; and while I cannot be sure that the very first are exact, I believe that they impressed themselves on my memory sufficiently to be essentially true. The first two events took place while I was yet being wheeled about in my pram –of this I am sure, because the memories were from places far beyond my ability to walk there.

I can remember being taken to Mr Gray's shop, the local general store, in the small village of Aberargie. There was a terrace, about 100 yards long, of single storey houses, whose small front gardens were fenced off from the pavement by cast iron railings. On this particular day the railings had gone. They had just been cut down by oxyacetylene torches for I remember seeing the raw sharp metal edges of the stumps of the railings in the sandstone flags, and lying on the pavement were the little black and dark blue globules of melted metal; they had not even begun to rust, so it was something that had just occurred. This drive for scrap metal took place in the summer of 1940. In another recollection I was just outside the baker's shop in Abernethy. There were only about five shops, and I can picture the location. I remember seeing the front cover (?) of a magazine – either The Picture Post or Illustrated. It was certainly a magazine with a photograph in black and white, and the title box at the top of the page was red with white lettering.

The photo was of a soldier in silhouette standing to attention with a rifle on some kind of balcony, while far below him there stretched a great river. I am pretty sure that this was some depiction of Die Wacht am Rhein (The Watch on the Rhine). This picture has somehow become fixed in my memory and has to date to sometime between late 1939 – early 1941. In 2012 I came across the very same or very similar picture that shows a German soldier overlooking the town of Coblenz just after the Rhineland was re-occupied; so, it is quite possible that the photo was used for propaganda in the early part of the War. The third memory was also from this time, probably during the winter of 1940–41. I remember asking my Mum why she was turning down our paraffin lamp, and she said, *"Listen to all those aircraft overhead."* Whether the aircraft overhead were German or British I do not know, but I could recognise the fear in her voice. I have since discovered, that the River Earn valley lay on the direct track from the Luftwaffe base at Stavanger airfield in Norway to the shipyards on the Clyde at Glasgow; this occasion probably dates from one of these raids on the docks on Clyde side in 1942.

By the summer of the next year I was old enough to accompany my Mum when she commenced to work as a "Land Girl." Thus, my recollections of '41 onwards, were associated with memories of Wellfield Market Garden, which was about half a mile from our cottage. This Market Garden had a number of large long greenhouses, each filled with tomato plants and other salad crops.

Any gardener will tell you that as a tomato plant grows it needs to have the side shoots pinched out so that the plant forms fruit trusses in an orderly succession. Even now when I smell a tomato plant it carries me back to that time, and the remembrance of my mother's fingers stained a vivid green from the tomato plant sap. In the summer fruit season, there were blackcurrants, strawberries, gooseberries, and raspberries to be picked. The raspberry canes were at least twice as tall as I was and were planted in rows some two hundred yards long and about three feet apart with the leaves on each row almost touching overhead. While my Mum and the other 'land girls' picked fruit and chatted, I wandered along the green tunnels between the rows of canes, far beyond the sight of my Mum and the other fruit pickers. At the far end of the 'tunnel' that I had started in I would traverse the ends of the rows until I came to the edge of the field and then return and try and find my way back down my original route. I felt like an explorer in the jungle. On one particular occasion, when I got to the end of the raspberry field, I discovered someone had set a rabbit snare, staked into the ground by the burrow. Now I had seen snares used and I knew what they were intended for. I tried the wire noose for size on my foot, but I somehow could not get the wire to release the way that I had seen it done. I was now far away from everyone, and no one could hear my cries for help. By the time that Mr Robinson the 'gaffer' came and found me, I was somewhat more than distressed.

Mr Robinson had a daughter, Anne, who was about my age, and we regularly played together while the grown-ups worked. The adults welcomed this arrangement, but we almost came to grief. We found a ditch full of water and were very soon engrossed in all the childlike games involving water. Unfortunately, the water had some dreadful contamination in it: I was very sick, but Anne Robinson was taken into Perth Hospital and was critically ill for a few days. Another memory of '42 was pasta! Our labour force at Wellfield had increased with the addition of about 6 Italian POWS –probably resulting from the British Army's successes in North Africa. I remember these POWS as happy cheerful men –glad to be out of the war. They were billeted in a small annex to the farm buildings. I was to them *"Il bambino"*, and I can remember their singing, and going into their accommodation –a semi converted stable - and seeing great strings of pasta hanging from some rafters near the ceiling. However, the greatest adventure in my early years was the autumn potato picking. Each farmer would assess how many people he needed for his potato harvest; word would go around the local area and at the appointed time transport would collect the workers. Work started at 8am sharp, so for this we had to get up quite early, dress in thick clothes against the autumn frosts, take a flask of tea and a pack of sandwiches and then wait by our front (and only) door for a truck to arrive. The flatbed of the truck was covered with straw and shielded with canvas in the manner of a Western prairie schooner, and inside there were crammed together the potato pickers. Sometimes the transport would only be a tractor and open trailer. This could be quite bracing on a cold autumn morning; fortunately, the potato harvest could only take place on dry days. The farms where we usually worked were to the west near Aberargie, not too far from the main Perth to Edinburgh railway line, and it was a splendid sight each morning not long after 8 o'clock seeing the great clouds of smoke going up vertically into the frosty air as a freight train powered its way up the incline to the Glenfarg tunnel. A potato field was the second occasion when I became aware of aircraft. I had just been watching a train when suddenly a single-engined aircraft appeared at full speed just above the tops of a wood not far from us. The pilot having spotted us, had dived down on the field and 'buzzed' us, and then pulled up almost into the vertical just above our heads. He caught me by surprise, and as I looked up and tried to follow him, I fell over backwards onto the ground. Thus, began my abiding interest in things aeronautical.

A Love of Books

There were advantages associated with my somewhat solitary existence. Of necessity I developed an ability to keep myself occupied. Modern children appear to become bored very easily and complain unduly unless they are stimulated by an excess of TV, computer games, and constant communications on their smart phones. Initially before I could read, I was given jigsaw puzzles and plasticine – modelling clay to keep me occupied. The only other 'entertainment' was the radio, but during my early years, the radio seemed to be dedicated exclusively to war news broadcasts, Workers' Playtime, or other adult programmes. I occasionally listened to Children's' Hour, but even then, I recollect it as being somewhat anaemic. It wasn't until after the War that children could listen each evening to 15 minutes of Dick Barton Special Agent, or when that wound up, Riders of the Range, and then Journey into Space. Later, in Scotland anyway, this older children's entertainment was replaced by 'The Mc Flannels' – a sort of Scottish urban comedy version of the Archers.

However, this dearth of amusement did allow me to discover the joy of books at quite an early stage. In my second year at Primary School, my teacher – Mrs Frazer, a quite stern severe old lady but excellent teacher, took note of this interest and let me take home an illustrated book on ancient history. It was full of the exploits of Alexander the Great and other such old-time heroes. In addition, she gave me a battered copy –which I still have –of Arthur Mee's The Book of Ten Thousand Things –full of interesting facts, such as illustrations of the Flags of the Nations; the Regimental Badges of the 196 different units, which at the time of the book's publication (1918) were mustered in the British Army; the sovereigns of Russia; scientific experiments that could be carried out at home, in addition to lists of interesting if somewhat trivial facts. To add to this miscellany, each year on Christmas Eve, my Mum's employment at Pitversie Nursery now included cooking the Christmas meal for the staff. During this time, Miss Dow, the proprietress allowed me to sit (quietly) in the lounge, in front of a lovely fire, reading, by real electric light, Arthur Mee's Children's Encyclopaedia. I eventually obtained the 10-volume set of these many years later. The smell of the imitation leather covers still reminds me of those Christmas Evenings. Mum also became friends with a lady called Kathie Martin who was housekeeper to a retired army officer – one, Major Othwaite. He lived in a bungalow across the road from Pitversie. He was a regular subscriber to the Illustrated London News, and after he had finished with the magazines, Mrs Martin passed them on to my Mum. The Illustrated London News featured extensive photographs of the progress of the War, so that by the latter stages of this conflict I was well up on the major campaigns, military personalities, and developments in weaponry. This may sound somewhat conceited, but when there was nothing else to read or to look at, this information stuck. I can still picture in my mind's eye a photograph of a phosphorous shell bursting on enemy lines during the battle of the Bulge; an artist's sketch of a British infantry man taking out a Tiger Tank at point blank range with a PIAT - an early form of bazooka; the great clouds of black oily smoke pouring out of the aircraft carrier the USS Bunker Hill after being struck by kamikaze planes; the full page diagrams and explanations of the V1 and V2 missiles, the Japanese 'Baka' suicide bomber, German midget submarines, snorkel apparatus, and the double page diagrams explaining radar and the Atomic Bomb. At the War's end, this magazine also featured pages of photographs of all the Allied and Axis leaders, who somehow, I had come to know from hearing their names on the radio so often. Even when I finally left Broadwell Cottage in 1960, I had a cupboard still piled high with those old magazines –and immaculate sequential copies of the Wizard and Rover comics. Unfortunately, while I was overseas in Malaya with the RAF, my Mum, who had decided to move to be next to her sister in Staffordshire, was left to clear up all our accumulated bits and pieces. I think that she got a bit low while trying to decide what to take and what to leave, and since by the time that she moved, I had been away from home for some 6 years, she gave away all my old magazines, comics, and boyhood collection of interesting things so that I had nothing to pass on to my own children.

Primary School

As I have mentioned, our cottage was isolated – there were no other houses or children nearby, and, as my father had died in early January 1940 when I was just over 1 year old, I had no brothers and sisters. Because my 5th birthday was at the end of November it was too late to begin school that year, consequently I didn't start school until August '44: thus, in my first 6 years I had a very sheltered upbringing; I was the archetypal reserved, painfully shy kid. I had one further disadvantage; my mother was English. Consequently, not only did I lack a Scots accent, but in addition, my mother having been a children's nanny to a family of the English-landed-gentry variety, (who, as I have mentioned, we visited quite frequently), I acquired – I was told – a very passable upper-class English accent.

It's been a while since I subscribed to the Beano comic, but I remember that there was a carton strip called *"Lord Snooty and his pals,"* which described the day-to-day adventures of an Etonian schoolboy who somehow co-existed amicably with a bunch of local lads. However, when I went to the village school in the autumn of 1944, I discovered that anyone who *presumed* to talk like Lord Snooty *didn't actually have many pals* at least not in my school! The past joint history of the somewhat fractious relationship between England and Scotland usually means that anything of a Sassenach nature is definitely squashed. In this particular case, there were about four kids, who absolutely abhorred anything English, and felt duty bound to beat this alien tongue out of me. Moreover, in any clash of interests, all my classmates, when the necessity arose and I felt driven to stand up for myself, seemed to have an elder brother of sister, or even the ultimate threat of *"I'll get my Dad to sort you out,"* to resolve the issue in their favour. There were days when I did not relish the thought of going to school at all. I was never conscious of lacking a father or elder sibling to defend me, but times like this hurt. In other words, I had a steep learning curve until I was fluent in the local patois and learned to look after myself. (I dare say mine is not a unique experience). Hence you can understand that I felt a certain amount of unease at the thought of the same cycle repeating itself in going up to senior school at Perth Academy. But by my final year at Abernethy all these issues were behind me; by a narrow margin I gained the top prize and was awarded a silver medal for my attainments. However, it was only my mother's insistence each evening that I had to complete my school home work that brought this about. She listened to my spelling of words that we were to be tested on the next day, helped me to be fluent reader, and corrected my basic maths. This supervision definitely helped me to gain sufficient marks to qualify for senior secondary school – i.e. a school that took pupils to the age of 18, as against a junior secondary school where the leaving age was 15. As a result of this opportunity, I was in a position to apply for university. It is to be remembered that my mother took on this task at the end of a full day's labour, cooking meals, the maintenance of our house, and all the other tasks that that entailed.

Over the Hills and Far Away

Another great compensation given to those who lived out in the country at that time was the freedom to roam. From the time that I started school until I commenced my secondary schooling, my after-school hours and weekends were dedicated to expeditions into the surrounding countryside; I can remember six or so of us –boys who stayed within about a half-mile radius of each other, wandering off during the summer holidays, playing Cowboys and Indians out in real wild country, making dens, camps, and wooden stockades à la Treasure Island hacking down young alder, ash, or sycamore trees to do so. I remember one particular summer's afternoon, while we were following a stream across the moorland on the south side of the Ochil Hills; it was hot and hazy, without a breath of wind, and no sounds except the calls of curlews and the occasional pheasant; it was if we were the only inhabitants in the world. Again, during the wheat harvest, we would follow the binder as it cut its way round the field, until as the last little bit of corn fell before the reaper, the rabbits would pop out and we would set upon them with clubs and dogs. Rabbit was a very tasty dish. We also explored streams, made dams with rocks and turf, guddled (tickled) trout, climbed disused quarries, burned whins (gorse), broom, gorse, ferns, and heather on the hillsides. Ostensibly this latter pastime was to help the farmers by keeping down such vegetation so that the sheep did not get caught in it. But in reality, it was as crypto-arsonists that we did it, taking great delight in watching the whole hillside erupt into flames and smoke. Unfortunately, I was away when some of my pals managed to attract the Perth Fire Brigade to extinguish a particularly well-developed firestorm!

On occasions our weekend wanderings could take us some two or three miles away from home from lunchtime until six or seven o'clock in the evening. My Mum was very understanding about this; by the time that I was 12, she appeared quite relaxed about my long absence. The only time that she really lost her cool was not long after I had started school. Just on the edge of Abernethy village, the road home from school crossed a stream – The Ballo Burn. It was not at all deep, but it held such interesting things as stickle backs, eels, and small trout. Arriving there about three forty-five one afternoon just after we left school in the early summer, three of us slowly played along the banks of this stream as far as the Perth – Newburgh railway line –this was about half a mile or so from the village. Since it did not seem a good idea to retrace our steps, we then walked alongside the railway –which was still in use, and finally back up a narrow country lane and across some fields to get back home. It had been a beautiful day, but by this time evening was drawing on –after half past seven. I was now about 4 hours late. My Mum by now was frantic with worry about me. She had no means of contacting anyone who might know where I had gone – no car, no neighbours, no phone, so when I finally appeared, I can remember getting a good scolding and a whack on my backside. It was a lesson well learned.

One other misdemeanour for which I was taken to task was being interviewed by the local bobby for stealing apples! He was the living epitome of Desperate Dan with an interviewing technique that went with his image. I didn't fall foul of the law again, or more correctly I didn't get caught for I remember on another occasion trespassing on railway property! The Glenfarg railway line that I had seen as a child was now within our orbit of operations. There were lots of wild strawberries growing along the cutting just where the line disappeared into Glenfarg tunnel. And yes, we did go through the tunnel, and we did not meet any trains, but neither did I inform my Mum about this escapade.

Other recollections of my boyhood involved Halloween and Guy Fawkes Night. We went guising, complete with hollowed out turnip lanterns, which was quite fun, but the big event – Bonfire Night – was even better. One of my friends – Ian Dougal lived with his little brother Eck (i.e. Alex), mother and her sister, and his grandfather in a cottage further up the Glenfoot road. His grandfather had been in the merchant navy during the First World War and somehow, I never found out how, he had been radically affected by Communism. He had lost an arm during his time at sea, and now he was running a croft/smallholding. I can remember that he had a complicated leather harness that he strapped to himself so that he could use a scythe, spade, and a gardening fork. His language was colourful even by the standards that I had heard from other farmers. His expressions of hate for Churchill, America and all things Capitalist were only exceeded by his admiration for Stalin, the Red Army, and Soviet Russia. Anyway, to get to the point, Grandfather Dougal's field was on the side of a hill about ½ mile further up Glenfoot from our cottage. Any bonfire lit there could be seen for miles, like a beacon used to warn of the coming of the Armada. Initially, our bonfires were just the usual household rubbish, straw, hay, paper, cardboard, and old wood, but on one of our scouting expeditions up the Glenfarg River, we had discovered that passing trucks and motorists were dumping their old rubber tyres into the river. It was some two and a half miles from where these tyres had been dumped to our bonfire site, but somehow, we wheeled them – including some fairly hefty truck tyres along two major roads – not much traffic then - and up the hill to the bonfire site. In our best and last, and biggest bonfire before we all split up in our teens, we based our bonfire round a large dead rowan tree. This particular fire still had glowing embers about 4 days later!

My other story concerning fires almost destroyed our cottage. January 1st 1948 was a Saturday. My Mum had left me in bed and gone to work at 9am to Pitversie for the morning. When I got up – sometime after 10am, I found that she had left the paraffin stove on to warm the living room. Just before I went out, I turned down the wick on the stove, blew out the flame, and turned up the wick just as I had done many times before, and went out to play. But a paraffin wick needs trimming every so often; otherwise an accumulation of carbon builds up on it and will continue to glow! On this occasion, although I had blown out the flame, the carbon was still glowing and eventually re-ignited the paraffin; the stove then relit giving off a heavy black sooty smoke. After a while, the wax tablecloth and linoleum floor covering commenced to smoulder, the table legs became charred, and the whole house filled with a dense cloud of sooty particles. Fortunately, the interval between my departure, and my Mum's arrival was not long. When she got off the bus, she looked up and noticed that the windows appeared black and wondered why I had drawn the blinds –we still had the old wartime blackout blinds in place. But the darkness was due to smoke! Any way to cut a long story short, my Mum managed to extinguish the stove, the smouldering articles of material and furniture, and remove the worst of the fire damaged things outside. I came home not long after, and I was given a close questioning as to how I had managed to almost burn the house down. It took many days to clean, scrub, wash and replace all the things that were fire damaged or soot stained.

A Farmer's Boy

From about the age of ten all children were expected to work in various part time jobs. I started earning money during the school holidays by picking raspberries, being paid one or two old pennies per pound picked, which meant that in a whole day it was possible to earn about 6 shillings, or 30 pence in today's money. Work at the potato harvest was harder but much more lucrative. On my first excursion into this job, I earned somewhere in the region of 8 to 10shillings (40–50p) for a Saturday morning's work!

However, there were some unwritten rules associated with potato picking that it was necessary to discover to avoid being taken advantage of. Each picker was given "a bit" –a length of ground that depended on the size of the field and obviously to some extent on the number of "tatty –howkers" that had turned up. As a lad under 12 you were normally expected to work "half a bit", therefore your pay was only half what a full bit would earn you. The farmer would start at one end of the field walking the length of the field along the potato drills with an armful of thin leafy ash tree branches and pace out the bit distance –dictated by the size of the field and the number of potato pickers, plant a marker, then step out a similar distance, or half that for a half bit, until he came to the end of the field, by which time if he had calculated correctly, he had also used up all his labour force. The tractor and potato spinner then started to uncover the potato drills one at a time, the pickers moved in with their creels – made of basketwork or wire grid, after which the tractor and potato spinner passed by again. But as the tractor progressed, it was necessary to move each ash branch marker further across the field. Ideally this was at right angles to its original location so that your original 'bit' remained the same length, but an unscrupulous person would allow his marker to drift towards his side. If each person either side of you did this, the two people either side of you could wind up picking less than they were paid for while you were gathering rather more than you were being paid for.

Still later in my early teen-age years, I regularly worked on Ayton Farm on Saturdays and during the school holidays. I have in my time gathered sheaves into 'stooks', forked sheaves up onto a trailer, cleared out stables and cattle sheds, spread manure, driven tractors, ploughed (briefly) with two Clydesdale horses, thinned fields of sugar beet; topped and tailed a field of sugar beet, turnips, and mangles (cattle feed) with a large cleaver. This was easy on a good day, but it was also a task that could be done in any weather, so in cold, wet, or frosty weather trying to hold a cold wet turnip covered in mud with one bare freezing hand, while holding the cleaver in the other bare freezing hand to hack off the leaves and the roots of the turnip without simultaneously removing one's fingers was quite a skill.

Harvest time
Although I had helped with the harvest previously, the culmination of my farming career came in the autumn of '55 at the wheat harvest at Ayton Farm, when a large steam engine arrived in the corn stack yard, pulling an even larger threshing machine. This old-fashioned steam traction engine –old fashioned even for the

1950s – drove the threshing machine via a large belt and rapidly rotating cast iron wheel. The mechanism on this Victorian traction engine seemed to be full of uncovered shining brass levers, governors, and pistons whirling round accompanied by steam and smoke, and hot embers.

Additionally, when the threshing machine was in operation, the wheat chaff, even though it was ejected some distance away by a long pipe, gave off copious dust that would blow back on the harvesters if the wind was in the wrong direction. On both sides of the threshing machine tractor-trailers laden with wheat sheaves were drawn up, and men threw up the sheaves of wheat with pitchforks to the men on the top of the threshing machine to catch, (who skilfully avoided impaling their hands on the tines of the pitch fork). At one end of the thresher the ejected threshed sheaves would also be pitch forked up to the men who were building a stack for bedding straw. At the other end of the thresher the harvested wheat would pour out into large hessian sacks to be loaded onto trailers. But in order to get the trailers as near as possible to these very heavy bags of grain, the tractor, with a trailer would be reversed down between the narrow rows of stacks. There was no warning about this, such as the reversing alarm that is now required, so anyone working there had to stay awake for the possibility of getting caught and squeezed between stack and trailer.

Thus in 1955, my 17th year, I was immensely proud to be asked if I would go up the ladder and work on top of the threshing machine. I was given a knife that had a short-hooked blade and a piece of cord wound through the handle such that the knife could be kept attached to the wrist, and up the ladder I went. The threshing machine was about 20 feet long, some 7 feet wide and about 10 feet high, while on the top there was a platform about 10 feet square, usually occupied by three people, (see photo above). The only concession to safety was a two-foot-high board round the edge of the platform, so you couldn't actually step off into space, but it was quite possible to trip over this safety board and fall to the ground! I had actually fallen backwards the year before off a sloping haystack, only stopping when my backbone painfully encountered the edge of a tractor-trailer.

When the threshing machine was in operation, with the platform vibrating and shaking at about force 8 on the Richter scale, the two receivers each grabbed a sheaf in turn from men on the trailers drawn up alongside. Then having got hold of the sheaf, we used our knives to cut the binding string, and pass the loosened bundle of wheat stalks to the man who fed the machine. In front of him there was a large gap about four feet long and one foot wide, inside of which could be seen the whirling blades that threshed the wheat. As I have just said, when being driven by the steam engine, the whole machine vibrated harshly, accompanied by a loud humming noise akin to a million angry wasps. There was nothing to stop anyone on the top of the machine from falling into it and becoming instant pulp. In fact, virtually all the machinery and equipment used in the harvest was alive with potential hazards. Nowadays, with the emphasis on health and safety, such machinery or practices would not be permitted; but in those far off days common sense and self-preservation were taken for granted!

Postman, Radio Ham, & Fisherman

My other summer job was as a postman! Before the War my Dad had made friends with a man who subsequently became our regular local postie – Davy McDougal. In the summer of 1955, when he went on holiday, he kindly asked me to stand in for him. I cycled on my own bike to Abernethy, collected the mail and the parcels, loaded them onto a really large and very heavy Post Office bicycle – with only one gear – so no easy hill climbs, and set off on my round. In the morning I delivered the mail to the outlying houses and farms to the east of the village, and after lunchtime, I did a similar round to the west, up and down and along farm tracks and minor roads before cycling home in the evening. All in all, I covered about 15 to 20 miles every day. The summer of '55 in Scotland was a really hot one, so I not only became very fit, but also got a tan into the bargain. That Christmas I took a job in the Perth General Post Office Parcel Office to help with the Christmas mail. This was my first night shift job –very exciting. The large bags for the parcels were hooked up and held open on long metal frames that ran down the middle of the sorting room; above each bag there was a name of each destination. In this way I became aware of quaint little places like Achnalt, Achnasheen, and Achnashellach, hitherto unknown to me along the northwest Highland railway. Old hands in the parcel office could unerringly aim a parcel to land in the appropriate bag, but this system was not fool proof. I can remember finding in a postbag a rather damp but solid parcel from which came the sound of broken glass and a strong smell of whisky – but we sent the parcel to its destination anyway!

Davy MacDougal was also instrumental in introducing me to short waveband radio. By the time that I was in my mid-teens, we had obtained a shed, which was originally intended for garden tools, but somehow it became my radio shack and finally my motorcycle garage. Many years previously my Dad had rigged up a 20 foot long copper wire radio aerial between two tall metal poles that gave a good signal for the normal BBC stations on the Long and Medium Wavebands, but I decided that in order to receive short wave stations from around the world, a vertical dipole aerial would be more efficient. To make this I used an old clothes pulley, an ancient way of hoisting wet or damp washing to dry by hanging it from the kitchen ceiling. The frame consisted of an eight-foot wooden pole, with two short wooden arms about two feet long at either end, each having a wire strung parallel to the long arm between each end of the short arms to hold wet washing. This apparatus with a suitable pulley attachment at either end of the long pole could be raised or lowered up to the ceiling. To make my aerial, I attached one end of the frame to a front set of bicycle forks which I had straightened, replaced the galvanised wire with copper wire and mounted it vertically on the shed roof, so that I now had a rotatable dipole aerial. I also managed to construct a couple of simple one and two valve receivers with the aid of a basic instruction manual, and I was very proud one evening to hear an American voice say amidst the static, "*Sky queen, sky queen, do not answer, do not answer. Identification X ray, Identification X ray.*" I subsequently learnt some years later that this type of broadcast was from a forward signals base in Scotland giving identification instructions to USAF aircraft returning from recce missions to the high Arctic off the northern USSR.

By this time, I had graduated to constructing a mains radio, without electrocuting myself, although I did have a faulty condenser short out and blow up quite spectacularly, but all in all I felt that I was getting along splendidly, until one particular Saturday morning, when a serious looking chap driving a black van drew up outside the cottage just as I came out of my radio shack. He asked me if I was a radio ham. I proudly told him that I was. We had a few more moments of chat about short wave radio before he casually asked me if I had ever done any short-wave broadcasting. I said no, because it was away beyond my capability. He then said that he was making enquiries on behalf of the GPO who were trying to trace the source of broadcasts that were being made on the BBC TV channel by some Scottish Nationalist supporters just as the BBC closed down each evening. I later found out that Davy McDougal had been involved in this. So, I had been fortunate that I had not inadvertently given him away.

My last temporary summer employment before University was with the Tay Salmon Fisheries. I had a motorbike by this stage – a 350cc Ariel Red Hunter, so getting about was no problem. This job during the summers of '57 and '58 paid an incredible £20 per week. It did involve living in a bothy - a small fisherman's hut - by the banks of the River Earn not far from where it joins the River Tay, sleeping on a straw palliasse, cooking your own meals, and working tidal six-hour shifts for a few days at a time. The river was about 50 yards wide down near Wester Rhynd in the lower Earn Valley. The water was also very deep. Something that I was aware of because I couldn't swim a stroke! There were two boats, and at the start of each incoming tide, one boat with two oarsmen – in this case myself and Roy Byres, a lad of the same age, accompanied by a tow man, would row against the incoming tide about 200 yards downstream and anchor at the river bank. Our tow man would leap onto the path along the bank of the river holding the ropes attached to one end of the net and set off down the towpath. When we heard a call from the gaffer, we upped anchor and pulled with all our might back upstream with the current while allowing the net, which had been carefully prepared in a special way, to unwind into the river from the stern of the boat. Prior to this, the tow man who had been hauling the other end of the net along the bank had also arrived and attached his rope to some large immovable object close to a mobile windlass. Eventually we arrived at the winch, which had been wheeled out on to a stony beach by the bothy, we would quickly beach the boat and attach the rope at the other end of the net to the windlass. We two oarsmen would rapidly wind in the rope using the two-handled winch, until the gaffer, Arthur Bett (another of my junior school contemporaries about 3 years older than myself), called a halt as the mesh of the net reached the beach. The current then swung the whole net upstream, but it was now in a long narrow funnel shape that was well into our side of the river. Four of us would then each take a rope – two large heavy ropes, that had to be kept down on the shingle, and two top thinner ropes that were held up above the surface of the water. When the whole net was pulled in there would be quite often some large or even super large salmon tangled in the net. A quick club to the head then disposed of these. Then while we re-laid our net on the stern of the boat, and the gaffer made repairs to the net, usually caused by hard old tree roots in some parts of the river bed, the other crew had already rowed off downstream ready for the next trawl.

Perth Academy

When I left Abernethy Primary School in the summer of 1951, it had five staff and about 80 pupils; Perth Academy on the other hand had 50 staff and over 900 pupils! A large proportion of the new intake in my year came from schools within Perth itself –Craigie, Cherrybank, Caledonian Road, Kinnoul, or even Perth Junior Academy, which was located next to the senior school. Thus, the move for them within the city up to Perth Senior Academy may not have seemed such a big step. However, for those of us who came from small village schools in the 'outback' of Perthshire, the transfer was awesome. It took me a little while to settle in and until I got to grips with the system my first year was nothing to write home about;

I did the work, I got by, but I didn't really get involved in what is termed 'extra-school activities.' I started my second year with much more confidence, and by the autumn of 1952 my class of some 30 boys had gelled into a unit. Many years later as a flying instructor in the RAF, I saw the same process take place with trainee pilots. Some courses worked together and played together and took care of each other so that no one fell behind. Other courses seemed to be made up of individuals, there was no cohesion, morale was quite poor and consequently there were more failures.

By my 2nd year I was confident enough to take up rugby and join the School Combined Cadet Force; (CCF) for this I am extremely grateful for the encouragement and persuasion of two 5th form lads, Sandy and Ian Miller – whose Dad I had worked for, and still worked for on Saturday mornings at Ayton Farm.

Combined Cadet Force

The CO of the Combined Cadet Force (CCF) was Colonel Grassie, who was also our PE Master. He had been an officer in the Black Watch in the First World War and had seen quite a bit of action in the trenches. The Cadet Force taught me much about basic military procedures: parade ground drill, rifle drill, how to command a drill squad, even simulating mounting an attack with a section of men with a Bren gun giving covering fire. Ultimately each cadet was capable of carrying out all the drill manoeuvres with a squad of some 30 boys from forming up, marching wheeling, and turning, full rifle drill, up to dismissal of the platoon. The rifles that we used were Mk1 and Mk 4 Lee Enfield .303s. We must have had about 100 of them stored in an armoury under the School, plus two Bren Guns, a few Sten guns, a number of .22 rifles, together with some hundreds of rounds of .303, 9mm, and .22 ammunition. The door to the armoury was just an ordinary wooden door, one set of keys to which was held by whichever senior cadet became the Quarter Master Sergeant. How innocent it all seems now.

Each summer the whole of the Perth Academy cadet contingent spent two weeks at an army camp. My first outing was to our nearest Army Camp some 25 miles to the west of Perth at Cultebraggan near Comrie (see below). This camp had been the largest German POW camp in the UK; it was now used for a similar purpose training National Servicemen; as an ex-POW camp the facilities were nothing to write home about: communal cold-water ablutions, and latrines of large diameter pipes that looked like long torpedo tubes with holes pierced in the tops, open cubicles with no doors were the height of luxury. If I had any residual shyness from being a single child, this surely eradicated it. We were given aluminium 'dixie tins' for our food. When we had finished eating, we sluiced them in a large metal container of hot water, and then rinsed them in a second similar container. By the time everyone had washed their dixies, the first container had the appearance of greasy soup – which, it was rumoured, was actually used as a basis for gravy in our subsequent meals.

In my 4th year – summer of '54, we travelled to Northern Ireland – to Magilligan Camp near Londonderry. This camp also became a prison camp a few years later for IRA prisoners. I can't remember the train journey from Perth to Glasgow, but I know that we sailed in the evening from somewhere among the extensive docks of Clydeside. It was as still as a millpond as we rounded the tail of the bank at Gourock. Some of the elder lads, free from parental supervision, and knowing that our three officers Colonel Grassie and two of our teachers, Captains 'Beefy' Stevenson and 'Doc' Anderson were probably partaking of a dram or two themselves, knocked back more than a few beers as we sailed down the Firth of Clyde. Unfortunately, by the time that we were drawing abeam Ailsa Craig the wind had risen sharply, and when darkness had fallen, we were beset by an incredible gale as the ship ploughed through the enormous seas of the North Channel. Our cadet force had been given space under the top deck right up in the forward bow –just where the seas hit the ship and the pitch was greatest. The beers so recently partaken of were now swilling around the deck. The heads (ship' latrines) were even worse. I did not suffer from any seasickness, but I eventually found a space right up on the top deck amidships, where the violence of the ship's pitching if not the rolling seemed least. I was very pleased that I found this place and had no trepidation until someone brightly remarked that it was near here in a storm that another ferry, the Princess Victoria, had foundered just over a year and a half previously with the loss of 128 people! It was a very sober ship that quietly slid into Londonderry early next morning.

One or two memories of this camp are worth recalling. On our first day, having bagged our beds in the inevitable Nissen hut, two of us went across some sand dunes to look down on a vast sunlit expanse of golden sand and fantastic breakers. We raced down to the water's edge. We hadn't been there more than a few minutes when we saw a figure waving to us from the top of the dunes. Although the voice was faint, we distinctly heard the words, *"Don't move; you're in the middle of a minefield!"* This was essentially true; for although the beach had been cleared of obvious mines, there were apparently still others deep in the sand. I can't remember how we were rescued, but there were no further beach expeditions. The second event also involved explosives, only this time it was even scarier. We had all been made to sit in a semi-circle, while being instructed in the art of firing mortar bombs. The sergeant had a 3-inch mortar and a crate of mortar bombs. He gave us a brief on how the army used such a weapon, and then dropped a round into the barrel of the gun. It made that hollow coughing noise a mortar gun makes; the projectile flew up and away and exploded –really exploded this wasn't a drill round – about half a mile away. The sergeant fired a few more to our great satisfaction, but on the last round the propellant explosive in the tail of the mortar shell did not function correctly, so that the mortar bomb only went about a hundred feet into the air and was seen to be tumbling over and over and was obviously going to land quite close by. No drill was needed; to a man everyone flattened themselves into the sand and grass. Fortunately, the bomb did not explode. Finally, to complete the litany of the dangers of allowing teenagers to become familiar with guns and ammo, the lad, who had gone with me down to the beach, almost became the first mass killer in modern British history. We were being instructed on the use of the Bren gun, which incidentally, before you were allowed to fire it, you had to be able to dismantle it, name the parts, reassemble it, (and on occasions doing this blindfolded), and deal correctly with all the known stoppages associated with the weapon. The Bren magazine held some 30 rounds. It could be used to fire single shots, or automatically. However, automatic fire, despite the examples of Arnie Schwarzenegger and other action-film heroes, was normally restricted to two or three rounds at a time. The training had been going well, until my friend lay down and got himself into the correct firing position. Somehow, instead of selecting single rounds to start he had selected automatic; and then having squeezed the trigger, he froze on it. The bullets hosed the wooden targets on the range some few hundred yards distant, and then as my friend didn't seem to have much control of where the Bren was pointing, it started to chop its way across country. Screams, horrible oaths, and blasphemies erupted from our Regular Army weapons instructor who managed to get alongside my acquaintance, prise him from the trigger, and make the gun safe.

One final peccadillo; The Camp at Magilligan Point, in common with all other Army and RAF establishments that I have ever known, was located out in the sticks/bush/back of beyond far from the delights of civilisation. Somehow the Royal Navy seems to have completely avoided this disadvantage since their ships have to tie up in harbours that are adjacent to cities. But although Magilligan Camp was sparsely supplied with diversions, just a mere nautical mile away across Lough Foyle that leads into Londonderry, the small town of Moville could be seen shining in the sun on the coast of Eire. In'54 there were no restrictions for British Servicemen travelling across the border. Two of our lads decided to sample what ever there was to see in Moville. Not far away, outside the camp, there was a little jetty and a small boat with a man sitting calmly looking out to sea smoking a pipe. The boys asked if he could take them across and how much it was to go across. *"Och, I'll take youse"* he said, *"It costs nuthin."* Sometime later, having spent a lot, but fortunately, not all their money, they returned to their boatman. But as they settled down in the boat, he said *"That'll be two pounds."* Looking pained, they complained, *"I thought that you said that it was free?"* *"Oh, I did indeed. Tis free to go across, but a pound to go back!"*

Many years later, Colin Gotts, a navigator on XV Squadron, related a similar tale of Irish logic after he had been on holiday in Ulster. He and his wife had stopped at a little country pub, so small that the front room was the main bar, with drinks being served through a hatch in the wall. They had scarcely begun to drink when the serving hatch shut. Colin said to his wife, *"We'd better drink up, they are obviously closing."* But just a minute later the hatch opened again. Colin, somewhat perplexed, asked the man framed in the little opening, *"I thought that you had closed?"* *"Oh, we had,"* said the man, *"The law says when we have to close, but they haven't said when we are to open again."* Would that this common-sense attitude was applied to some of the more nit picking and stupid rules that are made in this country today!

Just to round off my time in the CCF, our last camp in the summer of '57 was down in the Scottish Borders. This camp was so remote that I do not even remember the name of it, and not only did it feature all the amenities of the previous ones, but there was almost constant rain and low cloud as well. It was here that I took on one challenge but refused the second – so at least I was beginning to learn! Some of the younger cadets had been throwing some object around and it had landed on the roof of one of our Nissan huts. I volunteered to climb up and retrieve it, which I did. I was just about to climb down again when someone from the group of younger lads called out, *"Jump!"* Now by this time I had been promoted to Cadet

Sergeant Major (CSM), so to maintain face I accepted the challenge – I jumped, although the apex of the hut was some 10' off the ground. I landed OK, but my momentum carried me forward and I fell heavily on my left wrist. A sharp pain went up my arm. It did not go away, so I went off to sick quarters to see the Medical Officer. He diagnosed a fracture in one of my wrist bones. I was ordered to pack some overnight gear, given a rail travel warrant to the military hospital near Glasgow, and was told that transport would take me to the railway station. The system worked perfectly; I had an x-ray, had my arm put in plaster, stayed overnight in a ward and returned to my unit the next day. But that same day – our last full day – very late in the evening, some of my mates in our Nissen hut decided to go out and 'raid' one of the other cadet units. This was pretty much par for the course, but with my arm in plaster, I declined and went off to bed quite early. I vaguely heard them return. Next morning, quite early there was a thunderous hammering on the door of our Nissen hut; no one else moved, so I got out of bed, opened the door, and was confronted by what looked like a pit bull terrier foaming at the mouth dressed in khaki uniform. This was the CSM of the other unit that we had 'raided' who obviously felt that his honour had been besmirched. He demanded to know who was responsible. I honestly said that I did not know. By now he was poking me quite forcibly in the chest with his brass capped CSM's pace stick and was obviously spoiling for a full-scale fight. I waved my plaster cast at him and said that I couldn't help him any further. He continued to prod me with his stick, but as I refused to give him any names, or accept the 'dare' to a fight, he eventually had to back off while threatening to take the matter to 'higher authority.' In this I was rather fortunate, for he was built like a gorilla and would probably have sent me back to the military hospital for more than an overnight stay! Meanwhile, my 'mates' had lain doggo in bed until this confrontation was over. Thanks guys.

Companionship and Development

In my travels to and from school I was also very fortunate in that although some six miles out in the country from Perth, our cottage was situated on the main bus route for Alexander's Bluebird Coaches from Perth to Fifeshire, so that there were buses going literally past our door to and from Newburgh, St Andrews, Leven, and Kirkcaldy about every 20 minutes from early in the morning until late at night, which was great once I started going out with girlfriends from school! During term time, on arrival at the bus terminus outside Perth Railway Station, we were faced with a fairly rapid walk of about one mile through the Station and then uphill all the way to arrive in time for the School Assembly at 9am.

The whole school met in the assembly hall on the upper floor – the youngest class at the front, and the 6th form at the back. On the stage stood the Rector – John Kerr, and his deputies – Mr Stevenson for the boys, and Miss Young for the girls, together with the boy and girl head prefects on either side of the deputies, and at one side of the stage a lectern with a large Bible and the 5th or 6th form pupil (boy or girl) who would read a passage from the Scriptures. This duty alternated weekly between the boys and the girls. There were hymnbooks given out and the Rector would announce which hymn was to be sung –the accompaniment was by our music teacher Mr Frazer who was also squeezed onto a corner of the stage behind a grand piano. After the hymn, the Bible reading was given, and then the Rector would deliver a short homily, to be followed by special observations for the day, or warnings of impending doom for infringements of school rules, etc. There were four classes each in the morning and afternoon; occasionally there would be 'double' French for instance (groan), but we also had at least four PE periods each week and a games afternoon on Wednesdays. The Gymnasium, which was directly below the assembly hall, was divided in two by a heavy wood partition–one half for the girls and one half for the boys; on occasions – more of which anon – the partition could be pulled aside. However, my memory is clear on this, in our particular intake, from our 1st year right up to our 6th year –in whatever we were doing –in classes, games, sports, Christmas parties, there was a great sprit of unity and fun. During my subsequent adult working life, in activities and alliances that involved in any way the management of people, I have met a quota of mean, bad tempered, grouchy individuals: sad cases of people with abilities, but who fail greatly in their relationships with their fellow human beings. But I do not remember this occurring at any time, in any way while I was at the Academy! Secondly, although the staff contributed greatly to our success, our attainments at school ultimately depended on our own individual abilities. But our attainments in turn were also dependent on discipline – that imposed by the staff, and our own self-discipline.

Today, not only is there a serious shortfall in what is taught and how it is taught, but also there is next to no discipline, nor is any application of discipline allowed. Consequently, any pupil showing any aptitude and desire to learn quite often has to contend with those whose only aim is to cause mayhem and block the progress of those who do. Thus, many pupils, who have the ability, fall by the wayside through no fault of their own. None of us at Perth Academy between 1951 and 1957 had to combat this obstacle. We all had fun, but we all got on with the tasks we were given to do. Thirdly, behavioural scientists tell us that we are a product of our upbringing and our environment. I personally believe that my subsequent working relationships with those I encountered later in life benefited greatly from the years I shared at the Academy; we were poured into a mould that had a lasting effect. Finally, as mentioned earlier, since I had no brothers or sisters, in many ways my school friends became my brothers and sisters. I am being completely sincere in this; my personal circumstances were such that I couldn't have wanted a better start.

In summary, from being a very introverted shy kid in 1st year, I became at least a superficial extrovert by the 6th year, with the confidence to go on and become and do what I had decided to do.

Girls

The other great social grace that I acquired because Perth Academy was co-educational, was to become reasonably proficient in modern and Scottish country dancing. To be able to dance was part of the school curriculum, the classes for which were led by the girls PE Mistress. Thus towards the end of the autumn term, Colonel Grassie would open the wooden partition in the gymnasium that separated the boys' half of the gym from the girls half, and a crowd of noisy boisterous boys in their T shirts, shorts, and gym shoes would suddenly go silent as they confronted a group of girls in their gymslips who were glancing shyly at us and whispering among themselves —well we were all shy initially when we were in the first and second year; in the third year confidence and testosterone or testosterone and confidence were starting to have their effect, and by the time of the fourth, fifth and sixth forms, many of us had already been out with one or more of the girls or had even got to the 'going out regularly' stage and so we felt quite relaxed about meeting in such circumstances.

This was another hurdle that I was glad to have overcome. I remember one Christmas Party at Abernethy junior school, which consisted of a games evening of pass the parcel, musical chairs, etc. As I have previously mentioned, I was very shy, self-conscious, under confident –whatever social deficiency there was, you name it, when it came to mixing with other children, I had it. This party was probably in my first or second year, certainly quite early on, in which we played a game called "The farmer's in his den", wherein all the children circled round holding hands while singing, *The farmer's in his den, the farmer's in his den, Eey Aye my Daddio, the farmer's in his den,"* When the music stopped, someone was 'chosen' to go into the middle of the circle as the 'farmer.' The singing circle recommenced, only this time saying, 'The Farmer wants a wife'; and when the 'wife was chosen', the circle restarted, singing, 'The wife wants a child', then 'The child wants a dog', and 'The dog wants a bone', whereupon when 'the bone' went into the middle all the circling multitude fell upon and pummelled the person chosen as the bone. I, to my consternation, was selected to be first in the circle as the farmer. I had never felt so insecure, exposed, and embarrassed in my short life, for when my school friends stopped circling round, *I* would have to make my choice of some little girl to be my 'wife,' which I eventually did, whereupon the assembled multitude went *"OOOOOH"*, followed by nudge, nudge, wink, wink. At that point I wished that the earth had opened and swallowed me up.

Whether this was the reason or not, I did not go the first year Christmas party at Perth Academy. Each of the first and second years had over two hundred children, so the first-year party I gave a miss on the assumption that any party with this number milling round the assembly hall would be my previous experience greatly magnified. This assumption was proven when I went to the 2nd year party; it was ok – but only just.

However, in the last week of term in December 1953, I went along to the 3rd year party –which was on a Wednesday night. I know that this is so, because each of the 1st, 2nd, and 3rd year parties took place on Monday, Tuesday, and Wednesday of the last week of term before the Christmas break. The senior forms –4th, 5th, and 6th year, with markedly less pupils, amalgamated on the (last) Thursday night. A few staff, and all the prefects –boys and girls, oversaw each of the class parties. This was a great incentive to being elected as a prefect since if you *were* going steady by then and your girlfriend also was a prefect, you had carte blanche to be together four evenings in a row!

In those far off old-fashioned days, it was still the done thing for the boys to be ranged along one side of the dance hall, and the girls along the other. By the time that the party was drawing to a close I had decided to ask a little curly haired brunette if I could see her home, but it was not the done thing to ask *before* the last waltz. So, when the 'MC' said *"Take your partners for the last waltz,"* there was a scramble like the drivers at Le Mans racing across the track to make sure you arrived in pole position in front of your 'intended' before any other rival! This I did, I asked her and she said that I could see her to her house. I had to take a bit of a gamble on this, because if she had said that her house was at the far end of Perth, near St Johnstone's football ground, then I had about a five mile walk ahead of me to get back to the bus. Fortunately, her house was not far off my route to the bus terminus near the railway station. Having collected our coats, we met just outside the hall, and walked off into the night. As we both shyly tried a keep up a conversation, while walking down the hill from the school, I discovered that her name was Margaret and that she was not staying at school after the end of the third year. This was an option then; you could leave at the end of the 3rd year and commence some form of employment. Once we had crossed the Glasgow road, there was a long wide avenue with bungalows on one side of the street, and larger detached houses on the other. This side of the street was also interspersed with short cul-de-sacs, at the end of which was a narrow lane that ran parallel to the main avenue at the back of the houses. I knew that I wanted to kiss this girl, so I said, taking her by the hand, *"Let's take this way."* Some fifty yards along this dark lane, I stopped and pulled her round in front of me. She knew what was coming for her eyes were closed as she turned her face up to mine, and we kissed and clung to each other. There is something about your first love and your first kiss; something that either of us hadn't experienced before. We didn't, in contrast to todays 'anything goes' from square one, do anything else the whole time that we went out – except go to films, walk hand in hand, sit on a park benches, kiss goodnight; all very innocent and great fun.

There was probably an even greater reason to be circumspect. In the Fifties, if I remember correctly, there were three main reasons for capital punishment: regicide, high treason, and getting pregnant outside of marriage, since parental advice was of the *"If you get that girl pregnant; or if you get pregnant, I'll kill you!"* It is a sad reflection on the supposed progress of human sexual relationships, that what the liberal reformers have castigated as the so-called repressed attitudes of that time (caused by ignorance), have been replaced by them with a laisse faire approach where pre-teen children have a complex and more than required knowledge of human sexual congress in all its variations, but have been given absolutely no moral compass to go along with this knowledge. At least in the '50s families were very much more stable units, where the parents from all walks of life generally took pride in raising their offspring to certain standards.

But in my case, some supplementary information would have made life a lot easier. I suppose that in common with virtually every other boy, I discovered the pleasures of self-stimulation. This would have probably been of no great consequence, except for an inadvertent discovery. One day, when I was about 13 while at home by myself, I was searching for something, when I came across a book well hidden away in a cupboard. It was tucked away so I'm sure that my Mum had not 'accidentally' left it around for me to find. The book was an American publication and it must have been something that she had brought back from the USA in the 1920s. It combined a vigorous support for marriage with a denunciation of all the evils associated with illicit activities –adultery and fornication, tobacco, drugs, and drink. The sexual misdemeanours and the infections so contacted were particularly vividly illustrated by copious pictures of 'before' and 'after' – almost as if Charles Atlas reverted back to a 7-stone weakling; (You have to be of a certain age to understand this illustration!). The tobacco, drugs, and drink section I could not relate to, although the diagrams of a healthy liver followed by one taken from the corpse of an alcoholic were pretty convincing. But the diagrams of the degeneration of the sexual organs caused by 'self-pollution' were scary. The book did not actually spell out what this was or what level of sexual activity of any kind that caused one's sexual organs to atrophy and hair to grow on the palms of one's hands, but it strongly stated its case that abstinence from tobacco, drugs, booze, and illicit sex was the only solution. From hearing conversations of older boys, I knew the basics of how children were conceived, but where did that place the graphic cautions vividly portrayed in this book for 'actions' that were not directly connected with the propagation of the species? Such partial knowledge put me in a great quandary, whom could I ask about what was OK?

It's difficult enough for children to confide in their parents about such matters –and vice versa; In my case my Dad was dead, I could *never* have asked my Mum, I had no elder brother, and the thought of opening up my heart to one of my mates who would laugh and then go and tell everyone about my ignorance left me at a loss: so I lived with this dilemma; indulging my flesh when the pressure became too great, but suffering the accusations from my conscience afterwards. Subsequently, once I had started secondary school, I occasionally haunted the main public library in Perth, which featured a large medical reference section, tucked away down a side passage, where it was possible to browse without undue attention from the library staff. Considering that sex is a universal human activity, why is it that the wiring diagrams and the explanations of the male and female organs and their functions and malfunctions are always placed right at the back of the book? There are copious chapters on muscles, bones, skin, and every conceivable bodily purpose before there is any explanation (usually disguised in medical jargon) of how human beings procreate, and the variations thereof. It is akin to having the first chapters in a car manual describe how the window winding mechanism or how the cigarette lighter works, while consigning important information such as how often the coolant, oil, and battery levels need checking, and whether it's an automatic or manual gearbox to a few pages just before the index.

However, I digress; let's get back to the 3rd year Christmas party. Sometime over the Christmas holidays I took Maggie to a film – there were four cinemas in Perth then. But in pre-TV days since the cinema was universally popular, you normally had to queue to get in; eventually getting a seat half way through the 'big picture' and coming out when you said *"this is where we came in."* It didn't really matter that the film didn't really make sense, it was a rendezvous for courting couples, there wasn't anywhere else much to meet, so knowing the end of the film before you saw the start was acceptable. When I arrived at the bus terminal that Saturday afternoon, instead of her usual school uniform she was wearing a grey two-piece fitted suit and some make up, so she looked – well,

"Wow", older than her 15 years. However, I wasn't outdone. I was wearing an American Army officer's pale olive combat jacket. This had been given to me not long before by Colonel Mike Allan, the husband of one of Mum's erstwhile charges when we had last visited them in Edinburgh some years before. Nowadays, such casual gear is universal, but in '53, when it was almost de rigueur for young men to wear a jacket, this was very 'cool.'

Continuing on with the theme of coming home from school dances, the last bus from Perth that went past our cottage left the square outside the Perth Railway Station terminus at about 11:15pm, so it was quite possible to miss it. This would have been a bit of a restriction on my social life, but Perth has two large parks just at the edge of the old city by the river Tay –the North Inch and the South Inch, and at that time at the junction where my bus route cut through the South Inch, there was a large transport café, in an old variety playhouse called the Pavilion. I'm not sure how it started, but it became the custom after seeing our respective girl friends' home from the school dances, for all the 'lads' to meet in the large ex-theatre. The 'café' featured a very long counter, a very dusty wooden floor, a thick haze of cigarette smoke, and many tables and chairs, where we sat hoovering down large bacon and egg butties and mugs of tea, while swapping stories. Finally, about one or two in the morning, when things started to feel a bit flat, I would stand by the bus stop outside the Pavilion and thumb a lift with any large truck that was going my way. This was no problem, since all the southbound traffic from Dundee, Aberdeen, Inverness and other towns in the north took this route to Edinburgh. Normally, I would be dropped off at the Aberargie junction, and walk the last mile home, knock on the door and my Mum would let me in with a *"Where have you been until this time of the night?"* I only failed to catch a truck on one occasion; but Bill Calder, my closest school friend, had a solution. His Dad was a police sergeant, and on this particular night, he was on duty in the main police station. So, we walked round there, and his Dad very kindly put me up in an empty cell!

During my 3rd year I gained another companion on the bus journey into town – Jimmy Duncan, who came from Abernethy and who was two forms above me at school. After the Christmas break each morning along with the stream of other boys and girls going up to the school, if Maggie and I did not actually say hullo to each other, it was obvious to others that we were acknowledging the other's presence by shy smiles. Now Jimmy did not have a girlfriend, in fact I don't think that he had ever had a girlfriend at this point in his life and I think that this bugged him, for he regularly made sarcastic comments of various kinds to me about mine. This I ignored. But after the start of the 4th year in the autumn of 1954, Maggie had left school, so we only passed each other briefly in the morning going our separate ways – she to work, me to school. I don't know how long we would have continued in this arrangement, but it was decided very definitely one morning after Jimmy had bet me that I couldn't just walk past her without acknowledging her. Well I finally took up his bet and discovered the truth that Hell hath no fury like a woman scorned! The next day from her expression I knew that I had blown it for good! I felt really bad about it, but she never came that way again, so I was never able to apologise for my base treatment of her.

My 4th, 5th, and 6th years at school were super. I had found my niche, I had some good mates, I was promoted to corporal, then sergeant, and finally Cadet Sergeant Major in the CCF, and I was playing rugby. Unfortunately, in contrast to many of my friends, I stopped growing when I was about 16 (Maybe that American book was right after all?), for at 5foot 7inches tall and 11 stones in weight, I wasn't heavy enough to be a forward in the scrum, but too heavy for a fly half, and slightly too short in the leg to be a really fast wing three quarter. But school rugby was great, we travelled by coach to play teams from Aberdeen, Cupar, Dundee, Dollar, and Glen Almond: this last was a private all boys school not far from Perth. I don't know what they were fed on, but I never saw any team from that school that was not head and shoulders above any team that we fielded. There was always a sense of gladiators about have combat, especially when you stepped onto the pitch on a cold slightly misty morning when the temperature was just above freezing. Apart from Col Grassie the P.E. instructor, our other main rugby coach was one of our art masters, a man called J. Paterson Barkley, who looked a bit like the film star Stewart Granger, but twice as big – Mr Barkley, and that's what he was respectfully called by all the pupils, no one ever tried to give him a nickname, was an imposing figure who had once been selected as a forward for the Scotland XV some years before.

Another memory that comes to mind of this time was my one and only experience of water skiing – on the River Tay by the North Inch. At this point the river is a good 80 yards wide, shallow by the side of the park, but deep and swift on the far side. Some enterprising man had set up a motorboat with the basic water ski equipment by a small wooden landing stage, and for a nominal sum, he would take you on a racetrack pattern up and down the river before returning. A few of my friends were keen to give it a go, so not wishing to appear to wimp out, I went along with them one summer's evening after school. We got stripped off to our 'swimmies' and waited our turn. If I remember correctly, each participant sat on the small wooden pier, holding the towrope while his feet dangled in the water. When the rope tightened, as you hit the water, you were meant to straighten your legs out, and off you went. On my first attempt, I bombed into the water in the sitting position; on the second I got into an attitude where the skis were perpendicular to the direction of travel, such that my total drag almost equalled the maximum output of the engine and we were making all of about 2 knots. On the third tow I was successful; and I was off skimming across the water for a couple of hundred yards on the shallow side. Then the boat turned back. I had a couple of anxious moments negotiating the boat's wake, and then we were going at high speed along the deep side of the river. It was at this point I knew that I had to get it right. I couldn't swim a stroke. If I came off, I'd probably be in and under before the boat got back to me! However, after bouncing across the wake at the bottom end of the circuit, I made it safely back to the departure point.

In the meantime, during my fourth year I now had another girl friend – Jean. This friendship lasted until half way through the last year – coming to an end at Christmas time. In our senior years, we had formed a dance club, (see photo - I'm in the centre) called the Moncrieffe Club, which was located near the city centre in a small hall at a six-way junction just off South Street. I was on the committee of 12 – six boys and six girls; we had an electric record player that played – height of luxury – 78s, 45s, and LPS. It was really a reprise of the school parties, but the club regularly met every Saturday evening during the autumn and winter terms. We danced the usual eight some reels, strathspeys, dashing white sergeant, strip the willow, and the lancers, but we also had music for all the modern dances by bands like Joe Loss, Ted Heath, and Edmondo Ross for South American. Each Christmas, we held an annual dance in the ballroom of a hotel. By our last year, I suppose we were all getting ready to enter the adult world, but still being somewhat gauche, I never thought about the phrase *'the dress maketh the man.'* Thus, whereas quite a number of my friends on the committee had tuxedos – or at least had hired them, and others had suits; I did not have or possess either, so I arrived in a sports jacket that wouldn't have disgraced a bookie and would have gone down a bundle at anything but an evening dance. I don't know if this precipitated what happened next, but I suddenly found that my girlfriend of the previous two and half years had attached herself to another member of the committee. We didn't meet again until 51 years later at a school reunion!

The University of Glasgow

The next great adventure was University. By the summer of '57, both Bill Calder and I had decided to apply for Glasgow University. At that time if you wanted to go to University and remain in Scotland there were only four options: St Andrews, Edinburgh, Glasgow, and Aberdeen. Many of my contemporaries opted for St. Andrews or the other branch of it just across the River Tay in

Dundee. This meant that they could attend on a daily basis and travel home every night. Edinburgh University was slightly further away, but it usually involved coming home every weekend. Aberdeen was a possibility, but seemed too remote; therefore, for Bill and I Glasgow became our second home. I had decided to read Natural Philosophy or Physics as it is more commonly termed. This course in addition included Maths, Chemistry, Zoology, and Geology; all subjects that I felt that I could get along in. Bill and I were very fortunate in finding our 'digs' – 39 Park Road, Kelvinside, a mere half mile from the main university building. Our landlady – Mrs Fulton and her husband owned a second floor flat in a four-storey tenement block. She was the sort of person that you would wish to be your granny! She was in her late sixties; her family had all grown up and, in many ways, she adopted us as a second family. Although Bill and I usually ate in the Students Union Café – pie and chips with a beer most lunch times, Mrs Fulton fed us royally for all other meals, including the weekends. All this a weekly rent of £3.50!

Other than attend lectures every morning and science labs in the afternoon two or three times a week, our time was our own. Thus, we came to discover and investigate the other great university educational facility – extracurricular activities: Beer in the Students Union beer bar, jazz clubs down by the River Clyde, the latest films, student debates and Saturday night dances in the Students Union - and by association girls, and Glasgow University Air Squadron (GUAS). By this time, I had decided that I wanted to be a pilot in the RAF. Membership of the UAS was by selection only. You had to apply to join, fill in your reasons for wishing to be considered, and then be questioned by a board consisting of the Commanding Officer, his deputy - the Chief Flying Instructor, and a member of the University Staff. I found this quite daunting, I was nervous, and I was sure that I had not come across as very confident – in fact I was very confident that I had not been confident. However, I somehow convinced them that I was suitable material, and on an evening in early December 1957 I began a 45 year-long association with the Royal Air Force.

I'm not sure how cosmopolitan each year's intake usually was, but in '57 in addition to Scots, the UAS had some English, (to demonstrate how fair-minded Scots were), a Norwegian, a Ghanaian, an Australian, and a Mauritanian. One of the new UAS intake was a slightly older – and Oh, a so much wiser student – who had done his national service in the RAF after school before going to university. This was Ron Hepburn who became a close friend and our mentor for most of our remaining time at Glasgow – and initially in the real RAF. He was very much the guy who had been there, seen it, done it, got the ticket, or knew someone who had. He kept us clear of the many pitfalls that trap the unwary, such as volunteering before you had examined the consequences of so doing!

The day that Bill and I arrived in Glasgow - Oct 4th, the Soviets saw fit to launch their first satellite – Sputnik. I can remember the Glasgow evening paper being full of the enormous possibilities and dangers that arose from fitting nuclear weapons to powerful rockets. This fear generated lots of novels and science fiction books with variations on the theme of 'What were you doing on the Day' – the 'Day' being nuclear Armageddon. In a science fiction book of that era, Pat Frank's *'Alas Babylon'*, I was quite gratified when he quoted almost the same message that I had heard on my short-wave radio a few years before. But from then until the Christmas break there was much to do. Some classes –chemistry and physics were huge; about 200 plus students seated in great arcs that rose above the lecture platform. Some teaching was superb. Professor Gillespie, who taught pure maths, was a joy to listen too, and so easy to take notes from. At the other end of the spectrum, there was a young chap who spoke rapidly, did not seem to coordinate his words with what he wrote on the blackboard, and did not appear to be too fussed if he left the class behind. Just down the road from the main University building was the chemistry laboratory. There was a secret associated with this block, which I unfortunately missed, but Bill became privy to. Just a year or two ahead of us at Glasgow was a guy who had been a real 'character' and comedian at school in Perth –Jimmy Murray. On one afternoon when the lab was not in use, Jimmy, who had somehow obtained a key, opened a door at the back of the lab, and lo and behold, the gently sloping shaft of an old coalmine could be seen disappearing into the bowels of the earth. Jimmy also took Bill and me on an educational tour of some of the more basic entertainments to be found in 'Glesga.' Somewhere along Argyle Street was a little bar, very much like the one I previously mentioned my friend Colin had found in Ulster. This was called KO Curly McGregor's Bar, and their speciality was a substance called 'Red Biddy,' a mixture of red wine and meths that was reputed to make one literally 'blind drunk'. Needless to say, although keen to know where the cutting edge of avant-garde life was in Glasgow, we declined the invitation to partake of this fluid.

Our next news of Jimmy was connected with the infamous inauguration of Rab Butler as Rector of the University in February 1958. RAB, or R(ichard) A(ustin) B(aron) Butler, to give him his official name, was a Conservative MP, who at this point was Lord Privy Seal, and would ultimately be in the short list to become prime minister. It was his Education Act of 1944 that had made a university education possible to the less privileged (such as the likes of yours truly). The treatment that he was about to receive from those who had benefitted from his legislation must have caused him to reflect on the injustices of life. The official Glasgow University hand out notes of the time stated: *"The installation ceremony in February 1958 was one of the most notorious events in the University's history, as a small group of students caused an uproar and pelted the platform with eggs, tomatoes, soot and flour and set off fire extinguishers. The University reacted by fining a number of students for their bad behaviour, and by switching the venue for installation ceremonies from the city's St Andrew's Hall to the Bute Hall."*

The official reason may have been attributed to *"a small group of students"*, but this is far from the truth. The event was an all ticket affair, but rumour had it that Jimmy Murray our old school chum had apparently obtained an official ticket and then had some extra thousand tickets produced with bogus serial numbers. Hence on the day of the ceremony, many hundreds of students turned up and it was impossible for the ushers to tell who had been officially invited and who hadn't. I felt sorry for poor Rab by the end of the ceremony, he was covered in flour and the odd egg, but he had been fortunate in that he had avoided the full-size cabbages and cauliflowers lobbed at the stage. In addition to the above, there was a four-piece trad jazz combo in the balcony consisting of trumpet, trombone, clarinet and a drummer who kept the timing using his drumsticks on the wooden lip of the balcony, while someone else had had the foresight to flight test a radio-controlled model aeroplane in the ample space between the floor and the ceiling. To my shame I can say that I enjoyed it.

Rebellion

It's not surprising that behaviour such as this erupted at this time. The 'rock and roll' revolution had started a few years earlier in the USA. By 1958, the previous safe conventional music by the likes of Doris Day, etc., and films starring older father and mother figures, had been replaced by the music of Elvis Presley (Jailhouse Rock 1955), Bill Haley (Rock around the clock 1955), and films of teenage rebellion featuring the likes of James Dean (Rebel without a Cause also 1955). In my last year at school, some of my classmates had adopted the Dean slouch with turned up collar and a cool laid-back attitude and silent contempt for authority, (i.e. teachers). At that time, I thought this pretty immature, until I fell into the same mode a few years later under the spell of Dean's mentor, Marlon Brando, whose film, 'The Wild One' (1953), depicted him as Johnny, the leader of a black-leather-jacketed motorcycle gang. This film was banned in the UK for some years, but because the Students Union had a private film club licence, I saw it in the spring of 1958. I was particularly impressed by the scene wherein an upright teenager asks Brando, *"What are you rebelling against Johnny?"* Brando gives an insolent stare, and after a slight pause says, *"Whaddaya got?"* I feature in a number of photographs about that time adopting a similar mien! My own initial teenage rebellion started in a mild way sometime in my 13th year; I told my Mum that I no longer wanted to accompany her to our local church in Abernethy. It was many a long year before I attended church regularly again.

As I have already mentioned that although physical familiarity with the opposite sex may have featured in our thoughts, and to some extent in our liaisons, the ultimate consequences of illicit intimacy were usually enough to inhibit us at senior school. The whole time that I was at the Academy I cannot recall any girl going off unexpectedly to visit her aunt for an extended holiday. But alcohol was another matter. Scotland has a well-known (macho) tradition of celebrating Hogmanay – the New Year. Certainly, by the time that I was in my 4th year, as the old year of 1954 gave way to 1955, I travelled into Perth to meet up with my friends to have a beer or three, and a sup of the hard stuff; a custom we held to at the turn of the year in '55 and '56.

In the summer of 1957 as we came to the end of our school days, something changed again. In the evening on the day before the end of term, the school held the annual prize giving in the City Hall. I didn't get any academic prizes but I shared with Sandy Kerr the honour of being presented with the Paton Cup, which was given for all round excellence. That same evening, after we had dispersed, some daring souls climbed up on to the school roof and decorated it in whitewash with various cartoons and slogans. I was not party to this prank at all. It might have been because Sandy Kerr was a friend of mine, and therefore news would have filtered back to his father the Rector; or perhaps because I had been made head prefect half way through the year, and had now become, what is today termed, "an establishment figure." At the start of my 6th year I had been elected deputy head prefect, but sometime before Christmas, I was suddenly called to the Rector's study and informed that I was now head prefect. Although by now I gave the appearance of being relaxed and at ease in any company, subconsciously I was still quite reserved; so, when Mr Kerr told me this, I panicked at the thought of being head boy and the various responsibilities that this entailed and blurted out, *"I don't want to do this Sir!"* He said firmly, *"Well you are."* And that was it. I composed myself and took over. I subsequently found out that someone had dared George, the head prefect, to emerge in the buff from one of the changing cubicles in the Gym as one of the cleaning ladies was going past –though why a cleaning lady should have been anywhere near the rugby changing rooms at such a time I never discovered. Anyway, just as I had accepted the bet to walk past my girlfriend without acknowledging her; in similar fashion George accepted his bet, but the outcome for him was much more serious, in that the cleaning lady made a complaint, and George lost his position as head prefect.

Another thing that came into vogue at about this time was the 'all teenager party' devoid of the presence of any adults and an atmosphere far removed from wholesome fun of the 'Moncrieffe Club'. The first party was not that different: in that it was in the early evening at a house in Perth where lots of us from the senior years were crammed in to a couple of rooms with music, and drinks were mainly beers and lemonade, but one or two had smuggled in the odd small flask of harder stuff. But even this was quite unusual for the time. Just a few months later, I went along to another party, this time well out of town. Anyone who had transport was invited by the host, whose parents had gone off on holiday. Again, this is something that is quite commonplace today but a rare event then. The venue was at a place about 6 miles from my house, but by then I had a motorbike so that was no problem. Today such a party would be termed 'a rave'; I managed to get in the front door – just; there were lots of people that I hadn't met before, but also some school friends; the whole house, including the upstairs, was crammed full! Watching the amateurish, but excessive drinking, wild jiving, and fairly advanced smooching, was like arriving to take part in a game for which you didn't really know the rules and hadn't really had enough practice. If anything it opened my eyes up to the somewhat sheltered attitude to life that I had and prompted me to throw over any remaining traces of previous decorum, this was the event.

Thus, by the time of 'Rab' Butler's inauguration I had left my respectable moderately restrained behaviour behind. In fact, the University Rag Day the previous month had in some respects been a trial run for the inauguration. I had dressed up in a fairly nondescript but rainproof black leather coat – the day in question was steady rain or sleet. Over my head I had a mask made out of papier-mâché and painted black, a kind of Ned Kelly helmet/Man in the Iron Mask that looked (if I had known at the time) a bit like an early manifestation of Darth Vader. We collected our raffle tins and set off to scout round the plutocratic areas of Sauchiehall Street. On the way I came across a shop window mannequin – probably discarded from the floats that had paraded an hour or so before. The mannequin was a naked lady in the sitting position with her legs crossed. The previous owner had thoughtfully painted her nipples in a bright scarlet, and had also used some black paint to give her an ample display of pubic hair. *"Bonzer Wheeze, I thought!"* hoisting the model's bottom onto my left shoulder and holding her ankles by my left hand.

To be confronted by a masked man holding what to most people of the day was an obscene object was a tremendously effective way of making them cough up with the cash quickly to escape being caught by anyone who recognized them. Finally, however, the weather got through my covering and my mask was beginning to crumble, but before that happened, I caught the Metro back to the digs – the man at the ticket office was very understanding and didn't charge for my 'companion' – who I sadly abandoned on the subway.

Glasgow University Air Squadron (GUAS)

Ron, Bill and I had passed our interviews for acceptance by the UAS, so sometime in early November '57 we went up to the Headquarters, which at that time was in Bute Gardens – a terrace of lovely old four-story houses high up on the side of one of the many drumlins upon which Glasgow is built. We met Margaret Sinclair who had been the Squadron Secretary for many years, and was to remain so for many years more. She was a lovely person who put all us new boys at ease. We also met our future flying instructors, were told when to report for lectures (Tuesday evenings at 7.30pm), and sampled the delights of the cheap subsidised alcohol. We learned that the Christmas Camp would commence almost as soon as the term ended. This was particularly beneficial for me, since at that time GUAS aircraft flew from Scone – a grass airfield just a few miles from Perth. We travelled up to Scone in an RAF coach, each given a room in a chalet, issued with our uniforms and flying kit and awaited eagerly our taking to the air. However, we were also given some time off, at which point I caught a bus to Perth, then another home, saw my Mum for an hour or two, swapped any large washing that I hadn't done, collected some clean clothes – and a few pennies spending money, and returned to Scone.

The UAS flight accommodation was in a couple of long wooden 'SECO' Huts – the same style as the code-breaking huts at Bletchley Park – by the side of one of the hangers. We had, if I remember, about 8 De Havilland Chipmunk trainers to fly. We had only just missed flying the Harvard advanced trainer, which had just been withdrawn from service. My instructor was a young Flying Officer called Terry Saunders who had previously flown Meteors in the UK and Brigands in Malaya. Everyone who went up to the camp got cleared solo by the time the new term commenced. This was to be the first of many camps that I attended at Scone and subsequently in North Wales at RAF Valley, and RAF Thorney Island near Southampton. In all I flew over 230 hours in my two and a half years with GUAS.

I have been asked what prompted me to join the RAF. Simple – I wanted to fly. It was certainly more than a passing inclination, for from my early teens, certainly by the end of my 4th year at the Academy, I had made my choice of what subjects I wished to study in the senior years – this normally meant dropping some in favour of others. Although my maths and science marks were acceptable, I did not possess the analytical mind for the advanced pure maths of some of my contemporaries, but in order to apply for pilot aircrew I had to gain my Scottish Higher Leaving Certificate in Maths and Science. The other incentive came about because the '50s were also the time when Britain still appeared to be a major player on the world stage. We still had an Empire – of sorts, and the prototypes of new British aircraft regularly made headlines. It certainly sounded exciting and glamorous; but my choice was a disappointment to my Mum who hoped that I would become a Doctor.

Daft Friday 1

Meanwhile to backtrack a bit, as the first term drew to a close it was Christmas Party time again! Daft Friday was an all-night do, held in the Students Union, but being new boys; neither Bill nor I had any idea who we could take along. However, Ron was engaged by this time, and his fiancé's younger sister knew two girls who were in similar straits. So here again we accepted what was not quite a dare or a bet, but a blind date –enter Isobel and Helen. We all got along quite well for the 12 hours of the 'do' considering the circumstances. Bill continued to see Isobel – she eventually became his wife; Helen and I parted with *"Thanks for a nice evening."*

Philosophical Interlude

The first year ran its appointed time; but at the end I had to re-sit Physics and Chemistry papers. I remember that the summer of '58 was really hot and sunny; but for most of that time I shut myself up in my little bedroom with the skylight in Broadwell Cottage. All I could see of the summer was a patch of blue sky and the odd passing cloud while trying to get to grips with my subjects. I had a very definite motivation to pass my re-sits. If I failed, I would have been immediately called up to do my national service, and my short experience in the Army camps during my time in the Combined Cadet Force cured me of taking that option by default; neither was the Royal Navy an option, I didn't fancy being cooped up in a ship and weeks at sea. Instead, having listened to Ron's stories of his National Service, the RAF seemed like a better option in which to serve 18 months – if I had to! Fortunately, I passed my re-sits. I found organic chemistry a bit of a tough nut to crack, but I was favoured because one of the questions was for me a gift. I remembered the three-associated formulae; I had time for the other questions. I passed!

During the following two years student life continued its pattern of lectures, the odd geology excursion, dissecting various animals in the zoology lab, study time in the evenings; lecture evenings in the UAS, going to Edinburgh for the Rugby Internationals, and many weekends flying at Scone airfield. My life philosophy at that time was difficult to define. I can remember trying to explain to my Mum what I had learnt about evolution in the geology and zoology classes, while she held to a Biblical explanation. I wasn't atheistic, probably more agnostic; some years previously one of my aunts had asked me what I believed. I told her that I was fatalistic; you could do whatever you had to do to avoid your fate, but if a bullet had your number on it - that was it. I was quite convinced that since my father had died at the age of 43, that would be my fate as well. This attitude was well expressed by my favourite poet at this juncture –

A. E. Housman, with his somewhat morbid lines such as:

"When last I went to Ludlow amidst the moonlight pale,
two honest lads kept step beside me, two honest lads and
hale;
Now Dick lies long in the churchyard and Ned lies long in
the jail, when next I go to Ludlow amidst the moonlight
pale."[1]

And:

"Yonder see the morning blink:
The sun is up and up must I,
To wash and dress and eat and drink
And look at things and talk and think
And work and God knows why
Oh often have I washed and dressed
And what's to show for all my pain?
Let me lie abed and rest:
Ten thousand times I've done my best
And all's to do again."[2]

Somehow, through my second and most of my third year at university; but living a busy life with the studies and flying at weekends, I was without a regular girlfriend. Oh, there had been a few girls that I had gone out with for a week or two, but that was the limit. I remember asking a girl at the usual Saturday night dance in the Union if I could see her home. She mentioned that she stayed beyond Anniesland Cross. I knew that to be somewhere up the Great Western Road, but I said that's no problem. We left the Union just after 11pm, walked about a quarter of a mile to the Great Western Road, where we caught a tram. I used to love the old Glasgow trams with their slatted wooden seats, shaking jerky motion, and a suspension that felt as if you were directly in contact with the metal rails, but by the time that we got off I had had my fill of that, for we had gone about two and a half miles –and we had also reached the tram terminus. I then walked with her about another half a mile to

[1] When I Came Last To Ludlow by: A.E. Housman (1860-1936)

[2] May by: A.E. Housman (1860-1936)

her door, she said goodnight, and that was it. I raced back to the terminus –but trams there were none. It was now past midnight, and beginning to rain heavily. On my long tramp home, I composed the following:

> *Oh, Saturday night is over,*
> *The drinking and dancing are done*
> *Only the upturned feet,*
> *Of some drunks in the street*
> *Pay mute tribute to their fun*
> *Glasgow in the rain*
> *I hate the wet streets of black stone*
> *Dark canyons at night*
> *Of dripping neon light*
> *A wilderness far from home*
> *Rain like angry yellow tracer*
> *In neon light comes slanting down*
> *To explode on the street*
> *Like shrapnel round my feet*
> *And piercing me from toe to crown*
> *Oh, Sunday morning is dawning*
> *The faithful go to pray*
> *But for lazy sods who lie abed*
> *'Tis just another day*

There were another couple of verses that I intended to insert, but I never got around to it. However, short as it is, it expresses my attitude to life at that time exactly. Some 50 years later when I returned to Glasgow for a GUAS reunion. I could hardly recognize the town! All the black buildings had been sand blasted in the 1970s, and they were now in their original red, orange and yellow sandstone, and the sun shone the whole time that we were there!

Of other diversions there were plenty. I have already mentioned there were some good trad jazz clubs down by the river, including one that was right up in an attic complete with a bucket or two on the dance floor to catch the rain drips coming through the roof. The Students Union featured bands like Humphrey Lyttleton, and Glasgow's own renowned Forrie Cairns and the Clyde Valley Stompers; down town there were visiting jazz concerts by Count Basie and Kid Ory, but romantic attachments eluded me.

Forward Planning 1

My limited forward planning was not only in relation to girls. I can remember a number of my contemporaries at school who knew from an early age what they were going do for a career in adult life, either from their own choice, or under influence of a parent. The Rector, Mr Kerr sent a brief progress report to my Mum at the end of my 3rd year, in which he said I was progressing well, but that I had not yet shown any definite inclination of what career I wished to follow. Although, as I have mentioned, my Mum had a faint hope that I would take up a medical career, my choices of subjects from the 4th form onwards meant that I would be taking a science degree, for even then I had hopes of becoming a pilot. I remember one beautiful sunny morning after our final's exams in Glasgow, when a few of us were standing on the steps outside the Reading Room by the University, knowing that we had passed our degrees, discussing our prospects. Someone mentioned that the RAF was offering 5-year engagements as officer aircrew. I thought this a splendid idea, since I at that time still had hopes of gaining an honours degree and I reckoned that I could leave for 5 years, fly in the RAF, and then return and complete my studies. As I mentioned in my introduction, on such a whim was my future decided.

Subsequently, I have often thought how different my life would have been had my father lived. Because their fathers were manual workers, virtually every boy I knew at primary school left school as soon as possible at 15 and went into a trade. Would my father have let me do otherwise? Had my mother gone to stay with the Percy family, or married again, or returned to live with her own family in Staffordshire, what profession or occupation would I have followed? Providentially, my Mum had had a chance to encounter and to some extent experience, the vastly different life style of those who were very well off and educated, and selflessly decided that's what she wanted me to have.

Daft Friday 2

Then one evening early in December of 1959, a few of us were having a coffee in the Queen Margaret Union, the ladies Student Union building at the top of Gilmore Hill just opposite the Reading Room. There must have been some special function on, for men to be in there was very unusual. As we were chatting, I looked up to see two girls, one of whom was Helen, my blind date from the first year, making their way purposefully between the crowded tables towards us. Helen, who knew how to use her well-developed embonpoint to good effect, reminded me of a figurehead on an old sailing ship cutting through the waves. The upshot of this encounter was I found myself being invited to the ladies Christmas dance. I later found out that Helen had had some sort of falling out with her regular boyfriend, and so I became Hobson's choice to partner her to the ball. Still I wasn't complaining. I reciprocated by inviting her to Daft Friday in turn. This time our relationship blossomed. After the start of the new term, we commenced to go out quite regularly. Her father died soon after that and I was there for a shoulder to cry on and to try to be of some comfort to her. At the UAS Easter Camp at Scone she was among a number of girls who came up to stay at the airfield while their boyfriends flew. She now, to all intents and purposes, was my regular 'burd' in Glaswegian parlance. I was also aware that I was in my 22nd year and had not yet, as the Bible puts it, 'known a woman.' This was very much at variance, if they were to be believed, with very many of my contemporaries. They, on the other hand, assumed that because I had a regular girlfriend, I had consummated our relationship. As we went out more and more, I found myself thinking, *"I really fancy that burd."* At that point, that was about the limit of my forward planning. However, in mitigation, such interest was not all one sided! In a further homage to Housman's style, I wrote:

> *A girl to roll in bed with, a lively lusty pet,*
> *To pass the clock ticking hours, on Sundays when it's wet*
> (This really is disgusting stuff, the stuff that gets in print,
> Of a lousy no good student, and his lousy no good bint)
> *Thus, condemnation comes, from envious fellows who,*
> *On Sundays when it's wet have nothing better to do?*

Forward Planning 2

Unfortunately for my strictly dishonourable intentions towards Helen, girls mature much sooner than their male counterparts of a similar age in the subject of settling down to marriage, probably the difference between male wanderlust and maybe something to do with the female biological clock. This unconscious (certainly on my behalf) divergence of desires was perhaps the ultimate cause of

Helen and me going our own ways. There were a number of questions that should have been resolved between us but were not. For instance, when I phoned her to make a date, I had to walk about a quarter of a mile to the nearest phone box from my digs, to hear, *"Yes, no, or maybe,"* from her; the reason for this being that from time to time the previous boyfriend entered the equation and I didn't feature. I couldn't quite figure out whether I was being used as a ploy or a foil to cause him to come back to her, or he was being used similarly to encourage me to commit myself further. In fact, some months later, during vacation one Saturday afternoon when I was walking down the High Street in Perth, I suddenly met Helen and her on again off again boyfriend passing in the opposite direction. I just had time to say *"Hi"* as I walked past, before wondering why she would have brought him up from Glasgow to Perth? I decided to play it cool and act as if it was the most natural thing in the world – so I pretended that it hadn't bothered me, and I didn't ask, and she didn't tell me!

At this stage, during the summer of '60, I was in love with her to the extent that I wanted her without commitment. However, my failure to commit myself was not just caused by male egocentric selfishness, but probably stemmed from much more personal and practical reasons. My Mum had brought me up to be independent and fairly capable, but one thing she had not taught me was the necessity to make a rapid assessment of priorities. Probably as a result of being a woman on her own, she was a bit under confident and slow to come to a final verdict. How this equated with her previous ability to travel half way round the world by herself with two small children I do not know, but she had transmitted her hesitant disposition to me. Thus, in any big decision, I would always consider all the angles before I gave it my go ahead. This in turn caused me to contemplate where any future plans with Helen would lead us after we had graduated. Helen had applied to become an airline hostess with Pan Am– a very glamorous occupation at that time; while simultaneously, I was scheduled to join the RAF in September. But before I graduated as a pilot, I knew that I would have to pass through some 18 months fairly rigorous training. If I had committed myself to marriage and I subsequently failed to qualify as a pilot, what did I have to offer her?

Helen had been up to stay for a few days in Broadwell that summer, so she had no false illusions about any inherited wealth or status that I might have. Moreover, I couldn't see her leaving an elegant life as an airhostess to accept a reprise of the role that my Mum had played when she had left the 'High Society' to marry my Dad. But the death of her father had left Helen with the possible consequences of taking care of her aging Mum and a resident aunt. Thus, for her, marriage would have provided an escape route to freedom. However, during the summer of '60 I also had my own plans. The UAS summer camp occupied two weeks of June. For another two weeks during July – August, I, and a UAS friend –Peter Cameron, had planned to take a motorbike trip to the Costa Brava. Lastly, just before I joined the RAF, I was going for a few days flying at RAF Valley in late August early September for a final polish up of four of us from GUAS who had volunteered to join the RAF. All these various activities meant that we did not really give ourselves any time to clarify what we were seeking from each other.

Ultimately, Helen and I did become lovers over a period of a few weeks, and I found myself genuinely falling in love, while she on the other hand was probably hoping that I would ask her to marry me. We parted just before I left to join the RAF. We wrote and spoke to each other regularly almost right up until the end of my basic training, when suddenly it was her aunt who answered my phone calls, to say *"Oh Helen's out!"* When we finished our basic training at RAF South Cerney, we were sent on leave for a few days before commencing the next phase of our training. Each of us travelled by rail, dressed, by order, in our brand new No1 RAF Officer's Uniform. I did not go straight home but went via Glasgow to Helen's house. She was out –teaching at a local school. Her aunt said that she would phone her and let her know that I was coming. I went to the school gate and waited, feeling very much like an usher outside a cinema in my RAF uniform, but she did not appear. I went home. I was devastated. I tried to analyse where I had gone wrong. I finally took a very selfish and unreasonable way out, and blamed her. I wrote a vicious letter to this effect. She wrote back that she did not see it this way. Impasse! I went back to Glasgow to a party with some friends and got very drunk. At one point I was sitting at an open third storey (?) window looking out on *"the wet streets of black stone"* feeling very much as if my world had come to an end. In fact, I was almost at the place when I would have welcomed it. Fortunately, someone came in at that point and asked if I was OK. I'm glad that they did, for it broke my depressed frame of mind, and

I was steered back into the party.

I re-joined my course as we started our flying training at RAF Syerston, near Newark, in Nottinghamshire and tried to put all my sorrows away; but it was a while before I could put all these events completely out of my mind. A few years later I heard that she had married quite soon after we broke up.

Hasta La Vista

As mentioned above before my working life commenced for real, I took my Ariel 350 motorbike to the Costa Brava in Spain. I can't remember how this originally came about, but having packed what gear I might need, and having said goodbye to my somewhat fearful Mum (who probably imagined it would be my last goodbye), I went down to pick up Peter Cameron from his home near Ayr. We set off next morning and we hadn't gone a mile when on a bend on a wet slippery road the back wheel locked and we found ourselves sliding on our backsides on the road. Fortunately, I was only doing about 25mph at the time. Pete was a bit concerned about this, since we had some 1200 miles to go in each direction. I was non-plussed as to the cause, but tried to sound convincingly assured, and said, *"We'll be fine."*

That night we stayed at my Aunt's near Tamworth, and set off again the following morning. Then towards evening, somewhere north of London, which we were trying to bypass, we again came off for the second time at a corner on a wet road. Only this time the cover of the cast aluminium primary chain case broke. I now knew what the problem was. The linkage on the foot brake pedal to the back wheel had seemed slack, so I had adjusted it such that it appeared to be more efficient going over the back forks than under them, but I could not however find a use for a small strong spring that had previously been fitted. This was the spring that stopped the brakes from locking on! However, by good luck I had included it in my tool bag! We put together the pieces of aluminium and patched them onto the chain case with black 'bodge' tape. It seemed to work well and no oil leaked out. That evening while we waited for the ferry from Dover, I rearranged the brake linkage in its original form and we had no further problem with the brakes or the chain case all the way to Spain and back.

We had an uneventful drive down through France – Boulogne, briefly visited Versailles (having accomplished a quick and hazardous drive through the Paris traffic), Orleans, Limoges, Toulouse, and Perpignan; each night we stopped at Youth Hostels. Then exactly midway between the French and Spanish customs posts, the rear tyre went flat. So, in the burning mid-day sun we mended the puncture by the side of the road, while fleets of expensive cars of different European nations full of wealthy European holidaymakers, looked pityingly at the poor Brits.

We finally made it to a little seaside village called San Pol de Mer. We had a great time and then came back by the same route. The whole holiday cost us £40! Admittedly we ate quite sparingly – each morning after having had a fairly frugal breakfast in the hostel, we would stop at some local shop and buy a large loaf of bread, and a kilo of tomatoes. Then as I drove, Pete would feed me chunks of bread or tomato.

28th September 1960

Not quite a day that - to quote Roosevelt - *"would live in infamy"*, but a notable one for me nevertheless, for on that day, having travelled from Perth, I got off the train at the quiet little railway station of Kemble in Gloucestershire to find on the platform a company of other young men who seemed to be milling around looking a bit lost, acknowledging each other with a curt nod of the head. We were suddenly addressed by a very smart RAF SNCO, who said, *"Gentlemen, I am Sergeant Lister, I will be in charge of you during your time here at RAF South Cerney. Follow me,"* in a voice that we immediately recognised as one that was used to giving commands. So off we went like a flock of sheep being herded, 'baaa, baaa, baaa.' My RAF career had commenced.

Act Two

Basic Training

The two months of basic training at RAF South Cerney in Gloucester passed quickly. Well, as quickly as any basic training can do that is entirely comprised of drill, bull, inspections, service writing, traditions of the RAF, and how to *really be* an RAF Officer, (Photo below of Ron Hepburn 'bulling-up' his footwear); interspersed by a survival camp in the Welsh monsoon season, (Photo below of Graham Lecky and Bob Clayton in the mud); and liberally endowed with lots of other essential niff naff and trivia. I can remember only two minor amusing incidents while we were there. There was a real eager beaver Squadron Leader who was only a few years older than us, whose task it was to enforce correct decorum and manners at all times. Up to this point, this officer had only had to deal with recruits straight out of school, but hadn't encountered the more questioning ways of young men from university, whose attitude was more, *"We don't take orders, but we will consider suggestions."*

On one occasion he came into the ante-room in the Officers Mess to find the late Angus Clydesdale, or to give him his full title, Flying Officer, The Marquis of Douglas and Clydesdale reading the Times. This would have been quite in order, but Angus was sitting on the large table that usually displayed all the daily newspapers, idly swinging his feet and whistling while he did so. Enter eager beaver, *"Flying Officer Clydesdale, do you sit on your table at home while you read the newspapers?"* Angus looking up, completely un-phased, *"Invariably Sir,"* and then recommenced to peruse the paper. Exit eager beaver baffled.

The second bon mot also concerns Angus. When we had been brain washed sufficiently by our mentors at South Cerney not to let the side down, we were permitted to visit the nearest town – Cirencester, a beautiful place, but we had been given strict instructions that the correct walking out gear for officers –i.e. suits or sports jacket and flannels – was to be worn at all times. This walking out gear was to include a hat. We dutifully tramped off round to a gentleman's outfitter to find some suitable headgear. As far as I remember, no one bought a Homburg or a bowler hat; most of us went for a variation on something that Dick Tracy or Humphrey Bogart would not have been too embarrassed to be seen in. Leaving the shop wearing our newly acquired hats, and feeling very conspicuous, we met Angus and relaxed. He must have felt that as ex-member of Eton and Oxford, and a Lord of the realm to boot, it was a bit much for some minion to decree exactly how a real gentleman should be attired. He was wearing a superb tweed jacket, plus fours, woollen stockings and brogues, looking like the archetypal laird, but the whole effect was somewhat marred by his choice of hat – a cyclist's baseball cap, which featured a large amount of green plastic! Noting our amazed expressions, he said, *"We were told to get a hat, so I got one."* Unfortunately, his triumph over officialdom was short lived. A few minutes later, he literally bumped into Wing Commander Manning, who was in overall command of all student officers. In a brief one-way conversation, the Wing Commander refreshed Angus as to the correct interpretation of the order. But by the end of November our initiation rite was over and we were let loose for a few days leave before reporting to RAF Syerston, near Newark, Nottinghamshire, to commence our flying training on the Jet Provost 3.

RAF Syerston

My memories of No 2 Flying Training School (No 2 FTS) at Syerston in Nottinghamshire are also quite brief. The Jet Provost Mk 3 although a lot faster than the Chipmunk, was a relatively easy aircraft to fly. We were fortunate; the course progressed as planned with no hold ups due to the weather. I had no problem with the flying, and got an above average assessment at the end of the course. We visited Nottingham a few times, including a fascinating old pub – The Trip to Jerusalem – reputed to have been frequented by soldiers returning from the Crusades. The Christmas break was only for 4 days so returning to Scotland by train was impractical for those Scots on the course (the train journey effectively took a whole day each way), therefore we stayed for the Christmas Party and I won first prize in the raffle – a hamper of wine, food, and chocolate!

Other than flying instruction we were also given further survival training. The Officer who led us in this was a very much larger than life character; a Squadron Leader of mature years who rejoiced in the name of 'Black Tom'. His CV included interesting facts such as having force-landed a Canberra on a desert island during the British Atomic Tests a few years before, and he also kept two pet pigeons in a large, glass-fronted bookcase in his room in the mess. He was also somewhat of an alcoholic – but amusing with it. At the annual Cocktail Party, when the Station Commander invited the local 'big wigs' to the Officers Mess to smooth over any ruffled feathers caused by aircraft noise, or misdemeanours by young aircrew, Black Tom had occasion to meet a local Bishop, who was dressed in his traditional seventeenth century black coat, tight trousers and gaiters. Black Tom is reputed to have greeted the bishop with *"It's not fancy dress you know, Bish."* It may have been at the same party, or another at a later date, but the victim was certainly another bishop who was also bald, as was our hero, who when sighting the bishop's bald head, clapped his hand on it and declared, *"Snap!"* Such characters were not so rare in those days, but unfortunately in the much smaller RAF of today, more concerned with always presenting a positive public image and the prospects of promotion, such behaviour normally results in a rapid move into oblivion.

Just below the scarp, called the Trent Hills, on which RAF Syerston is situated, runs the River Trent. Black Tom, not long before the end of the course, informed us that on our next combat survival lesson, we were going to carry out a practical exercise, and therefore to be sure to bring some money. We imagined that we were to be dropped off at some distant point with the aim of making it back to the camp using only the money that we had, without being caught by some patrolling soldiers. But a few days later when he had gathered us together for combat survival training, he gave us two thin planks of wood and a used parachute to bring along, and declared that we were going to the far bank of the River Trent. We failed to see how this could be accomplished given the materials that he had issued us with and the fact that the Trent was a somewhat fairly fast flowing wide river. However, after we had crossed the airfield boundary and as we descended to the riverbank there was a field in which the hay had been cut and left to dry. Black Tom made us open out the parachute flat on the ground and told us the make a large doughnut of hay round the inside of the chute. He then got us to tie each of the rigging lines on the rim of the chute to those in the centre of the chute, thus trapping the hay. We now had what appeared to be a primitive form of 'bouncy castle' shaped like a doughnut, and the whole affair was finished off by tying a long parachute cord to either side of the chute. *"This will stay afloat for some time. So, two of you launch it and climb aboard, and use these two pieces of wood as paddles. Then when you reach the other side of the river, make sure you keep hold of one cord while we tow the chute back here."* There wasn't exactly a rush to be the first to test this rather flimsy contraption, but eventually two who reckoned that they were good swimmers set off, and quite soon they had paddled to the far bank. We towed the chute back. The hay was still dry, and being full of air pockets, only a little bit of water had entered into our doughnut. There was now a rush to be next across! If I remember, there were about two-dozens of us – including some Iraqi trainee pilots; by the time that we had all crossed the Trent, the 'life raft' was becoming distinctly soggy, but it still bore the weight of two occupants, albeit with wet feet. I was impressed with this use of a chute; and despite having later qualified as a Combat Survival and Rescue Officer and done a number of survival course in various parts of the world, I have never seen this trick repeated or demonstrated by anyone else. A further short diversion occurred on the far bank. One of the Iraqi students lost his watch just as he clambered ashore. Knowing the very dubious quality of the water of the Trent downstream of Nottingham, we assumed it had gone for good, but this lad, completely undaunted, stripped off, and dived under until he found it! Now that we were across the river it became obvious why our leader had told us to bring some money. Not far from our landing site on the far bank, there was an old Inn, where we partook of refreshment and treated our mentor until the RAF coach came to collect us.

RAF Syerston was bounded by the River Trent on one side and the A46, the Fosse Way on the other; the airfield and the Student Officers Mess being between the river and the A46, while the married quarters and the Officers Mess for the permanent staff were on the eastern side over the A46. There was a bar in the Students Mess that kept fairly tight (not a good word to use here), i.e., strict hours. One evening, one of our instructors, a young South African Flying Officer, called Dick the Yarp, who was the orderly officer for the day, came to the mess bar to check it out before he retired for the night. I don't know how it came about, but I finished up wearing his No. 1 Uniform jacket while he had on my civilian jacket. I may have been trying out my impression of 'Dougie Bader' doing his stiff legged walk routine just as the Station Commander, marched in. We all stopped and stood to attention. I was right in front of him. He glared at me, and barked, *"What's your name?"* Just behind me Ron Hepburn murmured sotto voce, *"Mud, Sir,"* just loud enough for a few of us to hear, including me. I laughed. This did not impress the Groupie, who put me on restrictions for three days. This was a form of punishment, in which the culprit had to wear his best No.1 Uniform all day, and report four times a day to whichever senior officer he could find to sign his restrictions chit. The next day, I did just that. The senior officer politely inquired why I was on restrictions, so I told him. He found this amusing, as did the other senior officers. It was not too long before my restrictions were cancelled, so I presume that the Groupie also discovered that his penalty had rebounded against him.

At Whitsun we were again given four days off and once again because the journey time to Scotland and back, two of us, both of us Scots, Don Dale and I, decided to remain in the mess. Fairly late on Friday evening, after a quiet day —I had no transport at that time; I went to try to find Donald who had spent the day doing some major repairs to an old soft top Riley sports car that he had driven down from Scotland when he joined the RAF. I finally managed to track him down at the car club, helped him finish off what he was doing just as it was getting dark; we cleaned up, and walked across the A46 as the station had gone into stand down mode and we had to eat and drink in the Main Mess. By now it was getting on for quarter to ten, and the bar was very quiet, nearly everyone who could had gone off on leave. I hesitate to use a now somewhat hackneyed excuse, but I can't remember what prompted us to ignore the usual, *"Would you like a beer,"* and instead set off on a voyage of discovery along the top shelf of the bar, the habitat of weirdly shaped bottles holding strange, outlandish liquors, the type of thing that is usually only found in cocktails. We commenced our tasting expedition, initially with discernment and aplomb, like an advanced wine tasting analysis, but at some point, before we reached the end of the top shelf, if we had been asked, we would have been happy to demonstrate our ability to walk like flies on the ceiling. I have never again tried so many exotic and different forms of alcohol in my life.

By closing time, just over an hour later at 11pm, we were well and truly beyond knowing or caring. We put on our overcoats – I remember that, got to the Fosse Way, looked in either direction, to see headlights blazing and cars whistling by, but we did not seem to be able to assess how far away the cars were in order to make it safely across the road. Finally, we broke cover and got across the road in the manner of a drunken game of chicken. It didn't seem to be a good idea to go back to our rooms the way our heads were spinning, so we set off on a walk round the airfield perimeter track – a good five miles at least. Neither can I remember much about this, except, having come to an intersection of the tarmac nor unsure of the way to proceed, Donald confirmed our position by operating his cigarette lighter. In its light we could read 25 written in large white numbers. *"We're at the end of the main runway,"* said Donald, *"We can cut across some fields rather than having to go all the way back through the technical site."* This we did, or at least I assume we did, for when I awoke sometime the next day, I found that my shoes and the bottom of my coat were covered in heavy brown mud; additionally, my coat was torn and I had also lost a part of the sole off one shoe.

It was late in the day before I felt well enough to appear in the Mess for a cup of tea and a slice of toast. However, there was one interesting effect that occurred then – the ability to foretell the exact time! Of this I am sure. During the day, each time that I awoke, I'd wonder, *"What time is it? I suppose it's about....,"* (whatever time

I'd imagined). I'd look at my wristwatch, and sure enough the time was just about what I'd thought. Over the next few hours, and after some more remarkable coincidences like this, while becoming quite sober, I could say, *"It's 14 minutes to 2, and the second hand is just going past 10 seconds past position"* – and it was! This effect stayed with me for some time. Many years later, at the start of a resistance to interrogation exercise that lasted all night, we 'prisoners of war' were blindfolded and had our watches removed. We went through all kinds of hardships and disorientation techniques, either in pitch darkness or under blazing lights to a background of 'white noise' for hours, before we were individually debriefed by one of the staff. In my case, just before the instructor handed me my watch back, in order to assess how well I had coped with this treatment, he asked me what time I thought it was. I said, *"It's twenty minutes to five in the morning."* He was impressed, because that is what the time was. At the end of the training at Syerston, our original course went its separate ways; some to fly transport aircraft with a view to take up a career in civilian aviation, and some to fly the Vampire, with the possibility of getting onto the fast jets such as the Hunter, Javelin, and Lightning.

RAF Oakington

Before the course commenced in July 1961 at No 5 FTS at RAF Oakington near Cambridge, I managed to take the train home for a few days leave, and go to see my Mum, who was coming up to retirement age. I still had my Ariel 350 motorbike stored in the garden shed. It would be invaluable when I started the new course because I would be close enough to Cambridge to use it, so I gave the bike a quick check over, re-taxed it – for some incredibly small fee, and drove off at the end of my leave for Cambridge. The motorbike did not prove to be such a great blessing, since all our expeditions to town were usually taken by car in the company of three or four other students. When we had started at RAF South Cerney, only four or so of us out of twenty owned a car, but by a year later I was one of the few who didn't. However, help was at hand. One of the guys on the course, Hilton Moses, a good friend of mine, took his life in his hands, and taught me to drive his Vauxhall. Having passed the test, we went looking for a suitable vehicle. Here again Hilton literally steered me clear of the traps and snares that I might have fallen into. There was at that time on the road into

Cambridge a large second-hand car yard run by a chap who was the archetypal Flash Harry spiv, *"Here's a nice little runner, guv', yours for a fiver!"* Yes, he did sell cars for some amazingly low prices, but as Hilton pointed out, as we toured his yard, he had good reason to. After looking at one particular machine and liking it, Hilton took me round to the rear and got me to look underneath at the rear suspension, which had been repaired by the insertion of a stout piece of table leg! (No MOTs in those days!). The other attraction was provided by a large selection of American cars.

Although Lease Lend had ended some 17 years before, the personnel at the USAF bases in East Anglia were now passing on their used automobiles; hence I drooled over some of the chromium plated, tail finned behemoths that Flash Harry had on offer. Hilton finally persuaded me to start my motoring with a modest Ford Anglia 100E. Unfortunately, it had a three-speed gearbox, in which the gear ratio was such that the engine had to be raced to change up from second to top to give any acceleration at all to a V max of about 50mph. Its other drawback was the pneumatic windscreen wiper system, for when overtaking, or attempting to overtake in wet weather, with the accelerator flat on the floor, the wipers slowly swept the windscreen about once every 5 seconds and forward visibility was almost nil. The only recourse was to take your foot off the pedal, at which point the wipers thrashed backwards and forwards sufficiently to give enough vision to continue to overtake! However, despite this disadvantage by November 1961 I now had wheels.

In the summer Cambridge was a wonderful place to be, although most of the student population had left town, there were still quite a number of foreign visitors. I went out with a very blonde Finnish girl for a few weeks, who was reading PPE; but since much of her conversational gambits included stuff such as, *"What do you think the chances of success for the rightist faction in the power struggle of the Central Committee of Upper Slovakia?"* and *"Have you read Keynes 'The General Theory of Employment, Interest and Money?'* To which I could only respond, *"Who?"* and *"No, I haven't",* our witty repartee was somewhat limited. And once the course started, I had enough studying and reading to do to get through the course without trying to assimilate the contents of Hansard, The Economist, The Spectator, and The Financial Times in order to keep her attention so we drifted apart. I found that the Vampire (see page 74) proved fun to fly, although it could do some weird gyrations when put into a spin. However, we were again fortunate with the weather. My logbook shows that we again progressed steadily through the flying programme.

Bubbles

By late autumn as the winter chill of the Fen Country started to make itself felt, any social activity was becoming confined to indoor functions. Thus, it came about, that one weekend when the Mess seemed a bit dull, some of us went into Cambridge to 'The Dorothy', a large entertainments centre that held different styles of dances on three separate floors: rock and roll, jazz, and modern. We opted for the modern dancing. It was as crowded and very similar to the school Christmas parties of yore, for, despite the advent of rock and roll, it continued with the tradition of the girls being ranged down one side of the floor and boys down the other. I had a few dances, before I spotted a beautiful little brunette in a cream frock. I asked her to dance, and we took off round the floor. Anglers will tell you that some fish will ignore certain bait, but will be unable to resist other lures. We chatted a few minutes, before she said to me *"What do you do?"* I replied, "What do you think I do?" She tilted her head slightly while looking at me coquettishly, half closing her eyes as if in thought, and said, "I think that you're a pilot." As I said some fish will find certain bait impossible to resist. Being very flattered, I bit hard on the bait, as I thought, 'What a discerning young lady.'

Sometime later, when Babs, or to give her, her nickname 'Bubbles', and I had been going out for some months, I learned that just before I had asked her to dance, I had been shooting a line about being a trainee pilot to one of the other girls that I had danced with, who just happened to be a friend of hers who had passed on the news. But by then I was truly hooked! Again, life appears to be largely made up of the Circumstances we encounter and the Choices we make *"What if I hadn't gone there that evening, what if she hadn't been there?*

By the time that we were posted to RAF Oakington, I had been in the RAF for almost a year without official leave, so not long after I got my car, we were given two weeks off. I decided to go back to Scotland again and bring back some more of my gear so make my room in the Mess appear a bit homelier. I still hadn't quite come to terms with my previous break up with Helen, which didn't improve when I reached Scotland. Consequently, my Mum did not have the pleasure of my company for many evenings while I was at home. Over a few evenings I decided to drive into Perth, and see if I could find any of my old school friends. I visited some old familiar haunts where my classmates used to meet after school, but just like swallows in autumn, they had all gone. I went to the Salutation

Hotel, which generally had a packed dance floor, but the only person that I knew was the girl who I had picked all those years ago to be my 'wife' when we were at Abernethy Christmas Party. We had a dance for old times' sake, and she commented on how English I sounded. This I found strange as all my contemporaries in the RAF said that my rapid Scots tongue was very difficult to understand. On another evening, there was a dance at the City Hall where we had had our School Annual Prize giving, but Perth was now in the grip of rock and roll and the hall was another dance hall full of Teddy Boys and their girls. Then on a third evening in a café cum bar with a jukebox I saw some young people dancing, and at the bar there was a young woman standing with her back to me. I was convinced that it was my former girlfriend from Glasgow. As I approached, the girl sensed my attention, turned around. I apologised for staring at her, and said that I thought that she was someone else. She must have thought it a corny line, but we got chatting and then started dancing. At some point my hand on her waist made contact with her flesh of her waist between her skirt and her sweater, but instead of drawing away she drew closer. And just as a jockey knows that his new mount has accepted him by her response to his placing his hand on her flank, I knew that this filly was going to let me gallop her round the paddock. I never found out her name, and she didn't ask me mine. She was about the same age as I was, she wasn't married or at least she wasn't wearing a ring, she had a nice flat but she seemed too nice and too young to be a lady of the night. Maybe she was just someone who had also lost out. Subsequently, when I thought about this encounter on my way home: this girl's flat was well appointed, a family home with a double bed, I felt my blood run cold! I suddenly realised that she could well have been someone's wife, and that I could have been discovered flagrante delicto. I shivered as I imagined the local newspaper headlines, *"RAF Officer- Ex Head Boy beaten up by errant wife's husband,"* which event would probably have not only resulted in the premature termination of my RAF service, but would have brought shame on all my family and the school. This close call together with my previous alcoholic haze at Syerston now became clear warnings that I had to apply much more caution to my adult amusements if I intended to survive life in general and my chosen path in particular.

I returned to Oakington with as much gear as I could cram in the car. I now had only some four months before I finished my training, and I proudly looked forward to wearing my RAF pilot's wings. Perhaps it was such thoughts as these that led me into the next great event in my life! Some two months later, I can remember one afternoon, a weekend I think it was, when I was in my room in the Officers Mess, prior to meeting Babs later that day, I was musing about our relationship. By this time, we had been going out for about 3 months; I was in my 24th year, she was just about to turn 18. I thought to myself, *'Pick someone your own age, you're a baby snatcher.'* But the upside of our relationship was, that compared to my previous experiences she was a poppet. She was just at the age where beauty and innocence are at their maximum, and incredibly sweet and trusting, which was very appealing and made me want to protect her and take care of her. Despite my previous limited experience as related above, in essence I was her male counterpart; I tended to trust and believe in those that I befriended. But was six years age difference between us too much? For instance, she was still very much the teenager with her main interests focussed on pop and rock and roll bands. My musical tastes had by now passed these modes by and were now focussed on trad and modern jazz. We went along to a pop musical film before I took her to one film that I really wanted to see while it was on in Cambridge – Haroun Tazief's 'Volcano'. This was a film exclusively dedicated to the geology, structure, location, and eruptions of volcanoes worldwide, very interesting and great photography, but not what might be termed, the average film for young lovers? I hoped that it wouldn't turn her off me, but she loved it and, as she told me later, thought, *'This guy is different!'* Hooray!

The Future is V-Shaped

Towards the end of our course, we were asked to submit our choices to the flight commander of what aircraft we wanted to fly. Naturally we all saw ourselves as fighter pilots –there were still quite a number of Hunter, Lightning, and even Javelin all weather fighter squadrons; but in 1957 the Defence Minister, Duncan-Sandy's White Paper had mistakenly forecast the demise of fighters for an all missile regime. And so even before we graduated our future had already been chosen for us and we were informed that all of us – apart from our top student Jerry Lee who was posted to Hunters, and Angus Clydesdale, who, as rumour would have it, just happened to be out playing golf with some very senior politician and had his posting changed to Canberras in Singapore –were destined for the V Force Vulcans, Victors, or Valiants. However, as a sop, we were told that we could have the V Bomber of our choice! I opted for the Handley Page Victor. At that time, the Victor Operational Conversion Unit (OCU) was located at Gaydon, not too far from Stratford upon Avon, and a mere 75 miles from Cambridge.

By the time that I left to convert to the Victor, Babs' Mum and Dad had moved back to the Cambridge area. Her Dad had been a pilot during the War and had retired as a Squadron Leader from RAF Oakington. They had somehow found it difficult to settle for any length of time after he had retired from the RAF. The normal RAF posting was for three years, and this was about the time that they stayed in one place before moving again, usually between Cambridge where he had retired, and Cumberland, where their roots were. After their latest move they had taken over a pub, called the Blue Lion, in the village of Hardwick some 5 miles west of Cambridge. Towards the end of our time at Oakington the Blue Lion became a favourite port of call for our course.

RAF Gaydon – Victor Operational Conversion Unit (OCU)

RAF Gaydon in Warwickshire had been a bomber base, which had been refurbished by the Labour Government during the cash strapped days after the War. This was pretty obvious. It had the overall impression of a large cut-price supermarket. Everything was functional, but definitely no frills. The accommodation was in the ubiquitous wooden SECO Huts. Living in such huts was no hardship, since they could be very snug, but in this case the water from the limestone upon which the airfield had been built had furred up and reacted with the plumbing badly, so the radiators were not only just warmish, but the water out of the taps looked like strong tea. Although it was only 75 miles between Gaydon and Cambridge, the main road network in the Midlands area was not at that time conducive to fast travel in east west directions, thus any journey between RAF Gaydon and Cambridge was along lesser indirect roads interspersed by many towns such as Daventry, Northampton, Wellingborough, St Neots, together with numerous villages. During one weekend my car broke down in Cambridge, but I had no trouble obtaining a lift back to base. The following weekend was different. No one else on the course was heading in that direction; there were definitely no train connections other than making a journey that took many hours and covered at least three times that distance, involving not a few changes. I decided that I would be quicker hitch hiking. At that time, it was quite common to see servicemen in uniform standing at the side of the road thumbing a lift. Moreover, they didn't have to wait long to be picked up. I set off just after lunch on Friday afternoon – in civvies; RAF Officers *did not* hitchhike, and certainly not in uniform. There were lifts a plenty, but most went only a few miles in my direction, before I was dropped off again. At one point I stood on the step behind the driver of a tractor; and I also walked through much of Daventry and Northampton. By the time that I arrived at the Blue Lion, it was just about closing time.

Of the conversion course I can remember but a little. There were a lot of systems on the Victor, and as a co-pilot I had to have at least a nodding acquaintance with them, but the co-pilot's main task was fuel management. The Victor had a fair number of fuel tanks scattered round the wings and the fuselage. Between the first and second pilots, recessed into the instrument panel, was a lap top sized tray covered in switches and magnetic dolls eyes associated with the fuel system. In order to maintain the aircraft in trim, by using the fuel in the correct sequence, the co-pilot monitored which pumps were on or off and how much fuel remained. I practised this drill in the simulator, which was very basic compared to the electronic state of the art ones of today, but very advanced for 1962. I was also given three sorties in the air consisting mainly of circuits and instrument approaches, and on the strength of that brief airborne acquaintance with the aircraft, I was signed up as a qualified co-pilot.

RAF Cottesmore – No XV Squadron

RAF Cottesmore, which was to be my home for almost the next three years, is situated in England's smallest county – Rutland. At that time there were two Victor squadrons at Cottesmore, and a further one just down the road at RAF Wittering, all armed with nukes. In addition, there was also a 'Thor' Intermediate Range Ballistic Missile site at RAF North Luffenham and a 'Bloodhound' Surface to Air Missile site at RAF Woolfox Lodge on the A1. Considering its small size and rural population, man for man, Rutland was one of the most heavily armed areas in the world. After a few beers, disconsolate souls would talk of Rutland seceding from the UK and becoming independent – who could stop us?

On the day that I arrived there, the CO Wing Commander Matthews and his crew had all bailed out and ejected when their aircraft had a four-engine flame out about five miles out on the final approach. This was not encouraging as I was scheduled to join his crew. Instead, I joined Jim Bowman's crew with John Williamson the navigator plotter, Steve Stevenson the navigator radar operator, and Dick Gommo, the air electronics officer (AEO).

There was a short period of 'running in', each crew member becoming proficient in carrying out specific exercises, after which we were given operational status. Being crewed up was a bit like being married. You all went everywhere together – we did target study together, alert crew duty together, (See photo, out at the aircraft in the winter of 1962), planning for each sortie together, ate together, and always as far as possible, flew together. In such circumstances we all got to know one another very well, and gain confidence in each other's abilities and become acquainted with mannerisms and quirks! Presumably, because my Scots nature could be a bit curt and terse, I was christened 'Cactus Jack'! However, on Fridays, this crew togetherness was carried to one further stage. Like all operational RAF stations, we had a Happy Hour in the Mess Bar –half price beer just after 5pm. It was essential to be there, because quite often, but not always, at some point the Station Commander would announce in a loud voice from the bar *"Produce your crew or buy a beer."* At which point each captain had to have his co-pilot, nav plotter, nav radar, and AEO line up behind him, as the Station Commander marched past each crew. The first crew that failed to tally five officers would then be invited to buy a beer for everyone else in the bar. Now, as I have said, since there were two Victor squadrons – each with ten crews, and each crew with five men, and in addition, engineers, ATC, and admin personnel – even at half price, the cost of beer could come to a tidy sum on each remaining crew member's bar book. On the following Monday morning, the absentee would then be asked to pay his share to the other four of the crew. This custom had repercussions for me. Nearly every weekend I went down to see Babs. The journey from Cottesmore to Cambridge was no problem, 55 miles, mainly down the A1, which even then was mostly dual carriageway interspersed with roundabouts. But I couldn't leave Cottesmore until the Groupie had found an under-strength crew – even if one of the crew had just left the bar briefly to go to the gents. Thus, by the time that I could leave I was definitely well over any legal limit. However, there was little traffic and I never came to grief.

Those with a statistical frame of mind have probably noted that this is yet one more of a series of stories that involve alcohol. I hasten to add that I was not nor did I become an alcoholic; and although I liked beer, I never had the ability to pour pints of beer straight down as some did. Secondly, after a bad experience with whisky during a visit back to Glasgow to see my old flat mate Bill Calder, and my previous experience at Syerston, (see above); I pretty much stayed off spirits as well.

There was an unwritten rule in the Officers Mess in the interests of camaraderie, unit morale, and cooperation that one never spoke about ladies, politics, or religion – different opinions on which could cause schisms. Therefore, alcohol was just a fact of life in the armed services then and now, and to be part of your team, the bar was where you went to let off steam about the sortie, the weather, (the forecasters), Air Traffic Control, the engineers, aircraft malfunctions, *and* line shoot. Because, after some hours being tightly strapped to an ejection seat in a claustrophobic, and at times highly tense atmosphere that could vary with the nature of the task, the weather, the serviceability of the aircraft, and the ability of the individual or the combined ability of the crew to accomplish the aim, almost inevitably carried out under the further pressure of a time factor that had to be adhered to exactly, then something had to give, and it was usually accomplished by sloshing down beer and getting involved in various mess games, especially on dining in nights, when the Mess furniture got some hard use, and one's mess kit – expensive even in those days – usually required some patching up at the end of the evening. As has been remarked, 'If aircrew do this it's called high spirits; when teenagers do it, it's called hooliganism!'

The Working Day

Our normal working day started about 7am, when the batman came into your bedroom with a cup of tea, *"Morning Sir"*, a concise weather report, and any major world-shaking developments, such as England having beaten the Aussies at cricket. This was followed by breakfast –cereal, poached egg on toast, coffee, toast and marmalade, with a quick scan of the daily papers; followed by a walk up to the Ops Block, which was about ¼ mile away. There I met the other crew members –all married men who stayed in the married quarters – discover what the task was, check the met brief for weather, winds, air temperatures and pressure, the length of the runway in use, the fuel load, weapon load, and hence the aircraft all up weight, then calculate the take-off criteria, which depended on these factors. Finally, find out from the skipper which bits of the flight he would (or might) hand over control to me. Then, when the rear crew members had finished their navigational and electronic plots, we trooped off to the aircrew feeder, for a mega saturated fat super cholesterol all-English breakfast of bacon, sausages, black pudding, beans, mushrooms, fried bread, fried tomatoes, with slices of bread and butter and a large cup of tea. Bear in mind that this was probably only about two to three hours after breakfast, but everywhere there were Flight Safety Posters with the slogan 'A GOOD FLIGHT BEGINS WITH A GOOD MEAL,' so we tried to be accommodating. Then, just in case one felt peckish during the four, five, or occasionally six-hour flight, we were issued with a can of a well-known brand of soup and a pack of sandwiches. During the flight, we ate the sandwiches, but avoided liquid, since the pee tube was down in the forward nose compartment, and this meant making the ejection seat safe, un-strapping, clambering down, performing, then reversing the procedure. As a consequence, we usually stored the cans of soup in our flying clothing lockers. By the time that Babs and I got married; I was able to bring her just about enough soup to stock a super market shelf. Then, after landing, and debriefing, we returned to the aircrew feeder and partook of another hearty post-flight meal. After this, if there were no further duties, sometimes it was possible to get back to the Mess in time for a cup of tea and toast, then wash off the sweat of the day in a bath, stop for a beer, have dinner, then return to the bar for a few more beers. No wonder Bomber Command was nicknamed 'Eating Command.' Strange to relate, I did not put on weight during my time on XV Squadron.

Unfortunately, in some respects, much of the flying was the least satisfying part of it. Although we quite often clocked up 30 to 40 hours flying per month, at 4 - 5 hours per sortie this amounted to only eight or ten trips. At other times the monthly total was much less –one sortie! Secondly, nearly all the sorties were of a similar type – a simulated war mission. This comprised take-off, climb to high level, a long navigational stage, with a final run in for a simulated weapon release against a ground target in which the results were calculated by ground radar in terms of timing and delivery accuracy; followed by a return to base, an instrument approach or two, and perhaps one or two circuits and roller landings. Since we had just finished over a year of training in which we had done lots of aerobatics, low level, and formation, such flying seemed like civil airlines without the comforts. Most of us second pilots (except those who had joined the RAF for a career and hoped to make air staff rank) were quite vociferous in our complaints, especially to any senior officers that we happened to corner in the bar after a dining night and a few beers, when I have seen a flying officer firmly prodding an Air Marshall in the chest on this topic. The great man took it in good humour and said that, *"It was government policy for the foreseeable future to focus on the V Forces, but the day would come when we would be let loose again to practice aerobatics, low level and formation flying."* But then he would say that wouldn't he? Very convincing, but was probably not true. But that's what senior officers get paid for!

QRA

Our other major task was the actual maintenance of a proportion of our strength to be always on 15 minutes readiness. All V Bomber squadrons maintained a QRA (Quick Reaction Alert) aircraft. During the normally 24hour duty, each QRA crew slept in separate rooms either side of a corridor at one end of an enormous SECO hut, (about 100 yards long dating from WW2), near the Mess – XV Squadron *always* took the rooms to the left and No.10 Squadron *always* took the rooms to the right of the door. Subconsciously, this reaction was programmed into my mind, so that even if half asleep, after a call out, I would exit my room and turn right. Some months later when 10 Squadron had disbanded, our crew for some reason occupied the right-hand bedrooms; thus, it was, when the alarm sounded, while still half asleep, I turned the wrong way and ran down about 50 yards of corridor before I realised that I should have gone the other way. When an alert was called, as it often was, in the middle of the night by the sounding off of a very loud klaxon horn, we would leap out of bed throw on our flying kit, pile into the QRA car –a Vauxhall Vanguard with a column gear change as positive as a ladle in a pot of porridge, finally find a gear, and roar off to the aircraft, where the crew chief had already started up the ground power unit. We climbed aboard strapped in, did the checks, while listening to the voice broadcast from HQBC (Head Quarters Bomber Command) at High Wycombe, *"This is the Bomber Controller, Exercise Edom, Alert State 05."* With our engines now running we could be airborne in 5 minutes. Finally, we would hear *"This is the Bomber Controller, Exercise Edom terminated. Revert to 15 minutes,"* and we would all return to our beds and try to go back to sleep. Many years later, I still had a conditioned response and would over-react when I heard a klaxon horn.

During the working week the QRA crew could wear flying kit and eat in the aircrew feeder, (aka 'The Greasy Spoon') in the Operations Centre, but which, unlike the Windmill Theatre, closed at weekends, stand-downs over Christmas, Easter, Whitsun, and on August Bank Holidays. Now the Station Commander Group Captain Bob Weighill was a really nice chap, but being an officer of the old school, he insisted on correct dress and etiquette from the officers under his command at *all* times, so no aircrew officer could appear in the Mess dressed in flying overalls. Hence, the QRA Crew had to wear No1 Uniform to appear in the Mess at meal times when the aircrew feeder was closed down. Moreover, if the alarm sounded in the Mess it was a gentile and discreet ringing of a bell –no need to disturb the other occupants even though you might be off to initiate a thermo-nuclear war by unloading a large H Bomb on someone –and, if for instance you were having a meal, then one was to stand up, muttering *"Excuse me, Excuse me"* to those to the left and right of you at the dining table, fold your napkin, push your chair back into place and leave at a brisk walking pace, while quickly picking up your light weight flying overall from the cloakroom, and slipping it on over your uniform en-route to the QRA car in a very Battle of Britain fashion, before proceeding as before to the aircraft.

I often wondered at the time about our chances of survival, especially in wintertime. By 1963 the Soviets had quite a good surface to air missile (SAM) system, so we would probably have been taken out before the target. Secondly, if we had taken a hit from a SAM, the chances are that the aircraft would have become totally uncontrollable. Many years later, one of our skippers –the late Keith Hanscombe was the captain of a Victor tanker when another aircraft collided with his Victor and took off the tail fin. The aircraft rapidly nosed dived, and only Keith managed to eject. Then even assuming that one did manage to leave the aircraft, it's a long way to the ground from 40,000+ feet wearing a light flying suit over an English summer's day uniform, with only black patent leather shoes on your feet; so the possibility of becoming an icicle was fairly high – and not really the thing to wear in the snow of a Russian Winter. Finally, on landing, having survived so far, one had the opportunity to try out one's basic Russian on the assembled Red Army reception committee, with *"Don't shoot, I'm a British Officer"*, at which point, being assured that you were a gentleman, they would shoulder their Kalashnikov AK47s, and escort you to the nearest Soviet Committee, where you would apologise profusely for having violated their airspace and reduced some half a million of their citizens to radioactive dust, but now you would like them to abide by the Geneva Convention, please.

Western Ranger to Offutt AFB Nebraska

Although the Victors of No 3 Group never quite emulated the Vulcans of No 1 Group who actually flew right round the world on training sorties –well that's what they called them, we did fly sorties that went far into the eastern and western hemispheres, which made up for the otherwise somewhat boring flying. Even though by the early 1960s, the sun having well-nigh gone down on the British Empire, Britain still had extensive bases across the globe, in places that had been ex colonies, such as Gibraltar, Malta, Cyprus, Aden, the Persian Gulf, the Indian Ocean, Singapore and Malaya, Hong Kong, Goose Bay, and the USA! Well, I did say ex-colonies and the Yanks were very gracious in permitting the RAF to keep quite a large detachment to service, support and maintain visiting RAF aircraft to Offutt Airbase in Nebraska!

On XV Squadron you had to have an indefinable quality to be chosen to fly a trip to the USA. Some crews seemed to go there quite often, others never did, which gave rise to the observation that "You couldn't go unless you'd been before!" a pithy observation with a Catch 22 flavour. Jumping forward a bit in time, our crew drew the lucky straw in October 1962 – just before the Cuban Missile Crisis. My memories of this event are brief: Goose Bay in Labrador was as icy cold as it was to be expected for that time of year; we had a super breakfast of bacon with flapjacks and oodles of maple leaf syrup. I was fascinated as we flew over Chicago. Looking down on cities in the UK from the air, you could see how a pattern of main roads was replicated on a smaller scale through smaller roads down to lanes like fractal geometry, but in Chicago all the streets were an orderly grid of streets going either north south or east west.

Goose Bay had been freezing, but in Offutt they were experiencing an Indian summer, which made us look rather foolish in our arctic flying gear. When we landed, we were directed to park our aircraft on a hard standing away from the USAF operational side. Our particular parking area held a B17 Flying Fortress, a B26 Invader, and a B29 Super Fortress, all of WW2 vintage, together with a B36, which first flew just after the War. I'm not sure if the USAF was trying to make a point about our Victor being somewhat old fashioned compared to their B47 Stratojets, and B52 Superfortresses. On the one-day stand down before the return flight, we hired a car from an entrepreneurial RAF ground crew guy who had foreseen the possibilities of making a fast buck by providing transport to visiting aircrew. As we drove off base to Omaha City, the second image that I had of the USA was how raw the scenery appeared. It was like being in a Western movie, and gave the impression that it had just been settled very recently – which it had of course since this part of the west had only really been opened up about 100 years previously.

The Cuban Missile Crisis

Sandwiched in between these travels was the other major event of the autumn of '62 – the Cuban Missile crisis. On Friday, the evening of 26ᵗʰ October, just as the Crisis was reaching its moment of truth, very much in the tradition of Drake playing bowls before sailing out to meet the Spanish Armada, or Wellington's troops going to a ball in Brussels before Waterloo, both squadrons at RAF Cottesmore were attending a dining in night. This function had been long planned, but no one had given any thought that the circumstances might require us to be ready to go to war. At the end of the meal, and before I adjourned to the bar, I went back to my room, and turned on the radio for the latest news, which was to the effect that the Russian ships were still headed towards Cuba and the USN had deployed their forces to stop them. It seemed a good enough reason to go and have a few more beers! However, the next day a heightened alert state was declared, and we were all commanded to bring our essential gear to the Ops Block and await deployment to our dispersal airfields. Since by this time Kennedy and Khrushchev had reached an agreement, this appeared to be a belated response to appear to be ready to do something. Both Squadrons aircrews remained crammed in the Ops Block for some hours before we were all told to return to our normal duties.

By the autumn 1962, Babs and I had been going out for almost two years, at which point I felt that it was about time to introduce her to my Mum and so I invited her to come up and see the family estate. For some reason that I can't remember, I drove home a few days before Babs, who would follow by train from Cambridge. She was a dental nurse, so it may have been impossible for her to get off work at the same time as my leave started. However, she rang me before I left Cottesmore and said that she would be arriving in Waverly Station in Edinburgh on a particular day very late in the evening. I said *"No problem; I'll be there to pick you up,"* but having calculated that after picking her up from Edinburgh we would not arrive at home before about 1 or 2 in the morning, I decided to get my head down for an hour or two and then get up in good time for the journey via the Kincardine road bridge to Edinburgh (no Forth Road Bridge then). Unfortunately, my alarm clock did not go off, but fortunately, my Mum stayed up, but not knowing how long it would take me to drive there she did not give me a call until 11pm. It's a good 50 miles from our cottage to Edinburgh, and my best average speed was about 35mph in my little Ford! By the time that I arrived at Waverly station, Babs had been there for about two hours. She'd had trouble with some drunks on the train, but managed to avoid them. The station at that time of night also had a good quota of the same. Fortunately, a guardian angel in the form of a RN rating told her to wait in the ladies waiting room while he kept an eye open for me. God Bless the Royal Navy.

Babs was a very practical and adaptable girl, so the somewhat primitive domestic arrangements at Broadwell Cottage did not faze her at all, and we had a great holiday, showing her Perth and the local area. But by this time my Mum knew that not only would I be stationed somewhere 'down south', but also highly likely that I would settle down there too, so it was highly probable that I would be returning home only very infrequently, and that for short periods. She didn't mention anything to me but it was about this time that she began to consider moving back to be among her family in Staffordshire.

RAAF Butterworth – Malaya

Those of us who can remember the winter of '46 –'47 may quibble whether the weather of '62 –'63 was any worse. I can remember '46-'47 well. I was off school with measles for two weeks as it began to snow. Then, by the time that I returned to school the rest of the school had been sent home not only because there was a general outbreak of measles, but with the continued fall of snow, food and coal supplies were getting short, and for those who had electricity there would be power cuts. I had a great holiday for two or three weeks sledging and making 'igloos' in the four and five-foot snow drifts. However, by the winter of '62 –'63 my boyhood love of snow had abated somewhat, so I was overjoyed to be informed late in December of '63 that in mid-January I would be going out to the Far East in advance of my crew who were bringing the Station Commander out to a conference at HQ Far East Air Force. The journey commenced from Stanstead, Essex, as a passenger in a Britannia - an RAF airliner, flying via Istanbul and Bombay to RAF Changi on Singapore Island, thence by Dakota up to Butterworth, the RAAF base on the mainland of Malaysia just across the straits from Georgetown on Penang Island. My crew did not arrive for about another 10 days, their aircraft having gone unserviceable in Cyprus, Aden, and Gan Atoll; I was in effect given this amount of time as unofficial leave, so I chose to explore my environment.

Georgetown, which could be reached by taxi and ferry, was a fascinating old place. At that time throughout Singapore and Malaya, there were very few skyscrapers and modern buildings, and the cities and towns were still very much in the colonial style, as was the attitude of much of the local population to the British. On recommendation, I visited the Runnymede Hotel, which was beautifully situated right on the edge of the straits, where it was possible to sit under the shade of the palm trees in the garden drinking a long gin and tonic, listening to the gentle lapping of the water on the sea wall, while savouring a feeling of pleasure commensurate with a nabob in his palace. In the early '60s, the hotel, still in use as transit accommodation for UK service personnel, was run in the best traditions of the British Raj. Fabulous meals were available in a large airy dining room, with only about two or three others residents as company, with about three times that number of waiters in attendance delivering an instant service. I also got great satisfaction in being able to exchange my British khaki drill shirts and shorts for some made locally. The KD shorts and shirts that I had bought in the UK from a well-known British retailer to the services, appeared to have been modelled on the style worn by Monty in 1942 –the waistband was midway between the breastbone and the belly button and the voluminous legs demurely covered the knees; while the shirts were long sleeved, and made of a material that stuck to the skin as soon as any perspiration occurred. However, the local Indian tailor, just down the road from the front entrance to RAAF Butterworth, made for me at some ridiculously small cost, two complete sets of Aussie style khaki drill shirts and shorts made from a material of a much stouter material that allowed the air to circulate freely.

Engagement and Holiday in Spain

After I returned from the Far East, Babs and I got engaged – she eventually consented to marry me, and in August '63 we went for a holiday in Spain – only this time by car – a Morris Mini. I'd recently sold my Ford, and had intended to buy a second-hand Austin-Healy 100/6 sports car, which was in my price range. But when I appraised the insurance company – General Insurance, with whom I had insured my motor bikes for some eight years, they pedantically pointed out that I was only 24 and that I was in the RAF, and that I was also a pilot to boot, therefore the premium would be astronomical. Retrospectively, their caution was probably well advised–so I abandoned this plan and bought a Mini instead which cost me all of £487 new! We drove down through France in beautiful weather, we camped, we met up with Babs sister Pat and her boyfriend Deryk, we toured with them, stopping at Tossa del Mar, before we headed back home via Andorra and Biarritz, detouring via the North coast of Spain to look at the Neolithic art painted on the walls deep inside the various caves.

RAF Tengah – Singapore
In December of '63 I went back to the Far East when XV Squadron detached four aircraft, together with a Britannia bringing the ground crew backup out to RAF Tengah on Singapore Island as a deterrent against General Sukarno of Indonesia at the time of Confrontation. In Malaya that time of the year is the northeast monsoon season, which means that there is less rain and fewer of the

enormous cumulo-nimbus thunder clouds ("cu-nims") around. Out in the tropics such cloud tops can reach up to 55000 to 60000 feet. I can remember on the leg of the outbound flight over the Indian Ocean between Aden and Gan on a bright moonlight night, John Williamson the navigator gave Jim a track correction of a few degrees. There were only scattered cu-nims around, but as we turned, in the far distance we could see that we were pointing straight at one. As we adjusted our flight path slightly to pass very closely by it, it was amazing to watch it visibly increase in height. Cu-nims have an awesome power and above this one gleaming coldly in the moonlight there was a pileus or cap cloud, formed by the condensation of moist air. Just the very next day we were to discover just how powerful such cu-nims could be.

I Learnt About Flying Through Cu-Nims From That

Even back in the 1960s statistics were becoming the dominant feature of life in the RAF; at RAF Cottesmore, the squadron crew status board was about the size of a billiard table lying on its side and completely occupied one wall of the ops room. (This of course was well prior to computerised records, and all stats were initially recorded on a large Perspex sheet with wax pens. As I have already mentioned, on XV Squadron there were 10 crews of five, and against each name were recorded details of every operational and training requirement and the date when each and every requirement fell due. Squadron Leader Howard, the Squadron Leader Ops collated information and assigned duties from that board with the fervour of Herbert Hoover who reputedly knew the whereabouts of every agent in the FBI in the world. Thus, it came about very early next morning on Gan Atoll, as I planned the fuel requirements of the next stage of our flight, that Jim my captain informed me that I, as co-pilot, would be doing the take-off to fulfil the monthly stats.

Our take-off time was quite early in the day, before the air temperature increased and reduced the thrust of the engines. This was necessary since the runway on Gan Atoll was only a few hundred feet longer than that required for our Mark 1 Victor to get safely airborne. Moreover, the atoll was so small that there was no taxiway round the airfield, which meant that we had to taxi out of the dispersal and onto the runway to backtrack to the take-off point. The weather was beautiful; a light wind on the runway, the visibility was unlimited and only the odd thundercloud dotted at wide intervals over the ocean. But, as we turned 180 degrees round on the concrete pan at the take-off end of the runway, we saw that there was a heavy shower cloud approaching the island at the other end of the runway, and I could just about see the farther horizon through the rain. (The following photo shows something of the intensity of rain that can be experienced in the tropics.)

Jim, my skipper ran up the engines, and said, *"I'll give you control at 90 knots."* During take-off, directional control up to that speed was through the nose wheel steering, which was on the captain's side. We started the roll, with one of the navigators calling out the various critical speeds. As the captain called out, *"You have control"*, the rain started. Jim switched on the windscreen wipers. No difference, the rain was coming down in stair-rods. The captain selected the higher speed on the wipers. Still no difference! It was going to be a genuine IMC take-off. IMC, or Instrument Meteorological Conditions, to give it its official title, means that because of cloud, mist, fog, rain etc., the pilot has no external visual reference, and can only use the cockpit instruments to stay lined up on the runway. The nav plotter called out *"Rotate"*, at about 138 knots at our weight to lift the nose off; then a few seconds later, *"Unstick speed"*, which was at 148 knots. I eased back on the control column and immediately we all felt the buffet, which heralded an imminent stall – and crash into the sea. The captain called out for me to lower the nose a bit (this being a euphemism for what he actually said). I then tried again, becoming simultaneously conscious that we must be nearing the end of the concrete – and Gan atoll, which only exceeded the runway by a matter of a few feet. I tried again to get the aircraft airborne, again the buffet. In the rear part of the crew compartment, the nav radar operator and the AEO, who could see the ruffled surface of the Indian Ocean through the side windows, screamed out that we were only just above the surface of the sea – and that's where we seemed to stay for an eternity.

The windscreen was totally obscured by rain, the ASI (Air Speed Indicator) was apparently stagnant at around 150 to 160 knots, the altimeter was on the stops, the buffet reappeared as soon as any back pressure was applied and the navigators, who didn't have any bang seats, were yelling out that whatever I did, I was not to ease forward on the stick. Jim my captain had been poised to take control all this time, but he too was aware that the control loads were so fine that merely by taking control would be enough to precipitate a stall or land us in the drink. Suddenly the rain stopped, and there was the vastness of the Indian Ocean before us, as calm as the proverbial millpond, with only the 'odd thundercloud dotted at wide intervals across the ocean'. The airspeed increased, the aircraft commenced to climb away, and we became aware of Gan ATC calling us, *"Mike Alpha Charlie Delta come in"*. They had been calling us since we had disappeared into the rain and had been transmitting this message at intervals. Even now the same call was repeated a number of times before the AEO confirmed that we were receiving them and we were continuing en-route as planned.

No one spoke for a long time. The first person to recover his composure was the crew chief sitting on a sixth seat placed just behind the pilots' seats, *"Anyone like a fruit gum?"* he asked. That broke the tension and we all expressed –one way or another –our relief at getting through the rainstorm. Subsequently, I read a lot about strong down draughts from heavy rain or cumulo-nimbus type clouds; in such weather conditions there is a massive down flow of air from the bottom of the cloud which can rush out in all directions – now known as a micro-burst. If the airburst is in the direction of take-off this has the effect of stagnating or even reducing the airspeed. I fully concurred with the advice contained in such articles never to fly in the base of heavy shower clouds at low speeds on take-off and landing. However, one thing continued to trouble me as we cruised across the ocean that was the non-availability of seats for the rear crew. It had been cynically said that the powers that be/ Government/ financial experts/Ministry of Defence had calculated that the estimated total cost of replacement for the losses of all the V Bombers, together with the cost of training new crew for those who had perished during the total time that the aircraft were expected to remain in service was less than the total cost of retrospectively fitting ejection seats for the rear crew in each aircraft! Whatever the true reason, a number of accidents occurred where the rear crew lost their lives but the pilots escaped. The most notorious of these was the Vulcan crash in short finals at London Airport, i.e. Heathrow, in 1956. Moreover, once the landing gear was lowered in the Vulcan, escape for the rear crew was impossible since the escape hatch faced directly into the nose-wheel undercarriage leg. In another accident, one of our captains, who was a very experienced pilot and instructor, delayed his ejection too late while trying to give his rear crew the chance to escape. Later in my flying career, I flew the Canberra B.I.8, which also had an ejection seat for the pilot, but the navigator in this particular mark of Canberra was expected to clip on a chest chute and dive forward out the entrance door. Here too there were losses because for what can only be called penny pinching reasons.

I had only been on Singapore Island for a few days when I met my cousin Gordon Dobbie, who I had last seen in Scotland in 1951 before he and his parents emigrated to Australia. He was now a Lieutenant in the Royal Navy, flying for the Fleet Air Arm off HMS Ark Royal. Meanwhile I had a super time deciding what exotic goods I would buy. I finally bought a Japanese transistor radio with eight wavebands, including FM – very up market for 1963, while my other purchase was a complete eight-piece dinner set of Japanese Noritake china, again for some incredibly low price, that included it being boxed up and shipped back to Babs in the UK!

One evening, having tried out a few beers down town, John Stansfield, one of the other co-pilots suggested that we also try out some of the local food on the waterfront. At this time the dimly lit waterfront in Singapore was not what might be termed a tourist attraction. Along one of the quays, the food stalls were little wheeled carts each lit by a pressure lamp and having its own hot grill, with all the basic raw ingredients laid out on one side. After a few beers one's gastronomic tastes were heightened while any sense of caution about inherent food poisoning was dismissed. I don't suppose that today's health and safety brigade would allow anyone within miles of these mobile delicatessens dispensing all manner of eastern grub. Whatever it was, it tasted absolutely delicious, but standing on the edge of the sea wall eating a morsel of some unknown meat wrapped up in what could be a palm leaf, and looking down into the water and seeing dead dogs, cats, rats, and other detritus, did make one wonder what bugs it was possible to catch?

I think that it was also John Stansfield who was involved in what could have been a very nasty accident. [If you ever read this John and it wasn't you, forgive me!]. Our detachment had been told to fly round Singapore Island on Christmas Eve in order to show the flag, but since this was to be at night, it seemed to contradict the aim. However, all aircraft duly got airborne at five-minute intervals and flew along in a steady stream at 1500 feet over all the main centres of population. Now if I remember correctly, Ken McLean, John's skipper, had decided to combine some pilot training on this sortie – as mentioned above, each crewmember had to complete a certain number of tasks peculiar to their role. On this instance, Ken had chosen to clear his requirement for flight under asymmetric power. The Victor, having the engines located close to the fuselage was no problem to fly when two engines on one side were throttled back to idle. However, during their stately progress round the Island, with the two port engines throttled back to idle, a fire warning light illuminated on one of the two starboard engines that were being used, (it subsequently transpired that an electrical fault had caused the fire caption to illuminate). Both pilots reacted. Ken shut down the engine that had the firelight, while on the other side of the cockpit; John shut the throttle of the other starboard engine causing the Victor to commence a descent, since the aircraft was now virtually without power. Some frantic increase of RPM on the two idling port engines and a relight drill on one of the starboard engines occupied the next few minutes, but the stats officer was happy since these actions accounted for a few more drills.

On another occasion, while returning to Tengah by taxi late one evening, my driver who was Indian, brushed against a cyclist who was Chinese, and caused him to come off his bicycle. The altercation between the two men rapidly attracted the attention of a policeman, who was Malay. After the Hindu and the Chinaman had attempted to fix the blame on each other, they and the policeman turned to me for the deciding vote. At this point I began to realise, that even at this stage of independence from the Mother Country, and even after the debacle of the British surrender to Japan in Singapore in WW2, they were looking to me as a representative of the 'White Sahib' to adjudicate. Fortunately, I was compos mentis enough to realise that whatever I did, I would arouse the wrath of the losing party. I played my best card, assumed the role of the Delphic Oracle, and gave a vague and ambiguous answer to the effect that I had been asleep and I was not sure what had happened. After a few more moments of multi lingual insults, we parted. When the driver dropped me off, he took my fare, but gave me a smile, so I reckon he was relieved not to have been charged.

RAAF Butterworth – Again

In January '64 the detachment moved up country to RAAF Butterworth, where I had been just a year before. However, this time, since we were a large detachment, we were given a formal welcome and pep talk by the Aussies. The Theatre Commander was an Air Commodore Ford, and the Station Commander a Group Captain Marsh, who was also the middleweight boxing champion of the Royal Australian Air force. He was reputed to have hair on his fingers right down to his nails, and certainly looked as if he could have given Mohammed Ali a run for his money. We all trooped into a large room in the Operations Block; the introduction went something like this: - *"G'Day and welcome to RAAF Butterworth. I am Ayah Commodore Fowd* [in a very pronounced Aussie accent], *and I am the Aaarea Commaaander*[ditto] *for all forces in Northern Malaaaya* [ditto]. *The Staaation Commaaaander* [ditto] *is Group Captain Maaash* [ditto], *and it's his staaation* [ditto], then turning and glaring at the Group Captain who was seated a few chairs away to his left, he bellowed], *EXCEPT WHEN IT'S MOINE!"* Having made this point clear, the rest of the briefing was quite normal.

The months we spent at Butterworth were in some respects quite idyllic. We had four aircraft and five crews. We always had to have one crew acting as duty operations personnel whenever flying took place, but we never ever had all the four aircraft serviceable at any one time. As there was no advantage gained by sitting around the ops block as against sitting around the Officers Mess, every morning very soon after the met brief it became de rigueur for crews not involved in the flying programme to return to the Mess. The main part of the Officers Mess at Butterworth was built in a T shape; the reception area, bar, dining room, ladies' room, billiards room, toilets etc. were joined together in a straight line, while the Ante Room, which was attached to the inner part of the reception area projected out almost to the edge of the sea. It was a large high-ceilinged room with many slatted doors –always open, while a similar number of electric fans stirred the humid air to little effect. Having returned from ops, we all split up into groups of four to play bridge –as per aircrew rules, which is not exactly in Omar Sharif style. From time to time we would order a plate of sandwiches and a coffee, adjourn for lunch –curry. In fact, you could have a curry every meal of the day, or partake of the Aussie meat allowance which was about four times that allocated to Brits. Play would resume sometime after lunch. We also had music in the background. It was always the same music; there were two LPs and only two LPs –Pepe Jaramillo and his Latin American Orchestra, and Richard Burton and Julie Andrews singing in the Musical Camelot. They were played constantly; at one time I could render every song from Camelot verbatim. At five PM, the bar would open for an hour. This was in deference to Sydney opening hours. There was an incredible crush to get served, and the glasses were small (about ¼ pints), so that no sooner had you obtained one and downed it than you had to fight to get another. If I remember the beer was also very cold and pressurised and served through hoses, so that the bar rapidly became waterlogged –well beer logged. After dinner, quite often, we would (knowing by then who would or would not be flying on the next day's programme) continue playing bridge until midnight or even one in the morning.

Sometimes, we would gather in the bar before an expedition to Georgetown. The Officers Mess bar extended the full width of the Mess building, with doors exactly like those in Western saloon; one side opening onto the garden, while the other gave immediate access to the car park at the front. One particular evening, we were standing round, when George Fewtrell, one of our captains, noticed among all the little wooden shields depicting the RAF and RAAF Squadron crests on the bar wall was one of No. 10 Squadron, which had been our competing sister unit at Cottesmore, but had just been disbanded. George, remarking that *"They're history"*, unhooked the wooden plaque from the wall, attached it to the darts board, and proceeded to put three darts into it, before going out through one of the swing doors heading for the gents. At almost exactly the same moment Group Captain Maaaash walked in through the other swing door, glared round. He was somewhat jaundiced towards Pommies, having already had cause to read the riot act to us about our casual dress. This was serious stuff when an Aussie complains about Pommies being scruffy! He then spotted No. 10 Squadron's shield pinned to the dartboard, and demanded, *"Who did that?"* We all effected surprise and amazement, saying something like *"Goodness gracious, how terrible,"* and that we hadn't noticed it. The Groupie, plucked the darts out, and then returned the crest to its place on the barroom wall before he departed out of one of the swing doors for the gents, just as George entered through the other door. Seeing the crest back in its place on the wall, before we could stop him, he proceeded to pin the crest back on the dartboard. We dumped our beers, grabbed George, and headed out into the night and piled into a taxi before the Groupie returned.

We had some good times and banter with the Aussies, although on another evening, we touched a raw nerve with one particular guy. I think that there were six of us altogether sitting round a table out on the veranda between the anteroom and the sea; three co-pilots together with some Aussies, one of whom was a helicopter Squadron Commander, and one of the other Aussies an army captain who had just returned from some weeks up country out in the jungle. He was covered in scratches and marks where he had been torn by thorns and bitten by leeches, looked quite gaunt, and his tales of hardship were impressive. By this time, having had more than a few beers, we were at the *"I'd like to drink a toast to...."* stage of the proceedings. The helicopter Squadron Leader said, *"I'd like to drink a toast to the Australian Army up in the jungle."* This was a fair request after what we had just heard. We chatted a bit more, before Bill Geveaux, one of the co-pilots, who was known for his Garry Larsen Far Side sense of humour, said in an early attempt at British sledging, *"I'd like to drink to Botany Bay,"* whereupon the Aussie Squadron Commander slammed his beer down on the table, stood up, and reached across the table scattering beers, before grabbing Bill by the collar with one hand, wielding a large clenched fist before his face with his other, while very forcibly expressing his sentiments, *"Say that again, and I'll give you a bunch of fives."* It took some time before feathers were unruffled, and explanations of British humour were attempted and somewhat grudgingly admitted.

On other occasions we went to Georgetown in the evening. We could take a taxi from the base to the ferry terminal, catch a ferry, and then take a trishaw to where ever we were headed. Coming back one evening, we each took a separate trishaw; with a wager that the last man to reach the ferry would pay for the lot. Our trishaw drivers keenly accepted to go along with this. Unfortunately, my man, although he peddled as best as he could, came in last. I felt in my pockets, but discovered to my dismay that I was short by a number of dollars. I thrust all the change that I had at them to sort it out and legged it for the ferry. By this time the 10ft high wire gates on the quay had closed, I didn't want to face the irate trishaw drivers so I had to haul myself over them. The ferry had just started to depart; I was conscious of the propellers churning the muddy water some fifteen feet beneath my feet as I ran and leapt over the intervening space with all my might to be caught by Steve and John Willie on the edge of the deck. On another evening, having missed the last ferry, the only recourse was to hire a motorised canoe. Getting into the canoe was no problem from the Penang Island side, but the canoe grounded some fifteen to twenty feet from the shore in a mud bank on the Butterworth side, with the result that I had to wade through this extremely evil smelling stuff to reach dry land.

Marriage and Honeymoon

The new 15 Squadron detachment arrived at the end of February, and our crews returned to the UK. I now had a month to get myself organised for our wedding. Babs had decided that she wanted to be married in her local church in Histon, a village a few miles outside Cambridge, where her parents had owned a house and close to the cottage that she and her sister Pat rented. This meant that I had to write to the vicar of the church to the effect that he didn't know me, and I didn't know him, but I would be coming along for a few weeks to his parish in order to fulfil the minimum statutory number of weeks required for the reading of the banns before the RAF whisked me back to the Far East. I was given a good send off on my bachelor night, so good in fact that Bill Izzard my best man spent the following morning driving me round in his Austin Healey with the top down while I absorbed lots of cold air to be in a fit state of compos mentis for our wedding..

After the reception we drove off for the West Country to our final destination at Hartland Quay, a hotel at the foot of the cliffs on the

Cornish coast. As it was still the end of March, the hotel was quite quiet, and we were the only young couple among some very elderly visitors. We visited quite a bit of the area, during which two minor amusing things occurred. Having stopped at a hotel for a drink prior to lunch one day, as I ordered at the bar, the hotel manager came across to me, and in a quiet voice, informed me that it was not legal to have underage girls in a public bar. I haughtily informed him that this particular girl was not-only-not under age but also, she was my wife. On the other occasion, we went into chemists to purchase some contraceptives. The lady behind the counter asked if she could help. Being still somewhat shy with Babs alongside and having to make my request to another woman, I mumbled that I would like to purchase some Durex contraceptives. She looked at me with an expression of amazement, wonder, and astonishment, before going away and returning with a fair number of packs of the same. I didn't like to make the error any more public, so we dug a bit deeper into our funds and left to a whispered, awed, and sympathetic conversation behind our backs among the staff. After our honeymoon, we moved into an RAF married quarter at Cottesmore. This, the first of over a dozen moves that we made during the time that I was in the RAF, was the easiest. I borrowed Babs' sister's car – a big old Rover, which easily held all Babs' worldly goods from her Mum's house in Cambridge. I also had a few suitcases of kit to bring from the Officers Mess; and there we were -A newly married couple.

At the end of May just before I went back to the Far East, we borrowed a tent from Babs' Mum, (the same old tent that we had used in Spain), and toured the west coast of Scotland, again camping in remote places. This subsequently became our mode of holiday once we had our children, so much so that the boys christened it *"Dad's annual survival camp."* We had idyllic weather, saw lots of seals, golden eagles, and camped just up from the beach on South Uist. One day while we were there, the crofter, a Mr McClellan, whose land we had unintentionally camped on, came across and we had a long conversation with him. Having then invited us to follow him across the machair – the strip of arable land between the sea and the moor, and watch him cut peat, at which we also had a go, he then reached under a clump of heather, drew out an old smoke blackened kettle, a battered aluminium mug, and a tin containing tea leaves. He then filled the kettle from a peat pool with some water –which already had the colour of strong tea, boiled the water on a peat fire, added the tea leaves, and proceeded to invite us to partake of this new beverage. After that, on our way back to the tent, he invited us round to his cottage for a 'ceilidh' (a social gathering). Babs and I duly presented ourselves that evening. The inside of his small cottage had pinewood panelling on all the walls, and the only ornament was a faded photograph of him when he had been in the Merchant Navy many years before. There were two other people present –his Mum and a neighbour, a Mr Munro, neither of whom could speak English to any degree, and both of whom could have been in their nineties. We had an interesting conversation –more like an interrogation really. He would ask us a question, about what we did where we came from, etc., etc.; we would answer and then he would translate this into Gaelic to the others, who would nod their heads at intervals. They would then ask questions, which he translated into English. We did the same, and at the end of the evening, although the old folks and ourselves none of us could directly converse, other than through the medium of the bilingual Mr McClellan, we felt as if we'd had a good 'ceilidh.'

The Far East Again

Unfortunately, all too soon I had to go back out to Malaya. As Babs was now pregnant it seemed like a good idea for her to return to her Mum's. This time I needed to hire a transit van to carry all our gear. On the morning of the day that I had set aside to drive down to Cambridge –I wasn't on the flying programme, Jim my skipper and the rest of my crew appeared on our doorstep just after nine am, and said that we had been tasked to go to RAF Gaydon for a simulator sortie. I told him that I'd booked, paid for, and packed the van and was all organised to transport our gear. Him said, *"Don't worry, we'll just go to Gaydon anyway, Squadron Leader Howard* (The Ops Sqn Ldr) *won't know."* But he did, because he rang Gaydon to speak to me, so Jim had to come clean, and we all got a flea in our ear because of this. The final three months in Malaya passed very much as before, only now we knew that as soon as we returned to the UK, XV Squadron was also going to disband.

The summer months are the Monsoon season in Malaya; the wind, now coming up from the southwest, brought an intensity of rainfall such I have never seen. It was always very humid, with a high likelihood of a thunderstorm at some time in the afternoon or evening. One Sunday evening, when all the officers had gathered in the anteroom to watch a film, we were very nearly wiped off the face of the earth. One of the RAF Javelin night fighters had been scrambled because radar had picked up what was thought to be an airborne intruder coming towards us from Sumatra. This turned out to be a false alarm, but on recovery, when the Javelin was on final approach, the electrical discharges from the thunderstorm not only partially blocked out the talk down radar, so that only intermittent echoes were obtained of the fighter, but also the torrential rain blocked out the pilot's vision. Moreover, he was short of fuel so at decision height when he should have gone around for another approach, he looked up and saw two red lights, slightly off to one side, which he assumed, was the runway threshold – but they were the anti-collision lights on the roof of the anteroom. At the last minute the Javelin pilot realised that he had got it wrong and overshot, but not before everyone in the room dived for the floor. The Javelin pilot now attempted a landing from a visual circuit as he had insufficient fuel for another radar pattern. Fortunately, the rain was very localised and the visibility had picked up enough for him to fly round the field, but on finals again he encountered the heavy rain, and although he managed to land on the runway this time, he was well over to the left-hand side so that his port wingtip caught the nose of each of the four Aussie F86 Sabres fighters parked on a large concrete pan by the runway ready for an immediate scramble. This made the RAF very popular with the RAAF!

Some who read this may also remember seeing a well-publicised photograph in the UK press of a Victor releasing a stream of 1000 lb bombs – 35 bombs in all, which was quoted as the Victor's bomb load. This was true, but what the papers did not say, if I remember rightly, was that this particular sortie, if I also remember rightly, had been carried out by a Victor with a very light fuel load, because the bomb load, the runway length, and air temperature, and engine power available all dictated that this was the only way for it to get safely airborne. With our recent experience on Gan, our crew wholeheartedly agreed with this, and watched this particular take-off with more than a passing interest. The aircraft took off in a northerly direction, flew up to Song-Song weapons range, only a few miles up the coast, released the bombs, turned 180 degrees onto the opposite heading, and landed on the reciprocal southern runway. However, the press release photograph looked very powerful and was no doubt meant to impress our Indonesian adversaries. But by early September we were all back in the UK, XV Squadron was disbanded on October 1st, and we all went our separate ways.

RAF High Wycombe Bomber Command HQ, Bucks

Simultaneously with the coming demise of XV Squadron, I was aware that only one year of my five-year commission remained. I was now married, and my wife was expecting our first child. Suddenly the thought of returning to university on a grant of £250 per annum did not look so attractive compared to my RAF pay, which was a heady £620 pa! I decided to apply for a permanent commission- well until I was 38, when I hoped to take the route of many pilots and join a civil airline. I was granted an interview very promptly, and during this interview I was asked how I saw my career in the RAF. Being somewhat naïve about what a career in the RAF really entailed, I replied that I hoped to continue to fly. This apparently was not the correct answer, as prospective career officers normally opted to be the officer in charge of various ground posts, pass promotional exams, apply for Staff College, and smoothly talk themselves into being selected as ADC to some big wheel, before becoming a big wheel themselves. However, before this extended commission was granted, I was posted on a one-year tour to complete my five-year commission to High Wycombe in Buckinghamshire.

At this point, just after my return from Malaya, I had a few weeks leave coming up, so we vacated our quarter at Cottesmore and stayed with Bab's Mum and Dad in Cambridge until I took up my posting to Bomber Command Operations Centre (BCOC) at High Wycombe in Bucks. Initially, until Babs had our first baby –Andrew, in February 1965, I drove between High Wycombe and Cambridge. It was a reprise of the Gaydon Cambridge run, across country and along back roads. Babs gave birth to 8 lb 9oz baby by Caesarian section, but she was only in RAF Ely hospital for a matter of days before she was sent home. Not many weeks later we moved into quarters at Medmenham, a lovely spot on the Thames. Unfortunately, it was only for a few months, for subsequently I was posted onto the Canberra; however, since the Canberra OCU was located at Bassingbourne, only 8 miles from Cambridge, we moved back to her Mum's house in Chesterton Road.

It's A Dog's Life

When Bab's was about half way through her first pregnancy, the thought of having a dog also entered our minds. It seemed just right for the well-rounded RAF family. It was, however, just a passing thought, but unfortunately Babs' Mum who was a very spontaneous person got wind of it, and very soon she had discovered a kennels south of Cambridge that was having a selling up and closing down sale. Now the house that Dad & Mum stayed in was a four storey Victorian affair on Chesterton Road, with a garden about big enough to swing a cat. On the day of the sale seeing that she was determined to buy a dog for us, I elected to drive her down there and talk her out of it. To cut a long story short we returned a few hours later with two quite small Harlequin Great Dane pups – both bitches. I suppose at about £10 each they were irresistible! But Bab's Mum discovered that a full-size Great Dane really did require room to move so after some months she passed her dog onto some friends. People have often asked me why I never made senior rank or even any promotion at all in the RAF. Well there are a number of very good reasons from the RAF's point of view, and one of them was connected to Suki as we named our hound. From being an ever so cuddly little pup that liked to snuggle up on your knees she grew into a pretty ginormous dog that still liked to snuggle up on your knees.

A few weeks after commencing my short 12 months tour at Bomber Ops, we were allocated a quarter at Medmenham. RAF Medmenham, which was situated near the Thames between Henley and Marlow, had been the home of the RAF Intelligence Branch during WW2. The Officers Mess (Danesfield House) was a pseudo-gothic castle built by the previous owner who made his money as a soap powder baron. This building was nicely situated in lovely parkland, which featured a café and an open-air swimming pool in the park. To travel forward a bit in time, by mid-summer, with Andrew now some 4 months old, in his pram plus carrycot, together with the dog Babs and I decided to stroll down for a quiet afternoon by the pool. At this stage let me set the scene: baby Andrew was out of his carrycot lying on a rug, Babs was chatting with someone or other while I showed off my Malayan suntan. Up to this point Suki had been well behaved sitting quietly with us. At this juncture I made a mistake. I decided to hitch Suki's lead to the carrycot while I went over to the pool. As I walked off, Suki got up to follow, the carrycot followed on the end of the lead, hit Suki's back legs, whereupon she leapt forward to be followed by another nudge from the carrycot. She now launched off into full racing mode. Babs looked up to see the carrycot performing as a hovercraft behind the dog, and forgetting that the baby was not in the carrycot but on the grass, let out a shriek. The dog hurtled past me straight into the pool. I followed her, dived in, and grabbed her before the carrycot could pull her under. As I reached the edge of the pool, I was aware of a very irate Squadron Leader in No1 Uniform with lots of WW2 medal ribbons shouting at me, *"You can't take your dog swimming in this pool!"* I promptly and bluntly informed him in no uncertain manner that I was rescuing the dog and not teaching her to do the doggy paddle.

How I (Almost) Started World War Three

BCOC – Bomber Command Operations Centre was situated down 'The Hole', the same underground ops centre that had been the habitat of 'Bomber' Harris during WW2. I held a unique role in that I was the only flying officer, while most of the other officers in the Officers' Mess were at least about four or five ranks above me.

Much of what we did down 'The Hole' was quite humdrum. But one particular incident stands out. There are still documentary films on TV that can be classified under the heading of *'Now it can be told'*, which related the hitherto hidden secrets of wartime operations. The events related in this article can be looked on in a similar vein as they occurred well over half a century ago. If you have ever seen the film 'War Games', you may remember that the main theme of the plot dealt with a super intelligent computer at the heart of the NORAD complex in the USA. The computer is programmed to examine the optimum response to every imagined scenario from local conflicts right up to full-scale thermo-nuclear war. Unfortunately, the computer opts to play the theoretical war games for real, with the result that all display screens in the defence centre show an apparent massive attack about to commence. Armageddon is only narrowly averted by superior human intelligence over computer logic. Having noted that highly unlikely fictional scenario, and bearing in mind that what follows was only about two years after the Cuban Missile Crisis, let me take you back on a nostalgic trip to the Bomber Command Operations Centre (BCOC) just about the time that Fylingdales, (see photo) UK's BMEWS (Ballistic Missile Early Warning Radar Site) came on line, and the V force attained its maximum strength.

At that time, the information in BCOC was limited to a simple large digital wall display which indicated, among other things, how many Soviet missiles were approaching the UK, and how many minutes one had before being able to fry an egg on one's head. In addition to the main display, to one side there was another neon lit status sign that showed whether the displayed information was **REAL** or **TEST**, which happened fairly regularly when Fylingdales notified us that they were going to run a test tape through the system to iron out any stray electronic bugs. On these occasions, Fylingdales would advise us on the telephone landline just before they were about to commence the test that we on the watch staff were to select the **'MANUAL'** display instead of **'AUTOMATIC'**; the status sign would then show **TEST** and all the other displays would show various test inputs until the end of the **TEST** tape. At this point, we would reselect **AUTOMATIC** display, and the status window would again show **REAL**. Apart from one hiccup shortly after its installation, the functioning of the display system had been without error, and it was, if I remember correctly, fairly user friendly and *"guaranteed never to go wrong in a million years"*. You may now speculate on what was about to happen.

BCOC worked a staggered shift system over a period of five days. The Watch on the first day took place during the morning 8am to 12am, and evening 5pm to 11pm, followed by afternoon 12am to 5pm, and all night 11pm to 8am on the second day. The third day was a stand down before the shift recommenced on the morning of the fourth day, followed by afternoon and night on the fifth day. Then we had a stand-down for two days, before running through the whole cycle again. Overall, it was quite a reasonable lifestyle but with a permanent amount of built-in jet lag. As a junior officer on a holding post, I was careful to follow the lead given to me by the senior officer of the watch, (a squadron leader), who occupied the ops cell next to mine, and who made all the policy decisions. The 'ops cells' -in appearance rather like a railway carriage - were interconnected along one of the long sides of the ops hall which had the dimensions of a small cinema; each cell consisted of a micro-office; containing a desk, phones, comms-equipment, chairs, and a Plexiglas window that enabled the watch staff to view and maintain the information on the big wall opposite. This information listed all the squadrons, serviceable aircraft, crews, and airfields (some dozen primary bases and two dozen secondary airfields scattered round the UK) that detachments of aircraft would hopefully be able to disperse to prior to the commencement of Armageddon. In my ops cell I also had an experienced Flight Sergeant who shared the main ops desk with me, and who gave me invaluable advice on the distribution of signals, files, and other paperwork, and who to contact in the Command hierarchy on various ops matters. In addition, there was a corporal and 3 WAAF personnel to complete the watch staff.

At times in BCOC it was very peaceful, no telephones rang, no signals arrived for distribution, and there was nothing to look at but the unchanging (we hoped) digital displays high on the opposite wall of the ops hall. At other times, especially during deployments overseas and exercises, the ops cells resembled the city editor's desk just prior to the final edition, with signals, orders, and instructions being received and redistributed to the various units of Strike Command. This was the situation on the particular day that this tale relates to; I came in for the morning watch, and fairly soon I was very busy shuffling signals to various departments, filing others, or sending them up the line to my ops controller. One signal was from Fylingdales. I hastily scanned it, noted that there would be a **TEST** tape running during my evening watch period, and assumed that they would, as per usual *let us know when that would happen.* However, what *I did not notice* was that on this occasion Fylingdales instructed BCOC to leave **AUTOMATIC** selected while they ran the **TEST** tape -*with no prior announcement!* But meanwhile, they *would* pass us periodic updates of genuine information on the telephone landline. What I, or anyone else, failed to appreciate was that with **AUTOMATIC** mode still selected, although it was a TEST tape, *A REAL STATUS WOULD BE DISPLAYED WHILE THEY RAN IT!*

The hectic morning watch passed. The evening watch was the opposite. No calls, no signals, no visitors. Inevitably after an hour or two of checking things over and tidying up from the day's events, we all gathered together in my ops cell and listened fascinated to some really hairy stories by the Squadron Leader Ops controller who had completed a couple of tours as an observer/bomb aimer on Lancasters over the 3rd Reich. Suddenly there was a gasp. All eyes turned to follow the gaze of the ops Corporal who was staring out through the Plexiglas windows of the ops cell. Across the hall, high on the far wall the infallible digital displays showed lots of incoming hardware arriving in the very near future with a **REAL STATUS** glowing malignantly alongside. There was a stunned silence for a moment, before the controller said to me, *"Call out the QRA."* I picked up the red telephone and said as calmly as I could, *"This is the Bomber Controller, Alert State 02."* No exercise code word prefix - just that brief broadcast. Bearing in mind, as I have noted, that this was only just two years since the Cuban Missile crisis, this brought every V bomber on the RAF stations that were on QRA up to runway readiness; with the first V bomber at each airfield on the runway with full power on the brakes, and the other aircraft closely following on the taxiway; each aircraft armed with A MEGATON NUCLEAR WEAPON!!

Now although the moon landings took place only a few years after this, the only communications that we at BCOC had at that time with the airfields that fielded the QRA force, were two 10-line Hadley telephone boxes, which were old fashioned even for that day and age. Each line on each Hadley box had a set of three-way switches, the status of each was indicated by three small lights: Red –meant you were being called; or, by selecting Amber –you put them on hold, and finally by selecting Green –you accepted the call. All 20 lines now lit up red simultaneously. I felt like someone who has just hit the jackpot on a fruit machine. Which one would I answer first? There were so many to choose from. I decided to proceed logically through them all. (With years of hindsight, I wish that I could have recorded for posterity the responses that I heard that night. However, with probable instant annihilation in the next few minutes, this was far from my mind at the time). The first voice said in a suitably Churchillian fashion, *"This is Wing Cdr S... here, my boys are ready"*. I selected another. A voice said, *"This is W.....* [Referring to a well-known East Anglian airfield] *Ops here. Do you mean to say that this is war???!!"* The voice rose to a falsetto shriek at the end of the sentence.

Fortunately for civilisation as we know it, our alert state 02 broadcast was also transmitted back to Fylingdales, who rapidly unplugged their tape and very breathlessly told us that I'd boobed, and would we please revert back to 15 minutes readiness immediately. I picked up the red telephone for the second time in minutes and ordered the QRA force to stand down. In growing realisation of my boob, I left out the correct code word, which the QRA crews also noted so they did not react until I had rebroadcast my message with the amendment. There were some interesting stories from the crews involved in that particular call out for as far as they knew the inevitable hot war was about to take place and adrenalin levels were about as high as they could go. At one base the Station Commander, who had by some coincidence been in the Ops building when the initial broadcast went out, rapidly got into his staff car, and drove out and parked next to the four aircraft on the ORP (Operational Readiness Platform – four concrete slabs next to the take-off point) just as the aircraft captains ran up to full power. He, having by now being informed that Fylingdales had reverted to 15 minutes standby, ran out onto the runway and waved his arms at the first crew motioning them to relax. In the cockpit, however, the pilots surmised that the Groupie was a Commie Sleeper, and if necessary, they would just drive over him on take-off. There were a few other similar stories. However, I will pass over, what in essence are just supplementary details, to the following morning.

Although I was not due on shift until lunchtime, I was ordered to report for duty nice and early in my best Number 1 uniform, for a little chat with the Group Captain in charge of the Ops Centre. I knew that I was going to get an almighty rocket, but I was also pretty certain that although the manual for Air Force Law stipulated the appropriate level of punishment for all manner of crimes by service personnel, none of the authors of that massive tome had anticipated the crime or punishment for, as the official legal service jargon might have phrased it, **"War, thermonuclear, inadvertent, causing of."** The Group Captain Ops – a Group Captain Griffiths – who had in his time played rugby for the RAF, was a large imposing man with a manner that matched his appearance! His conversation went something along the lines of.... *"What has just happened has shown us* (i.e., all the Big Wheels in the Ops Centre) *that the QRA system works just as advertised."* I mentally recollected this conversation when I watched the film, 'Dr Strangelove' quite soon afterwards. *"In fact,"* continued the Groupie, in his best steel in a velvet glove voice, *"the C in C* [Commander in Chief Bomber Command] *is quite pleased, for we would never have received political authorization for what you have just done." However,.."* He was now holding forth quite forcefully although I stood only a few feet from him, *"from the official RAF point of view..."* the memory of the next few minutes remained with me for some time.

By the 1960s, the Americans, with their experience of Pearl Harbour, realizing that a nuclear war might also come about suddenly and unannounced, ensured that each President of the United States was followed closely everywhere he went by an officer who had chained to his wrist an attaché case containing the authorisation and release codes for Strategic Air Command, the USN Submarines, and the Intercontinental Missile Forces. What is not so nearly well-known, is what procedures were in force in the UK at this time. In 2019, as I was completing my final revision of this book, I came across a publication entitled "Secret State – Whitehall and the Cold War" by historian Peter Hennessy; (published by Allan Lane, The Penguin Press in 2002). The author – now Lord Hennessy, noted that even with the completion of the Ballistic Missile Early Warning System at Fylingdales there would only be a few minutes warning of an attack by ballistic missiles. Lord Hennessy wrote *"It is amazing to discover from the files just how rudimentary, almost casual, were the arrangements as late as 1960-61 for the Prime Minister to authorize the ultimate retaliation"* (Hennessey op. cit.). In such circumstances the probability of contacting the Prime Minister and obtaining the relevant authorisation before the arrival of the enemy missiles would be at the best marginal. Therefore, *"authority for our nuclear retaliatory forces to complete their mission would be provided by somebody else.....In fact that somebody else was Air Marshal Sir Kenneth Cross, Commander -in-Chief of Bomber Command."* (Hennessy op. cit.). This additional information gleaned from the above book some 55 years after the event on who would have actually been the ultimate release authority in the UK, has finally clarified what I learnt during the one-way conversation from Group Captain Griffiths. The dressing down, which I fully deserved, was inevitable; but, with hindsight, I also realised that the Group Captain, or more probably 'The Big Wheel' at BCOC, (which by 1964 -65 was Air Marshal Sir John Grandy), had been extremely gracious to me by deciding to inform me of his (unofficial) satisfaction at the success of the (hitherto and previously forbidden – and never to be repeated) ultimate test of the QRA force. For I could have been given a flea in my ear and left to wallow ever after in my guilt and shame without being any wiser that my almost fatal error had resulted in a test of the system, just short of going to war, that would never have been countenanced by any Prime Minister and Cabinet; and moreover, that it *"had worked just as advertised!"*. This story is not an exaggeration. Although there were other safety checks before war commenced, I still get the shudders when I think what could have happened.

RAF Manby, Lincolnshire

As I neared the end of my initial 5-year RAF commission, and having been accepted to serve with the RAF until my 38th birthday, I was informed that my next tour was to be as a Canberra pilot; but before I could commence my Canberra conversion it was necessary to have a month-long refresher course. This I did up at RAF Manby, the College of Air Warfare and home of the Refresher Flying School, for pilots who were qualified but hadn't flown for some time.

RAF Bassingbourn, Cambridgeshire – No 231 (Canberra OCU)

The conversion onto the Canberra OCU (Operational Conversion Unit) lasted 6 months, including a one-month in ground school. Of all the courses that I did during my time in the RAF, I found this one the hardest, for a number of reasons. The Canberra was not a particularly difficult aircraft to fly on two engines, but when asymmetric it was a different matter. The engines on the Canberra were quite widely spaced, so that the loss of one engine caused a noticeable yaw, towards the dead engine, particularly so at low speed. In fact, once below 125 knots it was impossible to maintain straight and level. On take-off, this led to a fatal speed gap between lift off speed, around 110knots and minimum safe flying speed 125knots. A further complication occurred on an asymmetric final approach when full flaps were selected, since they produced heaps of drag, which rapidly reduced the airspeed. Hence it was necessary to have a minimum of 140 knots at 600 feet when full flaps were selected. Thus, the last part of an asymmetric approach called for quite a bit of fine judgement, because if for any reason a pilot got below the normal approach path with low speed, he was unable to apply full power, there being insufficient rudder force to maintain wings level while power was applied on the live engine in an attempt to climb away. Very many of the Canberra losses were directly or indirectly attributable to this cause. In fact, if my memory serves me correctly, although the losses of the Lockheed F104 Starfighter in the German Luftwaffe became very frequent –approximately 1/3 of the total of 913 F104s that were ordered; as a strict percentage, the losses from all causes of RAF Canberras over a somewhat longer period of service probably approached this proportion.

Moreover, today all aircraft have a simulator to practise all drills, but as we used to say, the only Canberra simulator was the T4, a converted Canberra B2, which had ejection seats for the instructor and student, shoe-horned into the cockpit. With two pilots on board, you were elbow to elbow with each other, some of the cockpit instrumentation was hidden behind the twin yokes, and the forward visibility was to some extent limited by the height of the instrument coaming, and it was impossible to raise the seat to improve the lookout because your helmet was already up against the Perspex canopy. Secondly, the Canberra Operational Conversion Unit (OCU) at that time did not give off good 'vibes.' Although many of the navigators on the course were first tourists, all the pilots had been on one or two tours before, and had quite a bit of service experience behind them. Yet the atmosphere was redolent of a basic training school. I do not remember the instructors having a 'getting to know you' in the bar. Moreover, tidiness and order in the coffee bar became almost a fetish that was insisted upon, infringements of which incurred penalties, and we had duty coffee bar rosters, including waiting for telephone calls such as, *"Bring another coffee up to my office,"* from the OC, a somewhat junior Squadron Leader.

My third observation is probably a corollary of the above, concerning the instruction given to the students. In my whole RAF career, I never felt that I needed to ask for a transfer from a particular instructor, but I did think about it at Bassingbourn. My instructor, who had been a pilot on Lancasters during the War, was very experienced. On the ground he was a really nice guy, but he was going through, what could be called a very messy divorce. This may have affected him in the air, for invariably, if you didn't comply with his exact requirements, he let you have a broadside of oaths, blasphemies and his opinion of how completely useless you were. On one occasion, a friend of mine, John South, an Aussie student, while flying a radar approach and being berated as per above, reached up behind this instructor's ejection seat and pulled out his mic-tel lead (the connection for radio and the inter-comm), thus cutting off the invective. I stuck it out until the end of the course, I passed, but confidence in my ability to fly this aircraft to any degree of skill was low. Eventually, I got quite blasé about whether I completed the course or not. On the day of my Instrument Rating Test, Dudley Brown, my 20year old navigator, and myself, together with the Instrument Rating Examiner, who was also known as a bit of a nit-picker, were driven across the airfield to the dispersal. It was in wintertime, and we had on our rubber immersion suits, so we were all hot and sweaty even before we climbed aboard. As we got to the aircraft, I realised that I badly needed a pee. I couldn't go back to the toilets by the crew room as that would have taken hours; there was nowhere else, so when the IRE told me to pre-flight check one side of the aircraft while he did the other, I paused by the starboard main wheel and peed on the tyre. As the IRE came around the tail and spotted me, I had the feeling that he was impressed and thought, *"This guy must be a real hard case to pee on the tyre before he flies, I had better pass him,"* which he did. I eventually passed the course, but for the first and only time in my career I was assessed as low average.

In addition to the above troubles, Babs and I bought our first house – a two-bedroom chalet bungalow in the village of Bourn, not far from Hardwick. It cost £3800 pounds total, of which I could instantly pay off £800 from savings of my RAF pay. Although we were posted within six months of buying it, we kept this house until 1979 and sold it for £25000. This was not planned, but each time that I wrote to the Inland Revenue and asked if I would be charged Capital Gains Tax if I sold the house, they wrote back to the effect saying, sell the house and we will let you know; which meant that we didn't sell it until Capital Gains Tax was abolished. In between, we repeatedly let it; in effect it helped to pay for the rent the RAF charged us for staying in Officers Married Quarters (OMQs). There was never any problem letting it, and Pat, (Babs' sister), who was in Cambridge very kindly showed the new tenants round the house each time it became vacant. In passing let me give credit to my previous boss at High Wycombe. This old Lancaster observer, Squadron Leader Georgopoulos Smith –his mother was Greek – was very clued up on finances and gave me some good pointers, one of which was the necessity of buying a house. Although financially it absorbed more of our spare income than many of my contemporaries, it paid off in the long run, when my contemporaries, having had a better social life than we did, were faced with buying a house at a very much higher cost when they were about to leave the RAF.

Act Three

RAF Laarbruch, Nordrhein, West Germany – No 16 Squadron

Babs and I had just over a week between the end of my course at Bassingbourn and the date for our arrival to RAF Laarbruch in Germany. RAF Laarbruch was part of the 2nd Allied Tactical Air Force (2ATAF) and the most northerly of the four RAF airfields situated in the Rhineland, which because of their close proximity to each other they were known colloquially as 'The Clutch Airfields." We still had the Mini, but with a year-old baby and a Great Dane dog –now fully grown, the Mini didn't really fit the bill. We had a look at a few other vehicles, including a super-sized American Chevrolet Impala –useless on petrol consumption, but that was no problem, as RAF personnel were favoured with subsidised fuel prices in Germany. But for some reason we decided against the Impala, and so our journey out to Germany was in the Mini. Somehow, we squeezed the carrycot and the dog together on the back seat, and set off (all our other belongings had been sent in crates courtesy of the RAF). At one point in the journey there was a squawk from our baba, and we looked behind us to find that Suki had stretched out a bit and Andrew's carrycot had shrunk a bit! We duly arrived the following day, after a rough crossing by ferry, at the Officers Married Quarters (OMQ) at Goch, a German base near Laarbruch. We stayed here for only a few weeks before reallocation to OMQs at Laarbruch. My one memory from Goch was in the bar one evening when we met a German Army officer who could not only speak English very well, but who could imitate perfectly every regional accent in the UK!

The conversion to the Canberra BI8 took no time at all, and in the first month I clocked up some 60 hours, and my self-confidence was much increased. But shortly after we arrived, one of the other new pilots who had been with me on the course at Bassingbourn had somehow lost control after suffering an engine failure at low level and the subsequent asymmetric problem caused him to eject: unfortunately, his navigator went in with the aircraft. He had only just newly married, and his wife came out for the funeral. Wing Commander 'Trog' Bennett, the Squadron CO, asked Babs and I if we would take care of her for a few days. Babs was excellent in having tremendous empathy to people who were hurting. Although Babs was only just 20years old herself, she took this young widow under her wing and really cared for her for the few days that she was with us.

I didn't think that this accident had affected me, but shortly afterwards, when I taxied out on my first night low-level sortie, I had a crisis of confidence and I found myself thinking, *"I can't do this."* The Canberra could be, as I have mentioned, tricky when coming in to land on one engine. However, I overcame this feeling and went on with the flight, and thereafter I did not encounter this fear again and by the end of my tour I had been assessed as above average as a pilot. One other thing that I was not aware of was just how much this fatality had affected Babs. I had told her that I had struggled a bit to pass the Canberra conversion course; this, together with the death of this young man may have given her cause to think that she could quite easily become a widow herself. She started to go quite regularly to the C of E church on the camp. Fortunately, the Vicar, Gerald Mungavin and his wife Margaret were genuine Christians, so the confirmation classes they held had real Biblical input rather than just a perfunctory attendance requirement. Babs did not mention anything to me about these classes –she probably quite rightly believed that I would just laugh and mock her, but she must have told the Vicar of my benighted spiritual state, for just before we left Laarbruch to return to the UK, he came round to our quarter and gave me a modern version of the New Testament which had a series of underlined verses pointing the way to faith in Christ; but I just thanked the Vicar and put his gift aside.

One evening, only a few weeks later, just after arriving in our married quarter in 12 Trenchard Drive, at about 11pm, there was a loud knocking on our front door. Babs had gone to bed, and I was just about to do the same. I opened the door, to find three of the bachelor pilots -Tom Eeles, John Saddler, and John South, standing on the doorstep with a stopwatch and a clipboard. As I opened the door, one of them started the stopwatch, while another announced that we were being 'TAC-EVALED.' Tacevel was the abbreviation for Tactical Evaluation; a no notice exercise that took place quite frequently during the Cold War at every NATO base, to ascertain how quickly, the base could get up to and maintain a war footing. Normally, TACEVALs were called at about 3 in the morning. In this particular case, it was the standard practice for bachelor pilots on the squadron to assess how quickly their newly arrived married colleagues could provide them a no notice beer and meal. I called Babs out of bed and she got busy with a fry up in the kitchen while I kept our 'guests' amused. After about two hours, they professed themselves satisfied with food, beer, and repartee. We were awarded a v. good rating, and they left.

There was plenty of low-level flying; i.e. about 250' above ground level, and much of that involved training to carry out Low Altitude Bombing Manoeuvres (LABS) using 25lb bombs on the Nordhorn Bombing Range, by the Ems River in Lower Saxony. The LABS manoeuvre was essentially a roll off the top (i.e. half a loop), the weapon being released by the navigator at the optimum angle as the aircraft approached a high nose attitude, while the pilot flew the LABS director on the instrument panel, such that if he kept two needles exactly in the middle of this instrument, he would pull the correct amount of 'g' and keep the manoeuvre in a vertical circle, hence the bomb would impact the target accurately. However, since the weapon to be used in wartime was a fairly hefty American nuke, straining for strict accuracy was probably academic. During the next few months, we practised the same manoeuvres out on detachment on two occasions to Cyprus (Nicosia), Malta (Hal Far), and Libya (El Adem and Idris). During one low level sortie over the desert south of El Adem as a pair with John South, a pilot in the other aircraft, we were flying abeam each other at what we thought was a reasonable altitude over what appeared to be semi-arid country covered in trees, until we flew either side of a couple of camels that were twice as tall as the 'trees'! The inaccuracy of the altimeter at very low level and the featurelessness of the desert had fooled us in believing we were much higher than we were.

During our stay at El Adem, the RAF base in Libya near Tobruk,

John South became friends with a major from the British Army detachment stationed there. The major invited him to accompany him on 'an expedition into the desert' the next day. The following morning, John joined a party of two army officers in one Land Rover, while another Land Rover with a Sergeant Major and two other ranks, plus a junior NCO with a dozen men with two three-ton trucks came behind. They drove for some time through fairly featureless desert until they came to a flat stone free area. The convoy stopped and the Major and the RSM both got out. The major said, *"This'll do Sergeant Major." "Very good Sir,"* replied the SM, while giving the Major a quivering salute. The army officers and John strolled off some way while discussing how rough it must have been for the 8th Army out in the desert during the last War. When they came back to the 'camp site', the men had erected a marquee, inside which they had placed three camp chairs, round a trestle table covered in a white table cloth, with proper silver cutlery. The officers sat down, and dined, on a fairly basic meal let it be said, before everything was repacked into the three tonners, and the whole party returned to El Adem. I think that the 8th Army would have been impressed; John certainly was with this whole episode. He reckoned that if any of us had tried that in the RAF, at best there would have been a mutiny, or at worst we would have been left buried up to our necks in the sand for the vultures.

In addition to practising LABS, nearly all our flying was low level round Germany, or Western Germany as it then was. The eastern half of Germany was very sensitive on border violations, so we were wary of infringing their airspace, since a border violation would at least involve being made to land at a Russian 4th Tactical Air Army base, or at worst getting shot down, and if one survived, spending a long time being interrogated in a Stasi prison. As a precaution against this, if at any time a NATO aircraft was seen to be heading east near the border, there was a broadcast on all VHF frequencies, *"Brass Monkey, Brass Monkey."* At which point everyone stopped doing whatever they were doing, checked their position, and if necessary, turned west. Accidental infringement of the Iron Curtain was not the only way to get noticed. One day, on a low-level sortie down in 4 ATAF (i.e. southern Germany), as we reached a turning point, Dudley my nav gave me a steer for the next leg, *"135 degrees"* (south east). Within a few minutes we found ourselves crossing Leipheim airfield, the Luftwaffe's main training base that seemed to be covered by acres of Fiat G91 fighters. As we flew over the seemingly endless ranks of aircraft, Dudley, realising his error said, *"Oh sorry I meant 315 degrees,"* whereupon we turned about and retraced our steps over Leipheim. We might have gotten away with this, but at that precise moment, Tony Hilton, one of our Flight Commanders had just landed and was about to make arrangements with the German Base Commander for a squadron exchange, but had to offer his apologies for our infringement instead. After this I surreptitiously took to carrying a copy of our low-level route with me in the front cockpit!

Squadron exchanges were of great value in seeing how the other NATO nations operated. I eventually went on one to Luxeuil in France. This was just after France had withdrawn from NATO, but exchange visits continued. Of all the countries that I have flown over, I found France the most beautiful of them all. We were treated royally, and did a low-level land away to Solenzara in Corsica. We had a French pilot along with us, and on the return trip he routed us over St Tropez – but we did not see Mme Bardot!

Sad to say, on many occasions duty and penny pinching seemed to dictate the level of hospitality offered by the RAF to other nations. When the German G91 pilots (10 of them if I remember) came up to Laarbruch, (some of our crews having gone to Leipheim), there were only two squadron members, Cliff Thomas and myself, from the *whole* squadron available to host the Germans in the bar; this was no problem, because all the drinks were on the Squadron bar book. But the absence of all the other pilots and navigators who were involved in night flying or in QRA, really did nothing to improve NATO inter-Allied cooperation. I felt that it would have shown much more good will if night flying had been cancelled for at least one evening. Neither could we take them out for the evening, for it was impossible to persuade the Motor Transport Officer to supply a vehicle of some kind with a driver, *"Who's going to pay for that?"* Again, full marks for careful accountancy, but zilch for co-operation and cementing relations. When our crews returned from Leipheim, extolling their hosts' largesse, which included a coach tour round the local area and a visit to a nightclub, I felt quite ashamed over our penny-pinching lack of hospitality.

Dudley and I discovered another aspect of Allied co-operation when we landed at Furstenfeldbruck, the Luftwaffe Air Base, near Munich. Such landaways were intended to exercise other NATO air forces in servicing and turning around unfamiliar aircraft. While we were checking our maps for the return route, planning by the aircraft as it was being refuelled, an open topped VW utility car stopped alongside. The driver, an oldish chap in his 50s in a casual Luftwaffe uniform, open necked shirt, battered forage cap but sporting no rank insignia asked us if we would like to go for a coffee. We said we'd be delighted; so, we let our driver (for that's who we thought he was) take us to the air traffic tower, while he asked us various questions about how we were enjoying our tour of Germany. When we reached the ATC tower we didn't go in the front door, but up an emergency fire escape staircase at the back of the building. As we followed him through the door on the second floor, it opened into a palatial office. At this point we realised that he wasn't a driver but the base commander, because hanging on one wall there was a full-dress uniform – complete with lots of gongs and gold braid.

On the other wall was a large picture of a German Bomber over London in the summer of 1940. This is now a very well-known photograph; it shows a Heinkel 111 over the East India Docks area of London and the Thames. Our 'driver' noticed our attention, beamed at us, and remarked, *"I also have visited your country. I was flying that Heinkel!"* We had a few minutes interesting chat while we had coffee with him. I did note his name at the time, but unfortunately, I have since lost it; subsequently I wished that I had had the 'bottle' to ask him to send me an autographed copy of this picture.

At other times low-level sorties could get quite 'hairy' in bad visibility, particularly since Laarbruch was not far from the Ruhr with all its industrial haze. On one particular misty wet day, towards the end of my tour, by which time we had three Canberra squadrons at Laarbruch – Nos. 3, 16, and 31, the station had been tasked with getting all three squadrons airborne as quickly as possible –to avoid the inevitable incoming Warsaw Pact heavy metal. However, the visibility was so bad that a normal 30 sec separation between each of the 36 aircraft on route would have been very dangerous. Therefore, the navigator leaders planned for each aircraft to turn right 90 degrees exactly 30 seconds after getting airborne and follow the right bank of the River Maas, which was just over the western airfield boundary. The first aircraft would fly north for one minute before turning and flying south along the west bank of the river; and each of the following aircraft would extend their northerly leg by a further one minute. This manoeuvre would get all the aircraft off the ground at 30-second intervals but give a two-minute separation along the route. The visibility was really atrocious, and it was even hard to see the river Maas, which is not that wide at this point. Consequently, every aircraft tended to hug the riverbank, but every so often would have to make a violent jink to avoid a previous aircraft that had turned round and was now coming south and who was also trying to keep visual along the opposite bank of the river. If I remember correctly only one aircraft made it round the route –and that was by an older pilot –Ray Offord who had flown over this area in Mosquitoes during the War. Everyone else pulled out at some point until we were able to descend again over the north German plain.

Although 16 Squadron's raison d'être was a low-level nuclear strike squadron, we did fly high level sorties in the wintertime, when the low-level weather was often unsuitable, but this came about by default. Each squadron had an allotted task of so many hundred hours to fulfil each month, but no squadron boss would admit to the hierarchy at HQ RAF Germany that his squadron had not been able to complete the task. Hence, we had a Standard Route 19, a 2.5-hour triangular navigational exercise (navex) round Germany that was only exceeded in boredom by another route that went north from Laarbruch to roughly the latitude of Bergen in Norway, across to the Faeroes, down to Lands' End, and back to Laarbruch. This took about 4 hours and was always flown at night at high level. It could on occasions have moments of excitement. On the final leg, when we were about to coast in over Holland, after about 4 hours of flying in the dark and boredom was really setting in, the Dutch Air Force used us to practice interceptions with their Lockheed F104 interceptors. They were on different frequencies so we were not aware of when they had made a 'kill', except when some of the F104 pilots would accelerate, pass underneath us, ease up in front at a suitable distance (but not too far ahead), and ignite the after burner. By this stage in the sortie the Canberra pilot had almost reached a comatose state, so to suddenly be confronted with what looked a fireball, and an almost simultaneously shockwave, he rapidly woke up. This was not the last time that I had the pleasure while flying a Canberra of a fighter pilot demonstrating the potency of his 'hot jet.'

It's a Dog's Life – Part Two

No 16 Squadron was a Tactical Nuclear Bomber Squadron, which meant that two aircraft were kept permanently on standby inside a wire compound. The 2ATAF version of QRA was similar to the UK set up; the aircraft, which could be airborne within a few minutes, were held in readiness inside a 12-foot fence, about 300m square, with barbed wire, searchlights, guards, guns, and the works. Each QRA crew of two did 24 hours as a duty crew, probably about once or twice a week. By this stage of our marriage, Babs had realised that taking care of a husband, baby, and dog -not necessarily in that order could be quite demanding. My working feeding and sleeping hours could frequently be very irregular; the baby's feeding and waking hours were somewhat similar; and these schedules were complicated by the large dog that insisted on a regular sleeping, feeding and walking programme. All this took an awful lot of her time and energy. Now comes the interesting bit. There was another pilot on the Squadron – Ken Lilley, who owned a Golden Labrador, and on certain days when his wife wanted to go shopping or to a wives' coffee morning, he took the dog with him to the Squadron or into QRA. Well wives talk among themselves, so it didn't seem any problem when Babs asked me if I could take Suki with me into the QRA site, while she could 'relax' with just our toddler to look after! The QRA site had two blister hangers each with a nuclear-armed Canberra and some 30 yards away a long low one-storey building that housed the pilots and the ground crew. However, because we were armed with American nukes, we also had to have an American officer who had to give the final clearance, and additionally, the blister hanger that housed each aircraft, was not only guarded by an RAF Police but also by an American GI; retrospectively, I'm not sure who was guarding who against what. Now on the day that I took Suki into 'the pen' (i.e. penitentiary) as the QRA site was termed, we had a call out. Just like the UK QRA, a call out was a no notice exercise; you could never know whether it was for real or just an exercise. The klaxon horn would sound off and each crew member would grab his gear and leg it to the aircraft and strap in and listen out on the R/T. At which point one hoped someone would say, *"OK chaps you can stand down."* Well on this particular day, I shut Suki in my bedroom and ran rapidly after Dudley Brown my nav. But sadly, I had forgotten to shut the window of my room. I had just strapped into the ejection seat of the aircraft when I was aware that a large slobbering dog was looking up at me through the open hatch, as if to say *"Can I get in this 'car' too?"* The reason for this particular call out soon became obvious. The Squadron Boss Wing Commander Bennet was handing over to the new Boss, John Newby and giving him a tour of the squadron. When Suki had arrived on the pan (i.e. the frying pan shaped piece of concrete that housed the hanger and aircraft), there were already the two guards - Yank and Brit, with Dudley and myself in the aircraft, so in doggy logic that was OK; however, when the two Wing Commanders pitched up, all hell broke loose, she wasn't going to let anyone else near the aircraft. She was a soft as a brush but had a magnificent and intimidating bark. Fortunately, both bosses saw the funny side of it (or so I am told).

On another occasion I returned from a sortie to be confronted by John South and Pete Izzard, his navigator, who shame facedly confessed that they had let Suki out of my car to take her to annoy the navigators. Suki, with some encouragement from John and Pete would leap up onto the large map tables where the navs were planning their next sorties and plant muddy paws across their maps. However, on this occasion she had decided to make for the pinewoods that covered large areas of Laarbruch to go after rabbits. After much whistling and calling I persuaded her to return from her hunt. Rabbits were not the only 'game' she went after. The semi-detached houses of the Officers' Quarters backed onto open countryside, which was on the other side of a high wire fence, but between the gardens of each married quarter there was only a low wire mesh fence. No problem to a large dog, in fact watching her jump fence after fence was like watching a horse in the Grand National, as she disappeared out of sight – well as far as the Station Commander's garden. Unfortunately, the Station Commander in order to emphasise his exalted status, shunned the normal household pets and had peacocks in his garden. As far as I know Suki did not physically molest any of his birds, but when Babs went to retrieve the dog and lead her back down the road to our quarter, Suki sensing retribution adopted a passive resistance mode as per Ghandi by lying down on the pavement and refusing to budge. It was impossible to get her to move until she had been reassured that she was a good dog, and ergo no punishment was forthcoming. Who said dogs are dumb?

QRA 2ATAF Social Life

Carrying out QRA in Germany was subtly different from that in the UK. The whole of the 24-hour shift was spent within the enclosed wire compound, and essentially in the QRA aircrew building, which comprised a lounge, kitchen, toilets, and broom-cupboard-sized bedrooms. When I first arrived there, food was delivered daily for the crews to cook themselves. As there were two crews, each comprising pilot and navigator, plus an American Weapons officer, almost invariably there was at least one person who could really cook. Thus, all our food requirements, which were, within limits, quite flexible, could be ordered in the morning by the oncoming crews from the cookhouse. A driver would deliver the goods in a large wicker basket, and the nominated cook would get busy in a small galley kitchen. At a suitable time, we would all sit down and dine quite well. Lunch was quite a la carte, but the evening meal on occasions might have made it into the Michelin Guide. Some cooks, were really cordon bleu, and some could not only cook well, but also did not burn the pots and pans or leave the kitchen looking as if a bomb had hit it. But after the meal, those who had eaten but not cooked were required to wash up all the used crockery, cutlery, pots and pans, and then attempt to restore the kitchen to a reasonable order of cleanliness and whiteness. After a few occasions of carrying out this onerous task, I made a resolution to become a cook. I got reasonably proficient, but unfortunately, I did not have long to practice this art, for a few months later, when the new boss John Newby, a South African, commenced to do his turn in QRA, by a strange coincidence he was paired for three times in a row with John Saddler, one of the squadron bachelors, and two navigators, none of whom could cook. As a consequence of dining on baked beans on toast for every meal each time he went into QRA, the new boss had an RAF chef deliver *and* cook the food. We still ate well, but no longer were there any budding Jamie Oliver's attempting some haute cuisine.

There was another occupant in the QRA living quarter – Charles Peace, the Squadron mascot, a green parrot that lived in a cage in the aircrew lounge. Occasionally when we got bored, we would let him out and he would fly the length of the room and land on a bookcase. Then with a wave of a tea towel he would be encouraged to make the return trip. John Saddler also tried the parrot's skill at night flying one evening by switching the lights out as the parrot was halfway across the room – this was less successful. Unfortunately, the next time this trick was carried out during the day, a window was open, and the parrot – who by then was probably nursing a grudge, managed to do a sharp turn in mid-flight, followed by an elongated glide in which he very nearly did a crash landing in the grass, but managed to reach the compound boundary fence and clamp his claws onto the wire mesh. Before we could get to him, he had clawed his way up the wire and taken off into Holland, and that was the last that we ever saw of him.

On another occasion while on duty on QRA, Squadron Leader (Sqn Ldr) Ike Dawson, one of our Flight Commanders, noticed that his watch had stopped and refused to start again. He rang the V and A (Valuable and Attractive items section of the Stores Squadron where aircrew watches were held). The conversation went something like this.

> Sqn Ldr Dawson: *"Hullo, Squadron Leader Dawson here in the QRA site, my watch appears to be u/s* (unserviceable). *Can you send another one across to me?"*

> Stores Wallah: *"The V& A stores are open for business only between two and four pm every Tuesday and Friday."*

> Sqn Ldr Dawson: *"I'm sorry but I am on duty in the QRA site, I can't fly my mission without a serviceable watch and I can't wait until then."*

> Stores Wallah: *"I am sorry too Squadron Leader, but those are the rules."*

> Sqn Ldr Dawson: *"OK, in that case I have no option by to inform HQRAF Germany that one of RAF Laarbruch's QRA missions has been aborted because the pilot does not have a watch."*

Long Pause.

> Stores Wallah: *"The trouble with you b****y flying types is that you think that the Air force runs for you!"*

A short time later a fully serviceable watch was delivered to the QRA site.

The last two stories from inside the wire both occurred on Christmas Eve. On the first, one of the pilots from No 3 Squadron felt that it would be a good thing to wish our opposite QRA numbers (and opponents) in the Soviet 4th Tactical Air Army a Merry Christmas. He picked up the phone and asked to put through to the exchange at HQRAFG, and then made his way successively through to some NATO telephone exchanges to Berlin. He then requested to be put through to the Soviet HQ. His request was accepted, but someone somewhere along the line must have feared about a possible breach of security and the line went dead.

We also had a TV set in the QRA hut that could receive only one station (from Holland), which broadcast programmes quite frequently in English. On Christmas Eve 1968, when the Apollo 8 spacecraft orbited the Moon, I was overawed as I watched the pictures of the moon and the incredible beauty and colour of the earth hanging in space, while Frank Borman, Jim Lovell, and Will Anders, the three astronauts read the first ten verses from Genesis. I had by now become somewhat fatalistic, and I didn't really believe in anything, but these pictures and the reading had a great and as yet unknown effect on me.

RAF Bad Kohlgrub, Bavaria – Winter Survival Course 1967

It was mandatory for new crews to attend the Winter Survival Course at Bad Kohlgrub, Bavaria. Consequently, at the middle of our first winter, the new boys, including Dudley Brown my nav and I were selected to attend. The initial RV for all personnel from RAFG and the UK was Monchen Gladbach railway station. The overnight train to Munich was the 2200hrs Rhineland Express, which would, with the well-known Teutonic efficiency, depart at 2200 hours. For this reason, it seemed an unnecessary caution for HQ RAFG to order all personnel to be present by 2000hours, thereby having to kill two hours on the platform. Inevitably, more than a few litres of fine German bier were consumed before the train departed. But as a bonus we all got to know one another, and having developed an instant camaraderie with the other aircrew, it seemed like a good idea when the train made brief stops further down the line at Koln, Bonn, and Koblenz to quickly get off the train, find the nearest station buffet and grab a few more bottles of whatever bier was on offer. It's amazing just how quickly 10 minutes can pass, and exactly 10 minutes after stopping the train began to roll out of the station. It was a *"damn close-run thing"* as Wellington said after Waterloo, but everyone managed to re-board the train just as the railway staff were insisting on closing the doors. Later while we were thundering through one of the tunnels along the Rhine valley, another 'sport' was accidentally discovered. Someone threw an empty beer bottle out the open carriage door window such that it impacted against the tunnel wall, disintegrated, and ricocheted back against the carriage, thereby causing an interesting phenomenon, for with practice, given the relative velocities of train, the width of the tunnel, and the force with which the beer bottle was thrown, the 'shrapnel' could be made to re-enter the train at another open window further down the carriage, where some of our mates were standing! Eventually we arrived in Munich about 9am, transferred to a slow local train and chugged our way up to Bad Kohlgrub; by lunchtime the long journey was over.

The course was divided into three parts; for the first week all personnel were taught or refreshed in the rudiments of skiing, and more importantly brought everyone up to a good standard of physical fitness before the second phase of the course. This was a four-day escape and evasion phase across some quite rugged country, as was emphasised to us at the briefing, *"If during night travel you see one metre pine trees ahead of you – Stop! There are no one metre pine trees in southern Germany; what you are seeing are thirty metre pine trees at the bottom of a twenty-nine-metre gorge!"*

There were about 30 of us on the course in total. The CO of the RAF detachment at Bad Kohlgrub asked if there were any who had skied before. About 1/3 raised their hands. He then asked how many of us thought that they could ski. About another third of us raised our hands. This was a good decision: those who had skied before went off and did just that. The third group who hadn't skied and didn't think that they could never really got off the nursery slopes. But those of us who had been optimistic enough to think that we could ski had a really marvellous time. The RAF ski students were dressed in an all-black outfit, which apparently was well recognized by the locals as saying *"These men are incompetent idiots, avoid them like the plague."*

Our instructor was a chap called Karl Wilhelm (centre of photo – I'm fourth from the left). On the first two days he taught us all basic techniques on some gentle slopes. Then on the 3rd day he took us to the ski lift that went up to the top of the local 'Alp'. At the top as the ski lift entered the terminal, some locals with a macabre sense of humour had nailed the remnants and detritus of failed skiers – boots, broken skis, ski sticks, gloves, and helmets to the wooden end wall facing the ski lift. Karl got us all lined up on what appeared to be a small car park that jutted out over the snowy hillside that sloped downwards at about 40 degrees. *"You will follow me,"* with that he launched off from the 'car park' onto the snow about two feet below him and cruised along at right angles to the slope. We all managed to accomplish this manoeuvre following his tracks, and pretty soon we were all strung out behind him. He then did the impossible and swung his (right) foot uphill – with ski attached – round so that it angled at the 2 o'clock to 8 o'clock position, and then smartly swung his other foot round to the 10 o'clock to 4 o'clock position and leaned towards the slope. *"Now we will all do this."* Well we did. No one disappeared backwards down the slope. *"Now we walk up hill."* Everybody followed. The slope eased off into a nice gently undulating snow scene bordered by large pines. *"Now we go back down,"* said Karl, for some reason smiling broadly. And there amidst the pines was a culvert shaped gulley about 10 feet wide of fairly compact snow. *"We will use snow plough ski position to slow*

down," advised Karl. Like a flock of sheep, we duly followed him. The snow gulley got steeper, the snow became firmer, then icier, the braking action became less, the gulley then did a smart left turn, which we all negotiated, but at the far end the pine forest ended and there appeared to be nothing to be seen but sky! First impressions were that we were about to launch out over the abyss. The snow slope did indeed drop very steeply. No one managed to stay on their feet, and pretty smartly there were some 10 bodies sliding down the slope in various positions. Karl thought this very amusing. We were now back on flattish area at the end of which was an establishment that served hot gluwien and bratwurst. A lunch break was deemed a good idea. After *'der kleine pause'*, and fortified by alcohol we had a confidence that enabled us to do things that we had thought impossible before. The remainder of the descent twisted down through the woods with quite a few steep slopes but by the time that we reached our starting point we had become quite adept at staying on our feet and stopping where and when we wanted to.

The next phase was escape and evasion. We were taken by transport to 'somewhere in Southern Germany' given instructions of where we were to make for, with lots of advice on what not to do, and let loose at discrete intervals sometime after sunset. Since there was lots of deep snow, and the air temperature was distinctly minus, some crews from the UK had brought the V Force bunny suit –a one-inch-thick head-to-toe two-piece cotton garment that could be worn under the rubber immersion suit. This suit was a brilliant solution for wearing under an immersion suit while sitting in a rubber dinghy out on the cold Atlantic, but it was an instant inbuilt sauna when attempting to negotiate deep snow. One or two of these guys rapidly came to grief, having to make a choice between sweating or removing the thick bunny suit and freezing.

As Dudley my navigator had opted to join the group three non-skiers, I found myself teamed up with Pete Jones and Tony Stevens, one of the other new crews on 16 Squadron. After a while, and getting somewhat tired of sticking to what seemed to be impenetrable woods, we came to a long valley between the forests on either side. Travel was easier and we made such good progress, that when we spotted a barn, we reckoned that we could ease up for a spell. We had been specifically warned not to lie up in such places, so we reconnoitred it carefully and established that there was no one else there, and got inside and lay down on a cold but dry floor.

Absolute bliss! A few minutes later there was an odd noise that went, "sshh sshh…sshh sshh…sshh sshh." *"What's that?"* *"It sounds like a mouse gnawing at the wood work."* But it wasn't, it was the sound of skis being used very quietly, for suddenly the door burst open and we were confronted by two SAS guys with torches and rifles. They pretty soon had us tied up, and roped together from neck to neck. I was in the middle, which was unfortunate for me for both Pete and Tony were taller than I was, and therefore took longer strides in the snow. If I didn't keep up, my neck got a tug from Pete in front, and Tony would tread on my heels at the rear. After the interrogation, we settled down to exist as best we could in the snow, knowing that we would have a few more days to ski before returning home.

The Red Arrows – Summer 1967

OK, the next few lines are a bit of an ego trip, but it's not every day that you get to fly with the Reds while they do a display! But that's what happened. When the Reds arrived at Laarbruch, I found that one of the pilots was Pete Evans, who had been on the Winter Survival Course with me, and who was quite willing to take me along in the back seat of his aircraft while they did a display over the base, at the end of which I got some super, if blurred photos as Pete departed at warp 9 about 20 feet above the station golf course. In the afternoon, the Reds gave another display at an air day at a local German civil airfield not too far away. This was even more interesting as this small grass airfield was located right next to an enormous grain silo. Pete was flying out on the tip of the diamond nine keeping his eyes on the aircraft next to him, but his peripheral vision picked up the silo as we flew incredibly close to it. I told him not to worry, as presumably the formation leader had made allowances for this.

The 16 Squadron Amstel Brewery Visit – Summer 1967

As a small recognition to the ground crews who worked on the line and in the hangar at all times and in all weathers trying to keep all the aircraft serviceable, once a year the Boss would grant them a day's outing of their choice. On this occasion they chose to visit the Amstel Brewery in Amsterdam. Now whether the lads were also given the choice of officers who were to be in charge (??) of the party, I don't know, but I suddenly found myself, with Fg/0ff Dave Wilby, elected to look after some 50 NCOS and airmen. Subsequently I realised that older and wiser officers on the Squadron who hoped for further promotion had concluded that being in charge of a party that could degenerate into something akin to the sack of Rome by the Goths in 410AD was not a good career move, hence the choice of two junior officers for the job, who with time, could redeem their fortunes! At this point I made the first of my only two wise decisions of the day. When we were all aboard the coach prior to leaving Laarbruch, I told the boys in no uncertain terms that the bus would leave from the drop off point in Amsterdam at 11pm – sharp, and if they weren't there, they would have to pay for their own return to base.

The day started fair and it did not take us long to travel by coach to Amsterdam – in fact we were there well before lunch –I'm not sure if this was what the brewery staff had intended. They had laid on a magnificent cold buffet lunch, after which we presumably were to tour the brewery, but, having arrived with lots of time to spare, there was no option but to take us on a tour of the brewery and the opportunity to sample lots and lots of Dutch beer on an empty stomach. By the time that lunch came we were well away.

As the gang fell on the food like vultures on a carcass, someone noticed that the 'dining room' was in fact up on the top floor of the brewery, and along one wall of the 'dining room' there were 'airport lounge' glass windows with a door giving access to a large balcony from which there was a panoramic view of much of Amsterdam. In the circumstances it was fortunate that the balcony had a wall high enough to prevent anyone falling over. On the other hand, it was not too high so that from one corner, one could peer over and obtain a view far below of a crossroads and traffic lights. I believe that it has been said that wars often start with an accidental discharge of firearms. On this occasion, someone 'accidentally' dropped an empty bottle – no sense in wasting good beer – over the edge of the balcony wall. From perhaps 50 feet up, the terminal velocity of the bottle when it met the tarmac resulted in micro shards of glass exploding in all directions. This seemed a good idea, and a few more followed. Fortunately, it was Saturday lunchtime and there were very few pedestrians and not many cars. Had the citizens been warned?

By the late '60s it had been some 20 odd years since the end of the 2nd World War, and although the Dutch people were still very grateful to the Allies in general for evicting the forces of the 3rd Reich and to the RAF in particular for the delivery of much needed food at the end of the War, I doubted whether their debt of gratitude would have extended to such an exhibition of drunken horseplay. I therefore made my second good decision of the day and quickly called the lads to heel, gave our profuse thanks to the brewery staff (who seemed not to have noticed our wickedness, and left for a safer venue –i.e. another bar, before wandering along another street until our progress was halted by a canal crossing us at right angles. Amsterdam is crisscrossed with many canals, and travelling by a canal bus is a great way to see the city. This became the next 'great thing' to do. The canal buses were boats, the interior of which (see attached picture) was just like a single decked bus with a Plexiglas roof just high enough to enable the boats to pass under the canal bridges. Also pertinent to what follows, the width of the canal bridges had been taken into account when the boats were designed; each boat having about a bulwark about 12" width on either side to protect it from collision with the canal walls, just sufficient in fact to allow the passage of the boats between the walls of the bridges. The group who had voted to *"get outside on the balcony"* at the brewery, now, noting the open section on each barge, opted for, *"let's get outside and sit on the deck and dangle our feet in the water."* Compared to the previous escapade, this seemed pretty harmless – until we came to the first bridge. The minimum dimensions between boat and stonework, meant that the nautical phrase, *"Repel all boarders"* swept the lads who had opted for deck crew into the canal. I can't remember if or how they caught up with us again, but all the seats on the coach were occupied when we left Amsterdam that night.

Water has a strange fascination for some people. In addition to the accidental immersions noted above, we had one lad whose determination to sample the waters, as it were, was much more deliberate. On the Squadron, this quiet shy young man was the office typist. However even here he exhibited the odd flash of rebellion. One of his duties was to type out Squadron Routine Orders each week; such things as

- ORDER No.1: All personnel are to ensure that a Security Pass is displayed in the car windscreen.

- ORDER No. 2: All Officers are to read Squadron Standing Orders on the 1st of every month.

For some reason, known only to him, this quiet retiring young man on one particular occasion typed an order that read.

- ORDER No. 3 'Squadron morale is to improve; otherwise disciplinary action will be taken.'

Now let loose in Amsterdam, fortified with 'pints and quarts of Amstel beer' to misquote A. E. Housman, this young man's 'doppelganger' resurfaced. By late afternoon, we had had enough – for the interim – of Dutch beer; the 'next great thing' was to view the sights in the Red-Light District. Sitting demurely by the window of each house of the street that we strolled along, was a 'lady', or 'ladies', who were ogled by the window shoppers. Meanwhile, our typist, so I heard later, noted that many of the local punters who frequented these establishments, arrived and departed by bicycle, which mode of transport allowed a relatively discrete rapid arrival and departure compared to parking a car or walking. The bicycles, left leaning against the wall or a tree, could therefore be instantly removed. This our lad did. His motivation was not however anything so base as theft, but so that he could pedal off, get up a head of steam, point at the canal, (there were no intervening walls between the pavement and the canal), and see how far he could travel before bombing into the water. I believe he did this not a few times over the afternoon. Funnily enough, no one came after him and asked for their bike back!

Well the day finally and thankfully came to an end. From being something like Mission Impossible, it had become Mission Accomplished: no one was missing; no one – amazingly – had been arrested; no one had been injured or admitted to hospital; and no one had been in a fight. On a personal note, on the following week, no one said thanks to Dave and I for our fortitude in the face of impossible odds, which is a pity because if there had been any unfortunate incidents, I'm quite sure that we would have carried the can.

Odds and Ends

Happy Hour at Laarbruch was also subtly different. The alcohol was very cheap. In fact, it was rumoured that it was cheaper to top up the windscreen wash bottle on your car with gin, rather than buy de–icing fluid from the NAAFI. In the Officers Mess bar there were two regular barmen –Gunter, a local German, and Franco, who hailed from Italy. The favourite squadron tipple at Happy Hour was Carlsberg, drunk straight from the bottle (remember we're RAF officers!), so once Happy Hour had been going for an hour or so most officers were becoming a little more than happy. (See photo. Author 2nd from the right) By this stage in the evening, each time Franco was asked for another bottle, he would flip off the metal top, then unobserved pour out a mouthful of lager down the sink and top it up with vodka. Hardly anyone seemed to notice this – until next morning.

As is normal in such inebriated occasions, the situation could get out of hand. On the far side of the entrance hall from the bar was the Ladies Room, which contained a piano. Having by now a basic skill in playing boogie and blues, I was invited to play, so it seemed a good idea to bring the piano into the bar. About six of us set about pushing the piano from the Ladies Room to the Bar. Unfortunately, unknown to us, one of the castors had partially broken off, effectively leaving two very sharp projecting pieces of metal, which divided the new hall carpet into three strips; two 10 feet wide pieces, with a one-inch strip in between. On the following day, having been told off in no uncertain terms by the station commander, the squadron was charged for another new carpet.

Detachments

There were frequent opportunities for visits to other Air Force bases. One of the first that I undertook was to the Royal Norwegian Air Force base at Sola - Stavanger. We arrived for an overnight stop with four aircraft, but on the following day my aircraft developed a fault and we had to stay behind. Fortunately, I had been given charge of the imprest – a cash advance for the detachment's expenses while in Norway. We didn't misuse the money, but on the second day of our enforced stay we met another RAF officer who was on a year's detachment to the Royal Norwegian Air Force. He confided to us that he yearned for some tasty food, as the Norwegians seemed to live on assorted pickled fish and various other very healthy foods but nothing approaching a good old 'British Fry Up.' In recognition of his plight Dudley, my nav and I took him across to the Scandinavian Airlines terminal, which was also located at Stavanger, and dined him out on the imprest. On return to Laarbruch, I took the remains of the imprest back to the Accounts Officer. He seemed a little surprised at the amount that just one crew had spent on food, but I was able to point out to him that beer in Norway was an incredible £5 a litre, and that we had been very good and stayed off the alcohol, the cost of which could not be deducted from the imprest, although this wasn't strictly true since the meal courtesy of Scandinavian Airways had included the odd glass of wine.

Another interesting excursion I made was courtesy of the British Frontier Service; an organisation that is no more. Initially this service was set up in the immediate aftermath of WW2 to control the flow of refugees and prevent smuggling between the Eastern and Western Zones. It was finally disbanded in 1991 when Germany was reunified. In 1968 I was detailed to visit them at Helmstadt, a city right on the East German border. It was fascinating to see the remains of vehicles that had been shot up and burnt and left since the immediate aftermath of WW2, on roads that were still blocked off; to see electrical pylons with severed power cables that did not carry power from east to west; and to stand next to a concrete post marking the East German border. On this post was a nice coloured shiny enamel badge, bearing the symbols of East Germany; and only two small screws held it on. My German guide quietly said to me *"Don't even try to touch it, you are probably already lined up in the sights of a guard in one of the watchtowers, and he will shoot with no questions or challenges beforehand."*

Squadron Exchange – Italian Air Force Base Ghedi Italy

The squadron exchange to Ghedi in Northern Italy in September '68 lasted two weeks. The weather was excellent, the food and wine –which the Italian Air Force served with each meal –was partaken of by all. Although there was some harrumphing by the wheels about drinking alcohol before flying, everybody was sensible enough to know when to draw the line. And in any case, there were lots of sotto voce mutterings about insulting the Italians if we didn't follow their customs: these last murmurings of discontent being enough to swing the argument. We made a memorable visit to Venice –nobody went canal swimming this time; and secondly, to the Italian Grand Prix at Monza just outside Milan. There was a huge crowd waiting to get in, but a kindly intentioned local racing fan led us round to a very high wire fence which proved no obstacle, and from there we proceeded to make our own mini-grandstand from two large oil drums and a long thick wooden plank to see over the heads of the crowd.

Flying round Italy during these two weeks was also quite interesting. Exploratory sorties were made by air through the Alps. On my first Alpine sortie, my nav for the day – Bob Latchem said he would take me up a valley where he had been by car and caravan the previous summer. The valley was steeply walled but wide. It got progressively narrower and more sinuous. I queried with Bob whether we were in the correct valley. He assured me that we were. But on rounding the next bend, the valley became what the Yanks call a box canyon, with steep mountains blocking the valley some two or three miles ahead. I now had the option of attempting a max rate turn and go back down the valley. But if I turned, I couldn't be sure how far the underside of the fuselage would be from the opposite side of the valley, while my wings were at a high angle of bank. The alternative was to go for full power, gain some speed and zoom over an intervening col between two peaks, hoping that we had enough energy to attempt this. This was duly accomplished with no great margin for error. I made a mental note not to trust Bob's holiday recollections again.

A few days later we launched two pairs. Pete Jones led the first pair, with Jerry Kingwell as his No.2; while I led the second pair, with Dave Ward as my No. 2 This time the route went south over and through the Italian Apennines, including an over flight of Florence and the tiny state of San Marino. At this point we need to record a little difficulty that Pete Jones was having. Jerry, his No. 2

was a very junior pilot on the squadron, but Pete had decided to give him the lead to gain experience at some point in the sortie –no problem really the weather was superb. Unfortunately, Jerry had taken the pair down a valley that was strung from one side to the other with high-tension electrical cables. Normally our aircraft flew above such obstacles, but in this case the cables were well above this minimum height over the middle of the valley. Jerry was oblivious of these and flew under them, but Pete flew straight into them –such cables are very difficult to see. The cables cut one engine out completely and partially severed the fuel line to the second engine, but the cut was so neat that sufficient fuel was still available to maintain sufficient power on one engine. Jerry returned to Ghedi and landed. Pete climbed to 5000' and got his navigator Tony Stephens to bale out. Pete then landed at Ghedi with some hundreds of yards of thick copper cable snaking about behind him. Pete's landing was OK, but the cable proceeded to demolish the runway caravan (sensibly vacated for the occasion), then the Instrument Landing System installation and the Radar truck, while the Italians in the control tower were finding it difficult to tot up the cost of the damage that now added up to billions of lire.

It was at this point that my pair of aircraft debouched from the mountains onto the plain of the Po River, 70–80 miles south-south west of Ghedi. We were at low level –250' so radio reception wasn't good. I made a call to Ghedi ATC that we would be with them in about 15 minutes. There was one RAF ATC officer in the tower to assist the Italians with the RAF R/T. He tried to pass a message to us that we were to divert to an airfield near Venice, but all we got was a broken message with what we thought was *"Steer 060."* This was the course ATC had calculated from our present position to divert to an airfield near Venice. We had expected a steer of about 020 east of north, and we knew that we were not that far off course –a steer of 060 would have meant that we were in the Milan Civil Air Traffic Zone –a very definite no, no, and this time Bob was adamant that he knew where we were and that our steer was definitely 020. Ghedi ATC was still pushing out some garbled message –using our section call sign, but now the message was in Italian.

As we joined the circuit our RAF ATC officer came on the air and told us that the runway was blocked; but by now we did not have enough fuel to divert the 60-70 miles to our diversion. There was but one option. About 3 or 4 miles to the east of Ghedi was Monti Chiari

-a disused airfield that had been a missile base up until a few years previously. It was now being grazed by sheep and covered in bales of hay. I lead my No. 2 there and turned down wind. As I started my downwind leg, Dave my No. 2, overtook me, declaring, *"I'm going ahead of you. I'm short of fuel."* He landed first, and cleared the runway of sheep for which I was truly grateful. About an hour later, just as the Italians had got the runway operational again, the new Boss Wing Commander Swalwell arrived from Germany so see how the exchange was going. The next few hours were interesting.

Squadron exchange visits seemed to invite the unusual. Sometime previously just before a detachment to somewhere in the Middle East, we were all gathered together for a briefing by the wheels on what not to do, which included the inevitable film and chat by the MO on the perils of partaking of the local food and talent, when the Tannoy suddenly came to life, *"Attention, Attention, there is an aircraft in the overhead with a double engine flame out."* To a man we left our seats, and ran outside. This was not just idle curiosity, but all of us knew that any officer who saw an incident could not be chosen as a member for the subsequent Board of Enquiry or Court Marshall. The pilot of the Canberra was John South, who had been practicing some wingovers and dive manoeuvres for conventional weapons (1000lb bombs) delivery. The Canberra normally had a fuel supply system that functioned under negative 'g', but on this occasion it had either failed or John hadn't switched it on. I think that he got one engine relit as he carried out a forced landing pattern, while furiously operating the emergency hydraulic handle to lower the landing gear and the flaps. On short finals, the main wheels had locked down, the flaps had travelled, but the nose wheel had not completely extended. John managed to hold the nose off while still pumping the emergency handle. Finally, the nose wheel came down just as the airspeed fell and the nose lowered. We all felt that he should have received some sort of commendation for this, but if I remember rightly all he got was a rocket.

Quite early on in the tour I had bought a larger car from one of the American's on the base – a VW Variant estate car that gave us lots more room. But I had to dispose of the Mini and because it was second-hand with a right-hand drive it had no prospects of sale. So, we drove it back to the UK, visited Babs' Mum and Dad, sold it, and for £147, bought a 1947 MG TC sports car. For that price it wasn't brilliant but it got us back to Germany – just. I then spent an awful lot of my spare time renovating this car. I spent a lot of time on this at weekends–with a lot of expert help from a Chief Technician who was keen on car repair.

Much of our leave was spent camping; hence we made a fair number of trips round Germany, Holland, France (to the battle field at Verdun), and Switzerland. With time our camping ambitions grew and we found that there is some vague law about one's possessions expanding to fit the space available, and although our VW estate car had a lot more room that the Mini, we still on occasion found it a bit of a tight squeeze to accommodate all that we wanted. In particular on a camping trip to western Holland, on the island of Walcheren, we not only had all our camping gear, our son Andrew, my Mum, who had come over on a visit, but also Suki the Great Dane, shoe horned in between the baggage and the roof. We had previously tried to leave her behind in kennels, but she pined and never ate, so that at the end of two weeks she was completely skeletal.

In February 1968, we had our second child – another boy who we christened Paul. Shortly afterwards we went on our final camping excursion to Scandinavia when Paul was only five months old! On this holiday with Vince and Christine Robertson and their children we had originally planned to visit Copenhagen, then Stockholm, and finally Oslo. But when we discovered just how much more expensive unsubsidised fuel was in Sweden, we headed directly for Oslo. This was a fascinating city; we toured Nansen's ship 'The

Fram' in which he sailed through the North West Passage, and Thor Heyerdahl's raft 'Kon Tiki', wandered for hours round the sculptures in the Vigeland Park, and marvelled at the Holmenkolen Ski Jump.

On our return, just as we got to the ferry at Gotenburg in Sweden, we saw banner headlines in a Swedish tabloid. None of us could read Swedish, but the pictures told the whole story –the USSR had invaded Czechoslovakia. We idly mused about remaining in Sweden a neutral country; since if this episode became a hot war, we were nicely placed.

Germany to Kenya and Back

The following article also appeared in the RAF Flight Safety Magazine 'Air Clues' in which I wrote, *"How often when it's all happening and your whole day is encumbered with multi-injects of the 'Do Not Pass Go, Do Not Collect £200, Go Directly to Jail" variety, have you felt tempted to press on regardless when common sense says STOP, SIT BACK, AND THINK THIS OUT? For those of you who do not subscribe to this defeatist view I submit the following odyssey dedicated to sufferers and inflictors of press-on-itis. "*

It was the custom on 16 Squadron, when a crew was approaching their tourex (tour-expiry) date, to let them loose on an Extended Southern Ranger Flight. This was a special bonus, a one-off sortie, which consisted of two three-day transits from RAF Germany to Kenya and back with a one-day stopover in Nairobi in between. (Let me say that in the days before wall-to-wall in-flight refuelling and high mach cruise speeds, three days each way to Nairobi was about the minimum time possible in a Canberra). Then as now with a shortage of crews and aircraft, the pressure was on to get there and back in time. Any delays that caused the loss of one day or more off the flight schedule meant that the Ranger terminated at the furthest point that could be reached within the original seven-day return schedule.

The morning of our departure dawned, a solid November Fog, the visibility down to zero and with no diversions anywhere. What's more, I had a raging sore throat heralding a possible cold, so I should by rights have declared myself grounded. However, the Met forecaster optimistically promised that the weather would improve, so arming myself with a packet of well-known throat lozenges; I presented myself to the Flight Commander for a final briefing. By lunchtime the weather had improved dramatically to a poor Amber (if I can remember the weather limits, this was a cloud base of about 300' and ½ mile visibility), with a dodgy No. 1 diversion airfield in northern Scotland. The Flight Commander, seeing my determination, consigned his immediate career prospects to fortune, extorted a promise from me to be back in seven days or else, and gave us the go ahead. As well as my usual nav Dudley Brown, I took along Jock Adams another navigator as a passenger.

Day one should have been easy even though we took off some four hours late, as we only had to transit to Nicosia in Cyprus and night stop. However, while cruising down the west coast of Italy at FL410 (41,000feet), the port tip tank would not transfer fuel, nor could any contact be made with any Rome ATC frequency because of a loud howl on the VHF R/T. However, I still had contact with RAF Luqa on Malta via UHF, so I elected to divert there to have the fuel problem solved, after which I could still make Nicosia in time to catch up with the flight schedule the following day. For those unfamiliar with VHF and UHF, VHF (Very High Frequency) radios which operate in the lower end of the radio frequency spectrum have a longer range than UHF (Ultra High Frequency) radios; but the characteristics of the higher frequencies of UHF radios make them more efficient in hilly or built up areas. In an emergency the pilot would normally broadcast on 243Mega cycles (Mcs) UHF – known as the Guard Channel, or on 121.5 Mega cycles (Mcs) VHF if in contact with a Civilian Airfield. But by the time that the ground crew had repaired the tip tank, but failed to find any fault with the radio, not only was the sun sinking over the western horizon but also there was a gale gusting above the crosswind limits on the main runway. (The Canberra had a crosswind limit of 25 knots, above which speed it was very difficult to hold the rudder to keep the aircraft pointing down the runway). However, with a nod and a wink to the resident duty pilot in the ATC tower, I showed him that RAFG pilots could fly to a somewhat higher crosswind limit than the Luqa Flying Order Book deemed prudent. I ran up the engines on the edge of the runway while pointing roughly into wind, which was at 45 degrees to the take-off direction, commenced the roll to let the air get established into the intakes (the Avon was prone to surge with a strong cross wind), then as the aircraft accelerated, pressed the port brake and simultaneously booted the rudder round to point the aircraft down the runway. So, we were on our way to Nicosia –that is until we ran into a really strong easterly wind. Regular Med fliers will tell you that the upper winds always blow west to east in the Med. Well, on that evening we found a 90knot headwind over a large height band and some severe Clear Air Turbulence to boot. Then one of the forward bomb bay fuel pumps packed up. Now, not only were we going to take a lot longer, but the aircraft was also becoming progressively nose heavy. I mulled over this new wrinkle for a bit before deciding that I could use the fuel in the forward tank by gravity feed once we had descended into Nicosia. By the time we had burned off the fuel (by flying instrument patterns at 2000' for 30 minutes) to put the aircraft back in trim, landed and explained the fuel and radio problems to the engineers, found contrary to expectations, that the Officers Mess had no accommodation (the Officers' Mess Summer Ball was in progress), ordered a taxi and reached the visiting aircrew hotel on the other side of town it was one o'clock in the morning. We had to be up at 5.30am. We could still hack it!

Day two was a slightly more demanding schedule. From Nicosia we were routing via Turkey and Iran to land at Bahrain in the Persian Gulf to refuel, and then, over-flying Sharjah on the tip of Oman, before turning for Masirah Island off the south coast of the Arabian Peninsula. The schedule was even tighter than this suggested, since Turkish diplomatic clearance for our flight expired at mid-day, and because of communications problems with Our Man in Ankara (the Air Attaché), no amended clearances could be obtained. Next morning, feeling distinctly seedy and experiencing that 'rusty eye ball' feeling, which comes from a lack of sleep, we yawned our way through breakfast wrung from a waiter with references suitable to Fawlty Towers, followed by a bellowed telephone conversation over a bad line as to why our transport had not arrived. Once more however, luck (?) was on our side, for on arrival at the airport we found that the unserviceable fuel pump had been changed, no fault had been found with the radio, and our aircraft was ready. We were still going to hack it –or so we thought until just after start up when the line chief looked through the entrance hatch and told me that there was a hydraulic leak. *"No problem. Sir,"* he said, *"we'll have it fixed in an hour or so."* We then sat on the rapidly warming tarmac, contemplating the prospect of a few days in Cyprus, and watched our diplomatic clearance tick away, while the transit flight team worked like beavers on the plumbing. At the same time as the aircraft was declared serviceable, we reached our latest time for a scramble take-off for entry, if not exit, into Turkish airspace while we were still legal. True we would not be at our planned cruise altitude but the flight wasn't in controlled airspace, there were no civil airways to cross, and the weather was excellent, so with a few replies of the *"Say again, you are unreadable"* variety to the Turkish ATC queries as to our exact flight level we surreptitiously climbed to height some three hours late but we could still make Nairobi.

The turnaround and departure at Bahrain were uneventful, if you discount being wrongly marshalled out of dispersal in the dark against a stream of large transport aircraft. However, we were soon cruising at height under a brilliantly starry sky, while far below the inky black of the desert was broken only by a few oil-well gas flares. We had decided that rather than fly the official dog leg route to Masirah via Sharjah's overhead, we would route direct to Masirah over the desert, since it was night and there were no ATC restrictions – or at least none that we would have to account for –and we would catch up some time. Incidentally, we hadn't actually been authorised for a night landing at Masirah. Sometime later I decided to try Masirah on the UHF radio and had been trying unsuccessfully for some minutes before there was a polite cough on the intercom from my nav, who said, *"Er, I think that I misread the opening times for*

Masirah in the En-route Flight Supplement. Since we are three hours late, they have been shut for two hours, and I don't think that they will have received our revised ETA on the departure signal from Bahrain yet." The next few minutes were somewhat confused, until the aircraft was heading back the way we had come while we decided exactly where we were (by dead reckoning – no navigational aids out there then), where our point of no return was, or had been, and how much fuel we had. Just as we rolled out on the return track, we heard a very faint call over the R/T from Masirah! They *had seen* a signal with a delayed departure time from Nicosia, so someone at Masirah with an IQ of about 150, had opened up ATC about the time he estimated we would be calling them. God bless all Air Traffic Controllers. We again reversed our heading and climbed to gain better fuel consumption, and finally saw Masirah's flare path and descended for a straight in landing – or we almost did – for at 500' the moist warm monsoon air in battle with the upper atmosphere cold soaked aircraft finally got the better of the demisting system and Masirah suddenly looked for all the world like a Lincolnshire airfield on a foggy day. After one or two IMC circuits with our spare nav wiping the Perspex on the cockpit, I finally got enough forward vision to land. Not my best landing, but we were down.

Day three; we were awakened early and on time. The sun shone out of a clear blue sky. The aircraft was ready to go. My ears would not clear! There were dark mutterings from the crew at the thought of sitting out my cold at Masirah, which is an island of sand and tarmac, sand, sand, and more sand, so I set about chewing some more of the throat lozenges and having a sniff of a nasal spray carefully and illegally hoarded from some previous affliction. After about half an hour I could successfully subject my Eustachian tubes to any number of no notice exercises and an hour later Salalah (another remote RAF out post of the Empire on the Omani coast) had faded into the desert haze beneath us. But about half an hour before we had to commence our descent, I began to worry whether my ears would still clear. We were at some incredible altitude, where the cruise speed, the critical Mach number, and the stalling speed all tend to converge –i.e. you can't go any faster, and you can't go any slower, and therefore the aircraft is very sensitive to control inputs. I carefully removed my mask, and took a sniff from the nasal spray, forgetting that it was still pressurised to sea level. I received so much decongestant down my throat that I almost drowned, during which the aircraft swung about a bit, disconcerting the navs somewhat, but after a few seconds I had regained control and got my oxy mask back on. After that I had no further problems with sticky ears.

On this leg we again suffered radio problems. It was now impossible to transmit on any UHF *or* VHF frequency, including the standby radio, without hearing an excruciating howl, however, we were VMC and the trouble cleared when we let-down to medium level. We turned around at Djibouti, a French airfield on the African coast the other side of the Straits of Bab el Mandeb from Yemen and Aden. We refuelled but had to leave for Nairobi without any possibility of being able to repair either of the radios. By now I was becoming physically and mentally exhausted from the combination of early starts, changes in time zone, late finishes, and our seemingly endless problems. Fortunately, the final leg to Nairobi went along well by previous standards until we tried to call Nairobi –once again that agonizing howl on all frequencies. What's more we had been flying over a seemingly endless cloud sheet and as we approached our destination, we could see some large civilian aircraft circling in the hold overhead Nairobi like fish in a pond. No chance of a free let-down this time and if this unannounced cloud was over Nairobi it could just as well be over our alternate. I reselected Nairobi approach and tried the RAF Speechless Aircraft procedure –using the transmit button as a Morse key in the hope that some ex-RAF controller might be sitting behind one of the radios; (previously Nairobi Airport had been RAF Eastleigh). After an age, a voice came back with the civilian equivalent of "Speechless aircraft, adopt the call sign Speechless 1." We were home; we had made it to Nairobi. We very nearly didn't make it even then. In our euphoria of establishing contact with Nairobi Approach and subsequently regaining use of the radio during the descent, we forgot about the altimeter checks and the height of Nairobi airfield (around 5000'). I was quite surprised to break cloud in a fast descent and see the ground appear only 1500' beneath us!

The next day, I felt absolutely dog-tired and ruefully opted out of our one day off sight-seeing Nairobi with both the navs, and chose to stay in bed. But sometime in the mid-morning I had a call from the RAF chief technician in charge of the ground crew, who asked me to come down to where the aircraft was parked. The good news was that they had repaired the radio – it had been a 'dry joint' a supposed good connection that became disconnected with a severe drop in temperature. However, the bad news was that the aircraft had been over fuelled. The outside air temperature was +40C. The fuel had expanded. The concrete on the dispersal was concave. The result – the aircraft was almost up to its wheel hubs in AVTUR fuel. The chief technician promised that he would try to get some form of towing tractor to move the aircraft while the dispersal was cleared of fuel. I consulted my memory for information as to what effect immersion in AVTUR had on the properties of rubber, but found it a conspicuous blank. Simultaneously, I was conscious that the crew chief was still hovering by my side rather in the fashion of the soothsayer about to tell Caesar to beware the Ides of March.

The gist of the problem was this. A large cartridge – about the size of a small artillery shell – 3inches wide and some 9inches long started the Rolls Royce engine. The Canberra BI8 had three of these cartridges in each engine nacelle covered by a fairing, with a further 6 or 8 spare cartridges stored under a hatch in the aft fuselage. The *normal* procedure on extended sorties such as ours was for each RAF station *en-route* to replace cartridges during each turn round from their *own* stores. The chief's doleful mien was now explicable. Some lazy erk or erks (i.e. ground crew) at one or more of the stations en-route had been using the spare cartridges from *our* aircraft, and now we only had 5 left in total. Nairobi did not stock Canberra starting cartridges; neither did the next airfield, the French base at Djibouti. We would need 2 cartridges to start at Nairobi and a similar number at Djibouti, before we got to Masirah where there were Canberra spares. Unfortunately, not too infrequently, cartridges misfired. This could mean that we were stuck at Nairobi – that would be OK, or Djibouti – not so OK. Moreover, it was impossible to have any replacement cartridges flown to Kenya, for although there were regular civilian aircraft from the UK landing every day at Nairobi; they were not permitted to carry dangerous air cargo, i.e. Canberra Starter Cartridges. The next RAF transport aircraft was not scheduled for some weeks. This was deeply troubling for me. My Flight Commander in Germany was not only a cynic, but in any disputes, he took no prisoners. I could not in my wildest imagination see him believing *any* reason I gave him why it was necessary to stay in Nairobi for the next 14 days. Perhaps Djibouti would be better after all. Using a French communication system via France, the British Diplomatic Corps, MOD in London, HQRAFG, and the squadron ops phone, we would be about as contactable as Dr

Livingstone had been some 100 years before.

Our best bet to make it as far as Djibouti was to have fewer cartridges in the port engine since that was always started first. Hence, if a cartridge misfired, we could always obtain a (i.e. the) spare cartridge from the still inactive starboard engine. At this point exhaustion set in again and I spent most of the remainder of my day off in Nairobi sleeping, although we did manage to have a quick tour and shop round town in the evening.

On the morning of our departure everything went as planned. We taxied out, did the checks, and obtained take-off clearance. Nairobi, as I have mentioned, is some 5000' high, we were full of fuel, and so I was determined to use every foot of runway available. At the take-off end just where the tarmac began, there was a 12' high wire mesh fence cutting off access to the airfield. As I eased the aircraft right up alongside the wire, I noticed that the fence was festooned right up to the top with the local young bloods sightseeing. This was probably OK when the aircraft taking off was a civilian prop or turbo prop, but I'll hazard a guess they rarely experienced the blast that comes from a pure jet on take-off. ATC didn't make any comment after the take-off, so I never did find out if we blew them all off the fence. Finally, some 20 miles out from Djibouti, we were cleared to descend through cloud down to 800 metres (roughly 2500'). Fortunately, Dudley my navigator was on the ball. *"I wouldn't do that just yet,"* he said, *"there's a 6000' mountain between us and them."*

The turn round at Djibouti had the odd moment. The non-English speaking lad, (and apparently non-French speaking as well, unless my French was a lot worse than I thought) who jumped off the fuel bowser onto the aircraft insisted on topping up the rear fuselage tank first – this would have resulted in the aircraft sitting on its tail. Somehow, after using the most expressive sign language I could muster, he got the correct idea. The departure from Djibouti was OK. We now had zero cartridges in the port engine and one in the starboard. Whatever happened we had to fly as far as Masirah. We stocked up again on cartridges, but no one could be found who owned up to servicing the aircraft on the out bound leg.

Well there you have it. When would you have called it quits? The base weather, the delays, the "unservicabilities" – nothing in themselves – but combined with an inflexible time schedule and a keenness to accomplish a 'one off task' made me take risks beyond the value of the exercise. I reflected much later on the risks that I had taken; the failure of the fuel tip tank, booster pump, and hydraulic leak were par for the course. If these had not been fixed, we could not have proceeded. Secondly, I'd seen other (more experienced) pilots get airborne in marginal wind conditions, so this wasn't too risky. However, Malta is a very rocky little island, and an engine surge that caused an aborted take-off at Luqa was very hazardous, since there was very little overrun before you encountered lots of solid Maltese stone walls. Thirdly, although I did not appear to have a cold, if I had not been able to clear my ears, that could have caused perforated eardrums and caused so much pain that I could have momentarily blacked out.

The failure to carry out the altimeter checks in the descent into Nairobi, (although caused partially by the radio problems and our fatigue was careless), as was Djibouti ATC clearing us below the safety altitude on the return leg. These are just some of the hazards of flying. The intermittent failure of the radios (UHF, VHF and Standby Radio) was potentially the most dangerous fault. Fortunately, all failed together in good weather approaching Djibouti, and became serviceable again on the descent. Since they could not be repaired, continuing on to Nairobi made good sense. Here too, by an act of Providence we were fortunate that there was someone who was familiar with the speechless procedure. The worst possible place for total radio failure to have occurred was inbound to

Masirah at night while over the desert. If we had been unable to contact them or find the airfield by dead reckoning in the dark, our only options would have been to abandon the aircraft over the desert (the Rub' al Khali –the Empty Quarter of Saudi Arabia) and hope to be picked up before we died of thirst; or to abandon the aircraft over the Indian Ocean and hope to make it into the dinghy before the sharks got wise.

By contrast on the return to Germany, we had no compulsion to get back. From Masirah we flew on to Teheran, and then to Cyprus. Things still went wrong, but now there was no press-on-itis so we took logical rational decisions in slow time. The weather in Germany was dreadful, so we had an idyllic week in Cyprus waiting for the weather in Germany to improve sufficiently for us to be able to fly home!

Tourex

By April 1969, my tour in Germany was all over. I had asked for a posting to Buccaneers, but I was informed that I would be going to the Central Flying School at RAF Little Rissington in Gloucestershire to train as a Qualified Flying Instructor (QFI). I saw Babs and the children off from The Hague; she took the VW on the ferry and was met by her Mum at Harwich. I returned to Laarbruch, tidied up the loose ends and came across a few days later in the MG. (We had already taken Suki across three months earlier, to the immigration kennels). I had one last decision to make before I left. Sometime earlier, one of the Flight Commanders, whose father had been in the Great War, wanted to dispose of a Mauser 'Broom-handle' automatic pistol before he returned to the UK, so I bought it from him for 20 Deutsch marks –an incredibly low price. This particular pistol came with some ammo and its original wooden holster, which could be attached to the butt of the pistol, which converted it into a small carbine rifle. One-day Babs and I took a drive round the airfield during a quiet weekend to try it out. There were always parties of huntsmen in the surrounding local countryside, so we calculated any shots from the Mauser would not be noticed. We parked by some fairly dense pine woods on the far edge of the airfield, I loaded up the magazine with a few rounds, pointed the pistol at a clump of pine trees, and pulled the trigger – *Bang! Bang! Bang!* On automatic fire it was very impressive. Unfortunately, a few months later just as I was returning to the UK, some incident with guns occurred in the UK which prompted the authorities to issue a weapon armistice, in which illegally held small arms could be handed in without penalty, but anyone caught with an illegal handgun would do time. I thought about secreting my Mauser in the TC, but discretion got the better of me, so I sold it to a local German gun shop in Goch for 275DM, a good price for the time, but I later regretted not keeping it, as they became a collector's item and incredibly expensive.

Act Four

No 249 QFI Course RAF Little Rissington, Gloucestershire

I collected my family from Babs' parents when I arrived in the UK, and after two weeks leave, we drove down to Chippenham in Wiltshire where we had been allocated a married quarter at RAF Hullavington, a mere 40 miles from the Central Flying School (CFS) at RAF Little Rissington in Gloucestershire. Fortunately, as there were four of us from RAF Germany on the same course, all at Hullavington, we were able to share the driving and the cost of the petrol. But as the lectures started at 8am sharp, this necessitated a very early rise to be up in time for breakfast and get there through the early morning traffic. Similarly, after returning in the evening, sometime after 6pm, we were usually required to do at least two hours study. Consequently, I had very little time with my family. This reminded me of a comment by a Canadian navigator on XV Squadron after an extended session of night flying, land-aways or detachments to other airfields, and QRA, all of which meant having to spend too long a time away from home, *"It's bad enough when you get home and your wife won't speak to you, and even your kids don't know you, but when your dog bites you, you know you've been away too long!"*

I found training to be a flying instructor challenging but fun. At one point I wished that I still had my upper-class English accent from my boyhood, for I was given extra instruction on how to moderate my high speed, strong Scots accent, so that *"Hoo noo broon coo"* became *"How now brown cow."* The course lasted until the end of September, by which time I knew that I was to be posted to the Refresher Flying School (RFS) at RAF Manby in east Lincs. The purist instructors on the CFS staff, tut-tutted, shook their heads and pursed their lips, and told me that I would have precious little opportunity of practising the *"Well Bloggs, notice as I pull back on the stick that there is an increase in buffet, while at the same time..."* type of thing. Which fact bothered me not at all, as I hadn't even volunteered for CFS in the first place. However, I digress.

RAF Manby Lincolnshire

A few days before the end of the CFS course, two of us, Martin Hands and I, both ex-16 Squadron, drove up to Lincolnshire, to Louth the local town to discover what private accommodation could be had for our families, as there were no married quarters available on the base – well there was one! RAF Manby had previously been under the command of an Air Commodore, and the now empty very palatial quarter was vacant just a few miles from the base. Martin and I looked at it – it was fantastic. There were paddocks for horses, large lawns and gardens, double garages, immense reception rooms, living rooms, bedrooms, and bathrooms galore – all kitted out with furniture and fittings commensurate with the requirements of an officer of air rank, (i.e., not the normal flat pack type of furniture, but real furniture). Our families could have easily shared it without getting in each other's way; in fact, we could have held the Officers' Mess Summer Ball or the annual Battle of Britain Cocktail Party without feeling embarrassed for space. The rent, although high, was quite acceptable when split between Martin and myself. However, RAF accounting was still firmly in the era when each mark, scratch, breakage, loss, damage etc. to Government Property would be charged for, and with four children between us and a dog, we regretfully declined it.

Martin settled for a nice detached house in Louth, the local town, but never really feeling at home in towns, I chose a place out in the country – Tathwell Cottage. It was called a cottage, but it was really, or had been quite a grand Victorian Farmhouse, with the wires for the original bell pulls (to summon the servants) still in place. It had been vacant for a while, but it was still furnished to a basic level. It also had a double garage, large garden, and a well, which I discovered accidentally by almost falling through a grass covered, rotten door placed over it. All this was ours for £16 a month from a Mr Whiteman, a septuagenarian, who drove a very smart Mercedes sports car and seemed to own much of the surrounding countryside! We made a few excursions round the local auction rooms to top up the furnishings with some good old Victorian furniture at a time when it was being discarded for modern chipboard! Shortly after we moved in there, Babs bought me a piano for my birthday from an auction room for half a guinea! (This is 52.5p in new money). I only regretfully relinquished it some forty-six years later. In addition, there was a village school just over half a mile from the house, which was very convenient as Andrew was just about school age. But in order to get to the school Babs had to walk through a field that occasionally had a bull in it. However, Tathwell Cottage was a splendid place for young boys to grow up in, it had lots of open spaces for games, more garden than I could manage, and it was also convenient because the base was only about 3 miles away so I was able to drive my old MGTC, or even cycle in good weather.

The flying instruction at Manby was certainly different from what I had expected. Most of the other flying training courses involved teaching students the absolute basics of flying; there was one exception - RAF Valley, which was *the* training base for pilots who were going onto fast jets such as the Lightening and Buccaneer. But at that time RAF Valley also operated according to a CATCH 22 rule that to become a fast jet QFI, *"You couldn't go there unless you'd been there before,"* i.e., you had to have been an ex-fast jet pilot yourself to become an instructor there. At RAF Manby, on the other hand, the students were all qualified pilots who had been off flying duties for some time. These varied from young students who had been on a non-flying posting for a few months after qualifying from other RAF flying training schools, or senior officers, such as Wing Commanders, Group Captains, right up to the next Chief of the Air Staff, all of whom had been on ground tours behind desks for a number of years and some of whom had not flown for a very long time.

The instructional skills required at the RFS were different from a basic FTS, where moulding the raw clay and supervising the growth of an ab initio student required an instructor to encourage his student to have confidence in his abilities, and know how long he can let him carry on before telling him quietly *"I have control.* This is an art that comes with experience. However, at the RFS, quite often your student would be a senior officer with lots of hours, (and very often still lots of confidence), but who hadn't flown for a long time, i.e. *"The last time I did a spin was in a Spitfire 30 years ago."* However, such older senior officers, many of whom had many more hours than their instructors had to be treated with kid gloves at times, since they were prone to believe the principle that once you could fly an aircraft you never forgot. Hence, they would declare *"This is how we used to do it, when I was on..."* whatever their aircraft had been, at which point you had to subtly inform them that things had changed. This type of student also had its problems, where criticisms such as *"That was bl**dy stupid"* which could be used with young pilots, with senior officers on the other hand, such reproofs had to be disguised as gentle tact, with the addition of lots of *"Never mind Sir, it will all probably come flooding back on the next trip."*...(while adding under one's breath).. *"I hope it's not with me."* I had one particular Wing Commander, who could fly quite well, but who consistently refused to learn his pre-flight checks. After a while I showed him what I had written about him in his course progress book – *"Wing Commander X <u>still does not know his checks</u>"* (written and underlined in red). I told him that in order to send him solo, I had to be sure that he would not omit anything. He said that he would endeavour to familiarise himself. This particular officer eventually arrived at RAF Chivenor in Devon – to refresh on the Hunter and re-familiarize himself on weapons delivery techniques. RAF Manby had sent the Wing Commander 's F5000 (Form 5000 – An assessment and a summary of a student's progress) of his time on the course at Manby, which included my remarks) to RAF Chivenor. When the Station Commander at Chivenor learnt of this officer's laid-back attitude to checks at Manby he was not impressed. He called him into his office for a dressing down, at which point the Wing Commander said that he wished to take out a redress of grievance against me! (Basically, a redress of grievance is a formal complaint by one member of the armed forces against another for something such as defamation of character that would affect his chances of promotion)! At this stage in my career this was a hollow threat, but nevertheless it would have been very serious for me if it had been upheld, as it would have resulted in some form of punishment. My boss called me into his office and put me in the picture, and said that I had better be sure of my facts. Fortunately, we still had the original flying progress records in which I had obtained the Wing Commander's signature stating that he had been shown my above criticisms. My boss said *"OK you can relax,"* and that's all I heard about it until many years later, when as a QFI at RAF Valley I suddenly met this officer who had now been posted to Valley – on a ground tour. We did not actively seek out each other, but when we accidently met, it was as two dogs that have no great liking for the other.

In addition to newly qualified pilots only a few months removed from completion of flying training and senior officers who had never left the ground for years, the other element of the student population was the young blood, the recently promoted Squadron Leader with two fast jet tours under his belt, a quickie ground tour, and was now about to be posted as a Flight Commander to the fastest thing that the RAF flew. This kind of refresher student presented a different problem. He looked upon being instructed by a new green QFI on a piddling little jet like the Jet Provost as somewhat demeaning but necessary evil to be tolerated before getting back into the real operational world. More often than not, I learnt a lot more about flying from such guys than they probably did from me, especially in things like tail chases where manoeuvres forbidden, or undreamt of by the authors of the Jet Provost 4 Flying Manual Air Publication 3225 could be observed at first hand and used to impress one's squadron mates later on. The great danger was yielding to the superior experiences of such a pilot who not only had more hours than you, but also had been on the sharp end, i.e., in Fighter Command, and that quite recently, especially when he presented his expertise with the implication that to forbid him to carry out his manoeuvre meant you were chicken.

This leads me on into the occasion of the following cautionary tale, which is instructive of the pressure that an instructor could be under with such a pilot.

I Learnt About Night Flying From That
We had been programmed to night fly. It was absolutely gin clear with a sharp western horizon and a three-quarter moon. I got airborne with my student –a Sqn. Ldr. Al Shepherd if I remember rightly, and we climbed up over Lincolnshire and admired the view.

"Have you ever done night aeros?" he asked, as we gazed over the lights of cities, towns, and villages of eastern England stretching as it seemed to the horizon. *"Well, no I haven't as a matter of fact."* And then with many other smooth enticing and seductive words, he spoke of the how easy it all was. At that point I should have bottled out, quoted night flying regulations, ignored my student's night operational qualifications and told him to go jump. But I didn't.

Well, we weren't entirely stupid. We selected a piece of sky that seemed to be clear of other flashing aircraft lights, switched all our navigational and anti-collision lights off so that our manoeuvres could not be seen from the ground, and made sure that we were far enough away from the Pundit lights of other airfields on the ground. (This being in the days when there were so many RAF stations night flying that you really had to know Morse to recognise which was your airfield - calling up for a heading to steer on such a night was not on). The aerobatics session went really well, and a great boost to my confidence. At the end of which we looked round, picked up the Manby Pundit, and descended to do a pukka join on the dead side of the circuit. There seemed to be only one other aircraft in the circuit, which was marvellous. However somewhere between calling up to join and joining the circuit we lost sight of him.

Then, just as we joined the circuit on the downwind, there was a momentary glimpse of some flashing nav lights extremely close and alongside us. Fortunately, we managed to pull away and recover our composure. *"The nav and anti-coll lights, we forgot to switch them*

on again after the aeros!!" My operational student pilot had just earned himself a beer by that remark; so quietly easing out of the circuit we lit up again and re-joined the circuit, this time making very sure that we had a good separation from the one other aircraft. We completed the necessary circuit flying, landed, signed in, and cruised casually through squadron ops. I sent my student off to do his solo and remarked that I was going for an early beer and slid out a wiser man. Waiting in the bar was my best mate, who said that he'd like a pint of the best beer going. I thought that this was a bit unfair, since, being there before me; custom decreed that he should have bought me a beer. It was almost as if he had been waiting for me to appear? *"You were flying XS....* (quoting my aircraft airframe number) *tonight, weren't you?"* he said. *"Why do you ask?"* I casually replied. *"'cos I saw your airframe number in my anti-collision lights when we did our bit of close formation down wind."* This last sentence was said with feeling. I owned up to him and bought him his beer and a few more, and his student, and then my student did the same for us all, so by the end of the evening we all felt quite relaxed again. But in the cold sober light of day, I thought about what could have happened and shivered. It also taught me that regulations and conduct of flights and rules of the air and all sorts of other things are there because they have been found to be the safest and most sensible way of going about the business of aviation. I also decided that no matter what the seniority, experience, rank of the other pilot, if I was the aircraft captain then I would make my decisions based on what I knew to be right, not on what the other man in the aircraft thought of me, whether good or bad.

More Detachments

It wasn't only illegal night manoeuvres in the air that were inherently dangerous; there were others on the ground that could have proved equally dangerous to my marriage and my career (such as it was) in the RAF. I had now been a pilot in the RAF for some twelve years and happily married for eight, but Manby was different in that going for a beer after night flying there were often a few young WAAF officers from ATC present in the bar, who were only too eager to listen to the hairy flying stories of their heroes the pilots. Male ego being what it is we were more than willing to embellish such stories for them and chat them up. Many years before the RAF 'wheels' had taken note of the potential dangers inherent in such acquaintances, for whereas differences of political and religious inclinations could give rise to a certain amount of reserve between those of different persuasions, any illicit relations with the opposite sex, whether WRAF officers, airwomen, or the wives of other personnel could lead to much greater repercussions which would be detrimental to the effectiveness, loyalty and esprit de corps of the unit. However, the RAF's solution to such situations was on a par with the KGB's treatment of those members of the CPSU who failed the system –they would simply disappear and it would be as if he had never existed. Thus, similar treatment was visited upon miscreants for any undue 'fraternisation' with the opposite sex; one moment the person was there, and the next no one knew where they had gone. You would notice his absence in the Officers Mess and on the squadron; if you inquired about his whereabouts, those similarly in the dark would shrug their shoulders, or say that he was probably on leave. Eventually someone would give you a sideways look and whisper out of the corner of his mouth *"Haven't you heard?"* The punishment invariably resulted in a posting to the equivalent of RAF Ultima Thule –some remote isolated backwater in the residue of the Empire, such as being the Officer in charge of a weapons range on the edge of civilization, where one's day was spent logging the accuracy of air discharged ordnance, counting seagulls, and contemplating ones fall from grace. Thus, although the system wasn't cast iron, it generally had its desired effect and kept the letter of the law if not the spirit of the law.

In association with this, another of our tasks required us to fly down to RAF Shawbury in Shropshire for a couple of days to give air experience to students learning to be Air Traffic Controllers; on each trip the ATC student would be strapped into the student's ejection seat while we as pilots flew the aircraft from the other ejection seat alongside. The student would listen to the R/T and try to collate the R/T instructions given by one of their controllers on the ground with the time our actions as a pilot took for a descent into a radar pattern. Very few of the students on each course had ever flown before, and none had ever been strapped into a 'bang' (ejection) seat, so it was necessary to give each one a standard briefing of what to do in the event of a major emergency. Then, to complicate matters, since there were no Jet Provost trained ground crew at Shawbury, when our student appeared at the aircraft, kitted out in a flying suit – together with the usual sick bag –each one would be strapped into the ejection seat by one of us.

To anyone unfamiliar with flying in a military jet, wearing a flying suit, a 'Mae West' life jacket, a helmet and oxygen mask, together with the R/T connection, oxygen connection, leg restraint straps, parachute harness, and full seat harness straps present a problem akin to a Chinese puzzle. This, together with the absolute necessity of removing and replacing the ejection seat pins in the correct place meant that before we strapped in, we had to, by necessity, adjust the straps and fit the harness round the student's arms, chest, abdomen, and thighs. This wasn't a task that was in any way considered onerous, particularly if the course included two or three WRAF students! In fact, it could border on a scenario from a Brian Rix farce or a Carry-On film, such as when prior to take-off or after landing the ejection seat pan handle pin had to be removed or replaced, a plaintive little voice would say, *"I'm sorry, I can't seem to find the pin,"* or *"I can't seem to put the pin back."* At which point Sir Galahad would graciously say, *"Excuse me while I reach down and I'll find it,"* while attempting to reach down between the passenger's legs with as much decorum as possible and avoiding any undue familiarity and eye contact.

On one journey down to RAF Shawbury, I led Ron Easton, who had been the pilot in the other aircraft during my night close miss, in low level formation across Lincolnshire, Nottinghamshire and part of Derbyshire before handing over the lead to him. We had agreed on this before the flight. It was the last trip of the day; we left Manby to arrive at Shawbury for tea. But sometime after I gave Ron the lead, he informed me over the R/T that he had mislaid or left behind the next part of his low-level route, and would I retake the lead! This might have been a smart move on his part, for, not long after I retook the lead, the weather closed down with bad visibility and low cloud; moreover, since we were now under the base of controlled airspace, we could not climb up very high. I called Shawbury for a steer; they came back with the comforting information that they had closed down their Direction-Finding equipment for monthly servicing and consequently they could do nothing for us. We were on our own. We had flown for quite a while at low level, and by now we didn't have enough fuel to return to Manby, I had to think of something quick. Just then I saw a gap in the cloud sheet that was over a large city or town. Normally, experienced pilots will tell you *"Never go down into a sucker gap"* usually because you don't know what you will find in the surrounding area, i.e. high ground, or obstructions such as TV masts, but on this occasion, there was no other choice. I found myself over Stoke on Trent, made a quick calculation and headed off southwest and found Shawbury some 30 miles further on.

Just a few weeks later I got a call from one of the other pilots on the squadron, who told me that Ron was in intensive care in a nearby RAF Hospital. He had had a few beers, got up out of bed in the middle of the night to go to the toilet, but while crossing the landing he had tripped and fallen down stairs. He did not break anything but at the bottom of the stairs the back of his head had hit the corner of a large central heating storage radiator. He went back upstairs and eventually returned to bed, but in the morning, he could not be wakened. The blow that he had received from the radiator had caused internal haemorrhaging. When I visited him, he was on a life support machine. I had never seen a dead person before, for although the doctors said that he was still technically alive – the medical apparatus was keeping his heart going, as I looked at him, I thought, *"The lights are on, but there is no one at home."* A few days later his heart machine was turned off, and his funeral took place shortly after.

I reflected briefly on the passing of my friend, but only briefly. There were fatal flying accidents from time to time – sometimes of people that I had known, but no one ever dwelt on them, in a sense one felt that it couldn't happen to you, and the usual recourse was to go along to the bar and have a beer or two in their memory.

RAF Gatow, Berlin

RAF Manby had a satellite airfield a few miles away at RAF Strubby, where other refresher pilots were trained on the Varsity twin engined transport. One of those pilots was Les Davies, who had also been on 16 Squadron with me in Germany. One day on the early winter of '71 he told Martin Hands and I that he had been authorised for a trip to RAF Gatow in the Western sector of Berlin, and that we were welcome to come along. Les duly got us airborne one cold Lincolnshire morning and headed out over the North Sea; we joined civilian controlled air space as we coasted into the Netherlands, and eventually joined the Air Corridor that led to Berlin. Here we encountered our first glitch. We were over 8/8th cloud and although the Varsity had a number of fairly basic navigational aids, on this occasion none of them seemed to be functioning satisfactorily. We were all aware that infringement of East German Airspace would be followed either by being shot down or being forced to land and become a long-term guest of the East Germans. Fortunately, the malfunctions were only short lived and we managed to make a normal approach into Gatow.

We had, if I remember, two days to see all the sights. To demonstrate their right to visit East Berlin under the post war agreement between the Allied Powers, the RAF regularly sent an RAF coach with service personnel aboard into the eastern zone – through Check Point Charlie. As we passed by the Vo Pos (Volks Polizei) we had to hold our RAF F1250 identity cards up to the window. I was a little bit nervous about this, since having had my photograph for the card taken some time previously, I had grown a handlebar moustache. I hadn't had an official new photograph taken in order to amend the card before I left for Berlin; so, in order to bring it up to date, I had used a black wax pencil to add a moustache to the photo. No problem – as long as I stayed in the bus and I didn't have it personally inspected by one of the East Germans! Once in East Berlin, we visited the main thoroughfare with its Stalinist government buildings and drab apartment blocks, then toured round the back streets, which were still heavily pockmarked from the onslaught of the Russians in 1945; at one point we were taken past a huge conical mound; this we were informed was made of the debris of bombed out buildings; we visited the Soviet Memorial and as we came out the front door we were snapped by some 'tourists' employed by the state security who photographed *all* military personnel who came to the East Zone. This would form; rumour had it, part of a large dossier of personal facts, likes, interests, foibles that you would be presented with if you had the misfortune to fall into their hands, so that they could start the interrogation with the time-honoured phrase, *"Vee haff vays of making you talk."* The very next evening we almost inadvertently proved the truth of this gossip. We went out on the town and sampled various German biers, in various bars, and finished off by partaking of a sauna to sweat out the alcohol. But since that was Germany, we should have realised that such establishments are not segregated as in Britain, so we were quite surprised to be suddenly confronted by the sight of some German fraus and mädchens au naturelle strolling past.

Having sobered up (to some extent) we decided that rather than take a taxi, we would travel by the underground back to Gatow. We purchased the tickets and boarded the next train. We had passed through a few stations, when I looked more closely at my ticket, and panicked. Berlin had two underground systems – the S Bahn and the U Bahn. In my befuddled state I could not remember which system ran through East Berlin. Although the East Berlin stations had been closed, it was not unknown for trains to be stopped for customs/security checks by East Berlin Officials/ Volks Polizei, especially at night. We had been warned never to travel through East Berlin at night, because there had been cases of Allied service personnel being removed for questioning. I told Les and Martin of our situation; none of us was certain whether we were on the U-Bahn or the S-Bahn. We consulted the underground map –a diagram similar to the London Underground, but still befuddled by the copious bier that we had consumed, we estimated that *if* it was the S-Bahn, the next stop was the last before the train disappeared into the Eastern Zone. We were in the middle of a carriage, which had doors in the middle and at either end. When we came to the station, the doors at either end opened, but not the door in the middle. We really did panic then. Literally walking over the top of the other passengers who were standing in the aisle, we managed to fall onto the platform before the train departed into the night, followed by the audible censures of the other passengers against the *"vertrunken Englander"*. We climbed up some steps, and looked in the direction of the disappearing train. We never did find out which railway system it was, but not so far in the distance was the wall lit up and guarded.

Low Level Training

By the early 1970's, the Avro Vulcan was the only V Bomber still tasked with an offensive war mission. But by now, such were the capabilities of the Soviet Air Defences, the safest way to get close enough to the target, was to remain at low level as long as possible. Although quite a number of Vulcan crews did low level training and took part in competitions with the USAF in the USA, the regular bread and butter low level route was one that went clockwise round the UK, over sparsely populated areas. Since some of our refresher pupils were destined for Vulcan squadrons, we decided to give them some preliminary training on this route, but as the Jet Provost could not cover the whole route in one hop, it was necessary to night stop once or even twice on route –which was the real raison d'étre for these sorties!

I took off on one of these sorties with Tim Delap a young squadron leader, who had an old friend who worked for the British Aircraft Corporation (as it then was) at Warton in Lancashire. We routed low level from Manby to Manston in Kent, refuelled, then along the south coast –this was the trickiest part of the route as there are lots of civilian control zones and weapons ranges, before landing at RAF Chivenor in Devon, refuelling again, then on to Warton. During each leg of the navex the student would attempt to fly a timed run from an easily identifiable IP (Initial Point) to a small target. They were often quite good at this, as we had previously trained them to carry out similar target runs in Yorkshire, using telephone boxes as targets; the catch was – and what we didn't tell them, in Yorkshire at that time the phone boxes for some reason were painted green!

However, because there was no Officers Mess at Warton, the Squadron Leader's old friend Alex put us up at his house and took us out for a magnificent meal and liquid refreshment. This went on until much later in the evening than I would have wished while they reminisced, for I was conscious that we had some fairly intensive low-level flying on the morrow. I couldn't relax into the mutual bonhomie and toasting, but I didn't really know how to excuse myself from mine host without appearing rude. Normally, on this leg we would have routed via RAF Valley on Anglesey in North Wales, where there full facilities for a pre-flight briefing, but Warton not being an RAF airfield, the next morning after the Met man had informed us that although the weather was OK for most of the route, north of the border it would be quite cloudy, there was no ops centre to check on the latest route info, and any Air Traffic restrictions. However, the route was quite straight forward. Our first stop was to be at RAF Machrihanish on the Mull of Kintyre, before, routing via the West Highlands, RAF Kinloss in Morayshire, RAF Leuchars in Fife, and then home.

The trip from Warton through the Lake District and Southern Scotland was great, but the visibility really started to decrease and the cloud base dropped as we approached the Firth of Clyde. We really wanted to stay clear of cloud, but if we tried to stay low level, we were going to pass quite close to Ailsa Craig, the rather hefty granite rock in the middle of the Clyde estuary, which was not a good idea since Ailsa is just over 1100feet high and we were at 250 feet above ground level in the now dreadful forward visibility. I was by now aware that we were flying under the Civilian Controlled Airspace of Prestwick International Air Terminal, so we were limited to about 1500' altitude, high enough to clear Ailsa Craig, but not really safe enough to clear the mountains on Arran just to the north of us. We tried a few times to contact Machrihanish ATC but didn't get a reply. I then called up on GUARD – the emergency channel on 243megacycles, for a steer, expecting to be answered by Scottish Centre since we were only about 15 miles from their base at Prestwick. I was really surprised to hear a faint voice from the London Military Air Traffic Centre inform me *"Aircraft calling on Guard, carrier wave only, no radar identification."* We were below the emergency radar cover and we couldn't climb, so we changed to Prestwick ATC and asked them for a steer for Machrihanish. *"Steer 285 for Machrihanish."* They also cleared us to climb a bit higher, but we were now completely in cloud somewhere over the middle of the Firth of Clyde. Apart from Abbotsinch (now Glasgow Airport but then a Royal Navy Base), Prestwick near Ayr, and West Freuch, a Ministry of Supply base down on the Mull of Galloway, southwest Scotland is not well supplied with alternate airfields. We tried Machrihanish ATC again and this time got a reply. We asked for an immediate recovery, only to be told that there was civilian BEA Viscount inbound on radar with a casevac (casualty evacuation) from the Outer Hebrides, which had priority. We would have to wait until this aircraft had cleared the radar pattern. We rapidly got back to Prestwick ATC and asked to divert there. There were very apologetic, but informed us that they were recovering trans-Atlantic traffic –which had priority –for some time. We rapidly chopped back to Machrihanish and informed them of our now increasingly desperate situation. Machrihanish said we could fit in behind the Viscount using the ILS (Instrument Landing System), which had just been declared serviceable. This was now Hobson's choice as we were running out of fuel, and although the weather at Machrihanish was down on the deck, there were no other options; we got ourselves into the ILS pattern, made a successful approach in dreadful weather, and touched down with the fuel reading about 100 lbs of Avtur! I later discovered from a note in small print in the RAF En-Route Supplement, "Difficulties may be encountered in contacting Machrihanish ATC when approaching from the east below 3000 feet owing to obstruction by high ground." I also subsequently discovered that there was a small but significant gap in the emergency radar coverage in South West Scotland over the Firth of Clyde just where we had been. I made a mental note next time to refuse excessive hospitality, even at the expense of ruffling mine host's feelings and secondly make more thorough planning ahead for the unforeseen.

The weather next day at Machrihanish was beautiful, but the rest of the country was socked in, with low cloud, rain, and fog. We walked along the beautiful golden beaches pounded by huge Atlantic waves, visited Cambelltown, went down to the docks, found an ex-RAF warrant officer who was in charge of the fish auction. He would have been quite happy to have arranged for us to have gone out on a fishing expedition on one of the trawlers overnight, but unfortunately our boss at Manby said that we had to be ready to return the next day in case the weather cleared; which it didn't. In fact, we were kept in enforced idleness at Machrihanish for three days, and each day we rang to enquire whether we could 'go fishing', but each time, permission was refused in case the weather improved.

RAF Gutersloh

Overseas detachments from Manby were very unusual, but in April 1972, we were tasked with taking two aircraft and four pilots to RAF Gütersloh in Germany, the home at that time of No 19 and 92 (Lightning) Squadrons, to refresh the pilots on the correct recovery technique for spin recovery. Since the Lightning pilots regularly practiced simulated combat manoeuvres, it was quite possible to get inadvertently into a spin, but as the Lightning was not really an aeroplane that you would want to deliberately put into a spin to find out if you still remembered how to recover it, we were sent out to refresh them on all types of spin recovery. The exercise went well, and as a bonus I got a ride in a Lightning T4 with a chap called Vic Lockwood who I had refreshed at Manby. I was very impressed, from take-off to 40000' seemed a matter of seconds. Vic did a supersonic run. I know that this results in a solid double bang at ground level, but if I remember correctly, we were pointing at East Germany so that by the time any complaints reached the west through 'the usual channels' we would be long gone.

The Officers Mess at RAF Gütersloh had formerly been one of the main Luftwaffe bases. In one of the rooms there was still a large framed photograph of Hermann Göring. We were informed that Göring, who was wont to come along to drinking sessions to impress the young pilots, would 'line-shoot' and as he ended, to emphasise the truth of his improbable stories, would look up at one of the beams of wood in the ceiling and say, *"If I'm telling lies, then let that beam bend."* The next time that he got involved in a 'line shoot', he was caught out –for some of the pilots had sawn it through and with a 'system of hinges, springs, strings, and pulleys' the beam was seen to bend!

Tourex

My 3-year tour as a Jet Provost instructor seemed to come to an end fairly quickly; I had amassed over 1000 hours and attained my A2 Instructor's rating, and was posted back to RAF Cottesmore this time as a QFI on No 231 OCU as a Canberra instructor. Both Babs and I, the boys, not to mention Suki the Great Dane and I were sorry to say good-bye to Tathwell Cottage. It had been a great place to bring up a young family, with plenty of space, and fields where we could exercise the dog. During our stay we also discovered that the cottage had one or two faults –it could be very draughty in certain wind conditions, the floor in the upstairs main bedroom had a pronounced slope, which required blocks of wood under the foot of the bed to prevent Babs and I sliding into a heap at the bottom, and when the wind blew from the southeast in winter –just the conditions in Lincolnshire for snow, the snow would enter under the roof tiles into the loft space and form a large drift. I can remember passing many buckets of snow down through the loft door to Babs to empty out of one of the windows.

RAF Cottesmore

This tour had two distinctive features: firstly, it lasted just 18 months, and secondly nothing happened very much. We took up residence at No 12 Zetland Square, just down the road from our previous quarter at No22. Both the boys Andrew and Paul now attended a school on the camp, so Babs had a bit more time to herself.

The instructional flying was quite straightforward – conversion onto type, asymmetric practice, navigational sorties, instrument flying including joining and flying in the civil airways system. I even applied for a set of notes on gaining a Commercial Pilot's License, so that I would be qualified when I reached my 38th birthday and retired from the RAF. In October 1973, I managed to wangle a weekend sortie to Cyprus, but we arrived there just as the Yom Kippur War started. I can remember going into the station ops room at RAF Akrotiri, on one wall were large-scale maps of all the nations surrounding Cyprus. These normally depicted the danger areas with their attendant height limits and times of operations, and civilian airspace reservations, but on this occasion some wag had outlined all the borders Lebanon, Syria, Jordan, Israel, and Egypt in red plastic tape with a prominent warning which said, *"Air to Ground, Ground to Air, and Air to Air Firing daily sunrise to sunset!"*

Early in 1974, I was overjoyed to hear that I had been posted to RAF Akrotiri as flight commander on the Canberra Target Facilities Flight (TFF) that was part of No 56 Fighter Squadron. Just before we left, we had received an invitation from Max Murray one of the navigators on the OCU; he had been in Cyprus previous to his posting to Cottesmore, so he asked us if we would like to see his slides and give us some background info.

Secondly, because we had a RAF quarter, we had to carry out the mandatory scrub-it-clean-and-have-everything-laid-out-and-lined-up for the marching out inspection on our last morning. On this last afternoon, because it was now impossible to prepare a meal or sleep in the beds, without disturbing the pristine tidiness, some other friends Noddy and Mo Brooke invited us to come and stay the night with them. They asked us if we were going for a meal with Max and Maureen his wife. We said, *"No, they just said come and see the slides."* With that we all drove off to a Chinese takeaway in Oakham the local town, and came back and polished off the take away just before we walked round to Max and Maureen's quarter. When we got there, there were another two married couples there sitting around in the lounge, drinking sherry. At this point I had a sudden dread that we were going to have dinner!

This proved to be true. As it was only March a hearty meal was appropriate; so, a farmhouse soup, followed by Hungarian Goulash, apple pie and ice cream, with cheese and biscuits were presented. Babs and I did our duty and ate. When it came to the dessert, we all declined an extra helping, but Max's wife must have felt that I was undernourished, and despite my negative reprise of Oliver Twist's plea, *"Please, don't give me any more,"* I was given another plate of pudding. Again, I did my duty. We adjourned back to the warm snug lounge, settled ourselves into easy chairs, the lights went out, the slide projector went on, and shortly afterwards both Babs and I fell asleep. However, they do say that the brain continues to assimilate information while we sleep.

Unfortunately, our posting to Cyprus involved leaving Suki behind. She was now some nine years old, and had been experiencing some failure in the muscles of her back legs, so that occasionally she appeared to have lost all use in them. We decided that not only would it be better to leave her behind, but that she would have to be put down.

We drove from Cottesmore up to Longtown, just north of Carlisle, to pay a farewell visit to Babs' Mum and Dad before we left for Cyprus. Babs' Dad very kindly offered to take Suki to the vet. I can remember on the day we left, as we drove off, Suki had her paws up on the windowsill looking out at us and wondering why she wasn't going with us. I couldn't help myself; I just cried buckets of tears as I drove off. The boys hadn't yet been told of our decision about the dog, so they kept asking Babs, *"Mummy, why is Daddy crying?"* It's crazy, but even almost 50 years later I still miss that great soft mutt of a dog.

Act Five

RAF Akrotiri, Cyprus – No 56 Squadron (Target Facilities Flight)

We flew to Cyprus in an RAF VC10 Transport in late March '74. Unbeknown to us, this was to be an even shorter tour than my tour on 231 OCU at Cottesmore. Our three-year tour was drastically curtailed following the minor war between the Greeks and the Turks that started in late July of '74. As a consequence of this the UK redeployed its forces in Cyprus and we returned to the UK in January of '75. Although it may have been a very short tour it made up for it by all the events that took place.

On arrival the organisation was good and bad! It was good in that as soon as we arrived at RAF Akrotiri we were met and taken straight to our hiring –a bungalow in Andrea Araousos Street on the outskirts of Limassol the local town, some 12 miles from the base. It was bad in that my Canberra instrument rating renewal was due the following month –April –hence no one including myself on 231 OCU at Cottesmore had thought to renew it before I left, assuming that I would re-rate after I arrived in Cyprus. But when I arrived in Cyprus my predecessor, Paddy Thompson, the outgoing Flight Commander and the *only* Canberra Instrument Rating Examiner (IRE) in Cyprus had already left for the UK – and the next nearest Canberra IRE was in Malta! So, having reported to Wing Commander Martin Bee the CO of 56 Sqn, I was ordered to get to Malta, A.S.A.P., to be re-rated. I found a navigator – Mike Hall who was willing to come along. It wasn't a completely wasted trip – since we also had to bring back one of our Canberras from RAF Luqa where it had been undergoing a major servicing.

Thus, it was early one morning Mike and I pitched up, in civilian clothes - fortunately in the light of later events, but with not much more than a towel, a razor, a toothbrush and our flying kit in a kitbag, to board an RAF Hercules that was bound for Luqa. Mike and I were the only passengers until shortly before take-off, when about a dozen or so elderly gentlemen in very smart civilian dress, armed with briefcases, boarded the Herc. We hadn't been long airborne when one of these chaps (who were in fact all senior RAF officers travelling incognito in civvies), went up to the flight deck to inform the captain of the Herc that he was to divert to Ciampino, an airport just outside Rome. These elderly distinguished gentlemen were a TACEVAL team on their way to Taceval RAF Luqa. Luqa *was* expecting a TACEVAL, but to allay Luqa's suspicions, the

TACEVAL team were going to arrive in Malta by civil transport from Rome; in this way they would be able to mingle with other civilians without being noticed and catch Luqa on the hop. Meanwhile the Herc, its crew, and Mike Hall and I would unfortunately have to spend some 24 hours in Rome.

The Herc crew were well versed in civilian airport procedures, and in no time at all after landing, we were all crammed into a minibus en-route to a nice hotel that they had previously used. Mike and I had been added to their flight imprest, hence the cost of all transport, hotel bills, and meals were already catered for. After a pleasant lunch, we joined the Herc crew (in our hired minibus) on a tour of Rome, and saw all the usual tourist sights, including the Colosseum, the Trevi Fountain, and a tour round St Peter's. Returning to the hotel, for a quick freshen up, we launched on a stroll around the streets, stopping only for a beer or three, after which we settled for a relaxing evening sitting out in a street café, having a delicious pizza washed down by a nice Italian red, while admiring the varied selection of Italian beauties that sauntered by. The Herc crew were in no hurry to return to the hotel, so a relatively short night's sleep was followed by an early flight to Malta, and then three sorties- my Instrument Rating Test, an Air Test of the Canberra that we were to take back to Cyprus, and a night Staff Continuation Training sortie with a QFI from Luqa. That night I slept really well.

On arrival back in Cyprus, I did a number of sorties to check out the two other pilots on the TFF and get familiar with the local area, followed by a run through on various target sorties that TFF provided for 56 Squadron. Meanwhile Babs and I were getting settled into our new accommodation. We only had the clothes we had brought in our suitcases on the aircraft, as all our other goods were being sent in crates by sea. Our car –a VW Passat estate was also coming by sea; and hereby hangs a tale. We should have sold it in the UK before we left, but Ted Heath's confrontation with the coal miners' union NUM was in full swing, the country was working a three-day week, and no one was buying cars. By necessity, I drove it down to somewhere near London and left it with a company that shipped cars. I was given a receipt so that I could claim my car in Cyprus. In addition, I received a very comprehensive document that listed the absolute right of the ship's captain to tip my car overboard if the need arose, abandon the said voyage and sail to anywhere else in the world, and a host of other exclusive clauses and causes that cleared the company from paying any compensation whatsoever. I despaired of ever seeing the VW again. But some two months later, I received notice that the car had arrived. I went up to Famagusta docks where I found the car with the remains of a thick rope hawser still attached to the axles. But at least mine was all in one piece, for alongside my car, a VW Beetle had been unloaded from the ship by passing a hawser through the open windows and hoisting the car onto the dockside; the roof now had a distinctly 'peaky' look to it.

The boys settled in, there were British Forces Schools nearby, and we acquired two cats, courtesy of Paul our youngest, who had found some kittens that had been abandoned by their mother in the 'bondu' – the scrub land that existed around in front of and behind much of the housing. When we moved onto a quarter on the base it was even better. For here there was an extensive scrub area, where all the children could play hide and seek and cowboys and Indians to their hearts content. There were also snakes, and the 'bondu' extended right on the edge of the sovereign base area where there were cliffs and steep paths that led down to the Med. But this was before the days of ''elf and safety' so no one worried and no one got hurt! At the other end of the airfield, the cliffs shelved away to a rocky beach, with a wooden raft moored about 100 yards out to sea. When we arrived, neither of the boys could really swim but by the time that we left, they were experts.

Practice Interception – Canberra B2 v Lightning F6
The main functions of No 56 Squadron Target Facilities Flight

were to provide a calibration aircraft for Gata Radar on Mount Troodos, and targets for 56 Squadron who were equipped with Lightning F6s. The Gata radar sorties were quite boring; we climbed up to high level pointing out over the Med, before returning and flying at a very steady height, heading and speed to allow the radar operators to calibrate their equipment; but the other type of target sortie –Practice Interception was much more exciting!

On a basic Practice Interception (PI) sortie, the target aircraft –a Canberra B2 or T4 flew at a designated height, speed, and track while the Gata radar operator on the ground vectored the fighter onto an offset but reciprocal course, simulating an attack in cloud/night conditions. At a suitable distance and angle off the fighter turned 180 degrees and rolled out astern of the target aircraft, whereupon the pilot of the fighter could acquire his target on the missile radar in the cockpit, close in to the optimum missile launch range, get a missile lock on, and simulate a missile launch. A number of these basic PIs patterns were flown by our Canberras for newly arrived Lightning pilots to build up their experience. But on later sorties, our target aircraft not only listened out on the Gata Radar transmission frequency, but also anticipated the incoming fighter's attempt to obtain an optimum offset, and so we varied the height and heading of the target aircraft to make life more difficult for the fighter.

On this particular day I was piloting the B2 with Mike Hall again as my navigator. Our Lightning opposition was flown by Steve Horridge. On this sortie our briefed attack profile for the day was to fly at low medium level, around 5000'. The day was standard for the Med in late summer – hot, a bit hazy, with about 4/8th thin stratocumulus cloud around 1500 to 2000'. We carried out a couple of warm up PIs before we went for our evasive manoeuvres. By this time Mike had made his ejection seat in the rear cockpit safe, unstrapped himself, and was sitting alongside me on what was called the 'Rumbold' seat – a flimsy aluminium rod and canvas contraption. This seating arrangement had the advantage that both of us could simultaneously scan for a visual on the fighter - I did the search radar mode left to right, while Mike did the nodding radar up into the vertical and high rear slant areas. We heard Gata Radar's instruction to Steve as he ran in, and at that point I shut the throttles, put the airbrakes out and descended rapidly to low level –about 250' above the sea. *"The target has disappeared off my radar,"* said the Gata controller, *"believed to have gone low level."* *"Roger, going low level,"* said Steve. I applied full power and we climbed rapidly and levelled off just above the cloud and haze layer. I put the Canberra into a steeply banked turn, and just down below me almost at sea level I could see the Lightning rolling rapidly one-way and then another, just like a shark looking for its prey. *"The target has reappeared, estimated at around 2500 feet,"* intoned the Gata controller. *"Roger,"* said Steve somewhat tersely. *"Tee hee,"* we said simultaneously, as we dropped back down below the scattered cloud to low level. *"Target has disappeared once more,"* said Gata. There was a pause, then a voice, that sounded really p****d off, *"It's all right, I have the target visual."* *"Uh oh!"* *"Where is he coming from?"* Mike and I went into frantic search mode but with negative results.

We should have known what was going to happen. A few weeks previously, Steve had been scrambled at night for real when the Turks had invaded Northern Cyprus, with their own air support. Steve had taken off in burner (i.e. re-heat) on the westerly runway at Akrotiri, hauled his aircraft round to point towards North East Cyprus, a track that took him across the town of Limassol. But by then the Lightning was going supersonic, and Steve had remained at low level so that the Turkish invasion forces on the north coast would not pick him up on their radar; the result was that a very loud sonic boom hit the town. The inhabitants must have believed that Judgment Day had arrived. I don't know how many windows shattered, but it probably didn't matter by then anyway, since the opposing sides had been machine gunning and sniping at each other for some days.

However, to continue with my tale, we were cruising along at around 270 knots at around 200 –250 feet above the sea, with no idea where Steve was coming from. With its plank wings, the Canberra could out turn the Lightning in the horizontal, so if we had sighted him, we might have been able to throw him off, but Steve came from behind us and flew directly underneath us at some speed greater than Mach 1. In a supersonic shock wave, there is a fantastic increase in air pressure for a fraction of a second. This shock wave hit us from the rear and travelled to the front of the aircraft. Apart from causing the poor old beast to shudder just as if it had hit a brick wall, the shock wave also punched up the engine jet pipes. In the cockpit the needles on both RPM gauges swung back and forth like a ship's telegraph going from full ahead to full astern. It was quite easy to surge the Canberra Avon engines in certain conditions, and I thought that we might have a double surge and or flame out. It's a moot point whether I'd have got one engine relit before Mike got himself strapped back in to his seat in time for an ejection, or before we hit the sea. Steve was retrospectively quite apologetic about this and bought us a beer each later in the bar.

The Turkish Invasion

About this time a new boss arrived on the squadron Wing Commander Al Blackley – who had been ahead of me by three years at Perth Academy and also in the Glasgow UAS. Whether this was instrumental in the next event I don't know, but in early July, he informed me that I had been chosen as a referee in a SEATO exercise in Turkey to sit in the back seat of a Turkish Air Force Lockheed F 104B – the trainer version while the pilots competed in the exercise. I was given $1000 US for expenses for the two weeks that I expected to be in Turkey. However, on the morning of my departure (Saturday 20th July 1974), on arrival at the DC3 that was to transport me, the pilot said there would be a delay, because of some minor insurrection among the Greeks and Turks; a not infrequent occurrence at that time; but on this occasion the Turks had invaded Northern Cyprus, and the island was effectively partitioned. I kept the $1000 for some weeks, but eventually I realised that my personal Turkish expedition was never going to take place, and so I handed the crisp brand-new bills back in to RAF accounts.

Just a day or two prior to the Turkish invasion, the RAF, (who must have had wind of this through intelligence sources), had carried out a practice evacuation of a *very limited* number of RAF families from Limassol to RAF Akrotiri, bussing in a hundred or so people to the Camp to test out the system. I don't know what the results of this trial were, but by the evening of the first day of the 'Cypriot War' everyone who had a car in Limassol, together with the whole fleet of RAF buses were taking people fleeing the town to the airfield; at that time there were probably about two thousand or more wives and children living off the base! It was quite chaotic. As the buses drove through the town, the warring Greeks and Turks were exchanging shots across the streets. The Limassol evacuation also showed up the usual human defects in an emergency; for while some personnel filled up their cars with those who had no transport, others insisted on filling up their cars with their valuables, leaving their neighbours to make their own way out. On the base, the sports fields were now rapidly becoming a vast tented encampment, where the evacuees were like sheep separated from their lambs at shearing time: wives and children sought their husbands, and husbands sought their families; this state of confusion went on well into the night. On the same day –we had been in our quarter on the base for just over a week –all husbands who lived in married quarters were ordered to take enough kit with them and share accommodation with about 15 other blokes in whatever barracks room they could find; while the homeless wives and children were billeted in the married quarters. In the evenings the husbands were allowed to visit their wives and families for an hour or two. When the evicted husband who rented the quarter returned to see his wife for an hour, it was quite normal to find that his quarter was now accommodating about four or five other husbands, who had also come to visit their wives and families. We had 4 wives and their children billeted in our quarter for some weeks. This system worked very well; each quarter received sufficient boxes of RAF rations –fairly basic food, but with up to six wives and a bit of ingenuity, I seem to recollect no one ever complained.

By now the fighting had spread to the countryside, and I can remember looking up at the Troodos Mountains, where we had some idyllic excursions, now had the appearance of a volcanic eruption. The forests had been set on fire and there was an enormous plume of smoke rising up into the heavens, it really did appear quite Apocalyptic. A few weeks after the start of the 'War', a detachment of six Phantoms from No. 6 Fighter Squadron arrived from the UK to bolster our forces. Each evening, as we gathered for a beer on the veranda of the Officers Mess, as we inevitably did, on the last sortie of the day, a Lightning followed shortly by a Phantom, or vice versa, would come roaring across the airfield just above the runway at low level as fast as they could without going supersonic, pull up into the vertical, engage reheat, and see who could reach the greatest altitude before running out of airspeed and control. *"C'est ne pas la guerre"*, but it was spectacular watching these jets climbing and contrailing up into the stratosphere. I managed to wangle a trip in the back of a Phantom. The first thing that I noticed was the size of the cockpit. I am at best of small to middling stature, but even allowing for this, most British aircraft seem to be designed by some mechanical bespoke tailor, and can only be entered by shoe-horning yourself into the cockpit; but the 'Tomb's' cockpit was positively huge. When I adjusted the seat so that I could see out, my feet were off the floor, and conversely, when my feet were on the floor, I could only just see over the cockpit coaming.

After the invasion, married men who had complained that they never got out to have a beer with their mates, now had this privilege every night of the week, and could only visit 'home' in company with other 'guests' for a short period in the evening. The universal moan now was, *"I'd like to be home with my wife!"* We continued in this mode of life for some weeks, before I was again given a new task. There had been a Cease Fire (and Peace Talks) of a kind going on in Cyprus between the two sides, with a British mediator, but now it was necessary to fly 'our man in Nicosia', in this case a Colonel Hunter to Geneva. The Colonel was carrying a detailed map of the demarcation lines between Greeks and Turks to the real peace conference in Switzerland.

Geneva Holiday

I had never landed at Geneva before and by the time that we had left Cyprus for Malta, refuelled at Luqa and got airborne again night had fallen. We were picked up by Geneva radar, and given a let-down. This was quite spooky; the descent path obviously was quite safe but necessitated a descent between high mountains that could be dimly discerned either side. When it came to doing a turn round servicing, we had a slight quandary about which fuel to put in; all the choices that the non-English speaking ground crew offered did not seem to match up our specifications. Fortunately, help was at hand. Next to us, was an RAF Comet 4 that had brought in the British Delegation (including Prime Minister Jim Callaghan); I knew that the Comet had Avon engines – the same engines as the Canberra, so I pointed at the Comet, and asked in my somewhat rusty French, what they had refuelled it with. They answered with something that I still didn't recognise, but I said in my best pidgin French, *"I'll have the same as him."*

The Colonel disappeared and Mike and I didn't see him for five days. Meanwhile we were billeted –which is the wrong word for where we stayed, in the Hotel Président right by the side of Lake Geneva. It was listed as five stars, an incredibly opulent and expensive place –or would have been if we had had to pay. To give a sense of proportion, the hotel charged £1 for a boiled egg! One could also order a Dagwood Special Sandwich. Dagwood was a cartoon character that had featured in an American strip cartoon in the nineteen forties. His special sandwich consisted of some 6 or 8 slices of bread with different fillings between each two layers. I do not know how much these sandwiches cost, but Mike and I lived on them. We also explored Geneva; there was some festival or other going on, with lots of marchers and bands and displays. We went to a super cabaret show that was a cross between Palace of Varieties, a Circus act and a strip show.

Mike had the foresight to bring his foreign driver's licence with him, so our next ploy to pass the time, was to hire a Citroen 2CV and drive to Mont Blanc (right), some 75 miles away. Having arrived at the foot of the mountain, we parked the car, took a chair lift to the summit, where there was a fully functioning restaurant with sightseeing facilities. Here we partook of a meal and a beer and walked through the ice tunnels to the Italian side, from where we sent a postcard to the Boss and all our mates living 16 to a room at Akrotiri, informing them of our hardships. This didn't go down too well, and we received a lot of grumbles from all and sundry when we returned. But by then the admin organisation had flown most of the dependants from Limassol back to the UK and I was able to return to my quarter.

The good life resumed, but not quite as relaxed as before; there were now restrictions on where you could and could not go, such as to the north of the island, across the demarcation line. It was fortunate that we had taken some leave for a camping holiday a month before the invasion and visited the beautiful town of Cyrenia and the nearby Bellapais Abbey. The only glitch had been during a visit to the beach by Cyrenia. Arriving by car one beautiful morning, we found a long beach that was quite crowded next to the somewhat full car park, but pretty empty further on. Spotting some vehicles in the distance, I opted to drive our VW estate car to this area. We set off, and had gone quite a way, before I realised that I was driving on softish sand. It shortly became a replay of the film 'Ice Cold in Alex' where John Mills, Sylvia Sims, Anthony Quayle, and Harry Andrews attempt to drive an army 4-ton truck across the Sahara. In short, we became bogged down. The 'cars' in the distance turned out to be four-wheel drive Army Land Rovers. The Squaddies, who came to our rescue, were delighted to tow out an RAF Officer's car – rear end first.

With these limitations, Squadron social life revolved more round the beach from just after mid-day. (The working hours were great - on the squadron from 6.30am until mid-day, and then all afternoon and the evening off, followed by about 5 to 6 hours sleep before commencing another 18-hour day! One evening some weeks after the Turkish invasion, the Canberra Flight, 3 pilots and 3 navigators, with our wives went to some Greek café at the far eastern end of Limassol. At the end of the meal, we decided to have a 'race' back to the base in our cars. Mine being a VW estate was not the sharpest machine off the starting grid, and consequently I was at the back of the pack in our race along the sea front road. At one point there was a roundabout, which had been partially blocked off by the Greek Cypriots, and in the middle of the roundabout they had rigged up a sandbagged defence point with a machine gun. Being suddenly confronted with a succession of cars going at high speed, breaking sharply to miss the blocking trees, and swerving round them with much screeching of tyres, had put them on their toes. By the time that I swung round them I was very conscious of being tracked by some itchy-fingered spotty teenage volunteer on the end of this machine gun.

The British presence in Cyprus had also been reinforced by the Royal Navy, so it came about one afternoon that our Squadron was invited to visit HMS Hampshire, a County Class destroyer. I remember that we were transported out to the ship by the ship's cutter sometime in the afternoon, for a very quick tour of the ship, followed by a long stay in the wardroom; I can only dimly remember coming home. Another visit to another 'ship' had almost fatal consequences. The RAF Yacht club had a largish yacht (40' or so) – The Lady Margaret, named after some Air Marshall's wife. I think that there were six of us, (including Babs), who went out in this yacht under 'Captain' Bob Cann one of our navigators, who had the requisite nautical ticket. It was a beautiful day, but the wind was too slack for an exciting sail, so we came to rest a few miles out in

Akrotiri Bay. At that point we started diving off the ship and swimming back and climbing on board. We were all doing this without a care in the world, when someone noticed that there was *no one* on board. If the wind had picked up, I'm pretty sure that none of us would have made it to the shore; the yacht would have become another Marie Celeste.

Another memory was a sortie with Ian Gristwood in the two seat Lightning T4. We did a recce over a Russian Krivak destroyer that was permanently stationed off the east coast of Cyprus. Ian had been warned about carrying out a low pass over this vessel, because someone had discovered that the Russian sailors regularly launched a hefty radio-controlled model aeroplane, which they flew above the ship in the path of any RAF aircraft that showed undue interest. A collision with this would have been terminal for both aircraft but rather more expensive for the RAF. On another sortie I had my first and only attempt at air-to-air refuelling in the T4 under the tutelage of Henry Ploszek.

In December '74, just before we returned to the UK, I managed to hitch a ride on a Hercules that was transiting out to Hong Kong. This jolly was an interesting trip for a number of reasons. One of the last archetypal outposts of the Empire we visited was Salalah, situated on the southern shores of the Arabian Peninsula. On the next leg, the captain of the Herc let me fly an ILS approach into Gan; but much of the time on the long ocean transits, I spent lying on one of the utility stretcher beds in the back of the Herc, with a pair of ear defenders to keep out the engine noise, while reading my way through all three volumes of Tolkien's Lord of the Rings, borrowed from the station library for this express purpose. We also called in at Singapore, before over flying South Vietnam. We had a two-night stop in Hong Kong, and once again I was impressed with a Herc crew who could instantly adapt to the ways and customs of whichever country they found themselves in. In the evening we walked to a downtown market area where you could buy and haggle for just about anything. However, the aim of this expedition was to have an evening meal at a 'restaurant.' This particular 'restaurant' consisted of plastic topped tables and wickerwork chairs set out in the market. The chefs were first class, their culinary delicacies were known to be exceptional, but were prepared with only a nod and a wink at conventional food hygiene. Here the worldly travelled Herc crew demonstrated their well-travelled experience. We all paid into the cost of the meal and the beer, and each of us was given a small bowl and two chopsticks, before the arrival of a huge platter that contained all the different dishes that we had ordered. Now by this stage in my life I could just about get by with chop sticks, but these guys were experts, so if I was going to have any chance of a reasonable portion of the food, I would have to acquire a greater level of skill very rapidly. Under this pressure, I did reasonably well.

On one of the return legs, the Captain let me land the Herc at Masirah – on the sand runway; and hereby hangs another tale. When Masirah was first being surveyed for development as an RAF Staging Post, (as someone once told me), one piece of vital information that was required was the direction of the prevailing wind. This was necessary so that the longest runway could be aligned with it. The statistics were duly sent off for analysis. Now Masirah, just off the coast of Oman, lies in the path of the Monsoon, so effectively there are almost six months of the wet south west monsoon, and almost six months of the dry north-east monsoon. Apparently, the information on the wind directions had been averaged out in some office, and instructions were sent to the work force to lay the runway southeast northwest, i.e. in the direction of the mean wind, which was of course at 90 degrees to the actual prevailing winds. Fortunately, just before work commenced, some bright chap noted this and the necessary corrections were made.

As already noted, Masirah did not have much to offer in terms of social life, however on our night stop we discovered that necessity is the mother of invention. In the bar there was a bucket that contained a number of hermit crabs –the kind that uses a seashell as a portable home. In this case each crab's shell had a white number painted on the side of it. After bets had been laid against the number on the shell, the bucket was emptied in the middle of something that looked like a large horizontal dartboard, which had a number of concentric circles drawn on it. The first crab that made it to the edge of the board was the winner. However, some unscrupulous punters were known to nobble the other 'horses' in the race by splashing beer or even more lethal liquid in the paths of rivals; the hermit crabs took it in their stride, and by the end of the evening, the punters were not the only ones who had sore heads!

Return to the UK

Most Brits in Cyprus usually bought a car out there – not only were they cheaper, but as long as you didn't sell your car for a year after returning to the UK there was no import duty to pay. But on this occasion, now that a very great percentage of UK personnel were returning, the second-hand car market had crashed –hence I was faced with the requirement to ship my old VW car back to the UK. We took our vehicles down to the docks at Famagusta, where they were lined up inside a high wire compound in very orderly rows and ranks prior to shipment. However, by this time many of the locals who had either been long-time supporters of General Grivas who preached 'enosis' or union with Greece, or who had since taken umbrage at the departure of the Brits and consequent disruption to their economy, were casually throwing stones over the wire, with a fair chance of getting a hit on someone's car! Early in the New Year Babs and the boys flew back to the UK, and I followed a few days later with the last Canberra out of Cyprus.

Act Six

RAF ST Mawgan, Cornwall

Our new home was at St Eval – a Second World War airfield a few miles up the north Cornish coast from St Mawgan. The day that we arrived –27th January 1975, the weather was down on the deck, the visibility obscured by sheets of rain, and the wind blowing a gale. The contrast with Cyprus could not have been more distinct. Viewing the desolate windswept married quarters occasionally veiled by the rain, I said to Babs, *"It looks like a scene from A Day in the Life of Ivan Denisovich,"* in reference to Alexander Solzhenitsyn's account of a Russian prisoner in a gulag camp.

After the somewhat frenetic activity that we had had in Cyprus, the quieter life in Cornwall was a welcome relief. I joined No 7 Squadron as a Squadron QFI and Instrument Rating Examiner (IRE). The other QFI/IRE was the instructor who had given me a hard time at Bassingbourn –however; by now he had remarried and was now quite mellow! No 7 Squadron had a number of different marks of Canberra –B2, T4, TT18, and T19. This last mark of Canberra had originally been fitted with a radar device in the nose cone; but when the equipment had been removed, in order to keep the aircraft in trim a suitable weight in the form of a large block of cement had been added. Hence it was rumoured, to keep Russian intelligence guessing, it was put out that this aircraft was now equipped, (in deference to a well-known cement manufacturer), with a new secret 'Blue Circle Radar!'

No 7 Squadron's main task was to provide towed targets for various Royal Navy and Army exercises and weapons ranges. Apart from the usual drogue target, the TT 18 was equipped with a Rushton target drone, which could be launched from the parent aircraft and then towed at the end of some 30 thousand feet of cable, allowing live firing. There were regular detachments up to RAF Kinloss on the coast of the Moray Firth in Scotland, whence we flew across to the Outer Hebrides, for target practice for the Army on Benbecula. Some miles out over the Atlantic, the target aircraft would deploy the drone, fly towards the target, and on reaching the target, the aircraft would initiate a turn outbound back over the sea. This turn had to be carefully judged, since too tight a turn would cause the thousands of feet of cable between the aircraft and the target drone to become slack and drop. This happened once to another pilot, with the result that the wire made contact with some power cables and the island's electricity supply was cut off!

On another occasion I was told to hold off for some 40 minutes while the Army solved problems with their tracking equipment. As I hadn't deployed the target and it was one of those beautiful days that the Western Isles occasionally experience in exchange for the many days of storm, wind and rain, we decided, rather than just orbit round we would fly out to the isle of St Kilda, some 50 miles to the west. We stayed at low level, the visibility was excellent and we could see the top of the hill on Hirta the main island from a fair distance. I should have been warned, for there was a smallish cap of cloud sitting just above the summit, a sign that there was a good breeze blowing over it. The wind over the ocean was steady, but just as a rock in a river creates rapids, so the hill on the island was creating quite a lot of turbulent eddies downstream. This became very apparent when our aircraft started to shake, roll, and buffet while we were yet a few miles from the islands. I abandoned our low-level recce, selected full power banked away and climbed out. After my experiences on take-off from RAF Gan, and getting 'bounced' off RAF Akrotiri I had no intention of finding out how good my relight drills were at low-level 50 miles out over the North Atlantic!

Summer Mountain Leadership Course – Gautestad, Norway

The information in the Ministry of Defence NOTAM (Notice to Airmen) said that a two-weeklong course on summer mountain leadership would be held in Norway. Although I was now in my 38th year, I reckoned that I was reasonably fit: I cycled 5 miles to work each day (In Cyprus from Limassol to RAF Akrotiri it had been 14 miles each way), and I had done a short jungle survival course, a winter survival course, and the usual sea survival courses. This would add to my collection. Travelling from the tip of Cornwall – RAF St Mawgan, involved an MT truck to Truro; by train up to London; across London by Tube; RV with some of the other course members; Night stop in a hotel, bus to Luton, flight to Hanover; day stop in an army barracks to pick up more members of the course; bus to northern Denmark; steamer to Kristiansand; MT truck up country to a remote little place on the southern edge of the Hardanger Plateau called Gautestad –the British Army's training centre in Norway. By the time we got there I realized that I had made a dreadful mistake. **ALL** the other members of the course (apart from one Sergeant who was in his late 20s') were 20 –22-year-old para-troops who were straight out of basic training and had the appearance and physique of trainee gladiators. My previous estimate of my fitness was light years removed from these guys. But having spent 24 hours getting here, there was no way of opting out.

As soon as we arrived, a very military Sgt Major type told us to get our PE kit on, form up in single file and commence a run up a path with an appreciable uphill gradient. Having run for some distance, the lead runner was commanded to stop, bend over locking his hands in his ankles, thereafter the subsequent runner was to vault over him, run forward a few paces, and then also adopt the same position. Ultimately, the whole line carried out this manoeuvre until everyone had vaulted over everyone else –while running up hill. I didn't manage to measure my heart rate but I believe that it must have approached that of the American astronaut Alan Shepherd during his Moonwalk. Then we all ran downhill again changed into our 'swimmies' and dived into a lake whose water temperature would have been quite suitable for polar bears. The next few days – I think – My memory has been mercifully erased –proceeded along similar lines. Other pastimes included abseiling –something quite new to me, and orienteering on maps that were akin to the POW escape and evasion variety, through country that was bog, lake, birch, and rock repeated ad infinitum, all overseen by a staff of PT fanatics. Then came the highlight of the course; we piled into Land Rovers drove northwards for some time into the Hardanger Plateau. Meanwhile the cloud thickened, and the rain began in earnest. Eventually we stopped by the side of a very steep slope covered in birch trees. Our party got out, the Land Rovers departed, we hoisted our Bergen rucksacks swung them onto our backs, and adopted an attitude leaning well forward to prevent toppling over backwards. *"Right,"* said the leader of our party, *"we go this way,"* and without further ado, started to climb up the 45-degree slope by grabbing the slender trunks of the birches. We followed. The rain came down. We sweated copiously. The trees thinned (above the tree line?) And then horror of horrors; the slope continued up at the same crazy angle forever until it disappeared into the cloud. We struggled on. The slope eased off to a mere 20-degree slope, but now it was covered in a glacial scree composed of large boulders, which were progressively wet and mossy, wet and slippery with lichen, and finally just wet – on top of melting ice. I felt that should one slip and damage a leg or ankle, the ethos of this party would probably require one to do the right thing and say, *"I'm just going to proceed at my own pace, I may be some time"* in the manner of the late Captain Oates. Eventually we cleared the boulder field, and arrived at the snow line and the edge of an ice field where we proceeded to make camp.

The next day the expedition continued in pouring rain and low cloud across the same rugged country. My strength was holding up, but I had developed huge blisters across the back of my heels. On the third morning, the sun was shining and everything looked really great. We roped up and spent some time crossing the Breidfonn Glacier. At one point we came to a large pool formed from the outflow of water from under the glacier. The water was exiting from a cave cut in the ice. Some brave souls decided to explore this by edging along the ice. Fortunately, they hadn't gone far when a large chunk of ice peeled off and almost washed them away in a mini tidal wave. An example of global warming from 1976! Meanwhile great sheets of cloud had been building up, and more torrential downpours accompanied our final day and descent off the mountain. At the end of the course, I was definitely fitter – but this didn't impress the Directing Staff, who, although they didn't actually imply that I had been malingering and lagging, consequently marked me down for failing to display the aggressive leadership to the young paras such as would have been expected from an Army officer of the equivalent rank. I didn't shame the RAF by informing the DS that I was probably much fitter than the vast majority of my contemporaries back home.

Signing On
I had joined the RAF initially for 5 years, with the intention of returning to university, but, by the end of the 5 years I was married with one child, and the prospect of returning to live on a student grant didn't seem so good. As I have also already noted, I had decided to leave the RAF to apply to join the civil airline world when I was 38. But by the time I was 35, the thought, despite the money, of sitting for hours flying airline routes, transporting passengers caused me to ask for an interview at MOD, with the intention of remaining in the RAF until I was 55. On the day of the interview I was ushered into the office of a young Wing Commander –younger than me by a few years, and who was a navigator to boot! He knew I was coming so he had already familiarised himself with my file and taken note of my service with the RAF, but he probably wanted me to convict myself out of my own mouth, before he gave judgement. He politely asked me what I had done. I informed him

that I had flown this...flown that...flown here ... flown there...and...He interrupted me at this point and asked whether I had had any staff jobs. I said no. He perused a few more pages of my file and then asked me what I wanted to do. I said that I would like to remain in the RAF until I was 55, and I was wondering what chances there were of a career and further promotion. He took a further look at my service history, and then said words to the effect, *"Dobz, if you were to leave the RAF at this point and take holy orders, you'd stand a better chance of making pope!"* But not long afterwards, I was informed that my application to extend my service to the age of 55 had been accepted.

Although my tour in Cornwall lasted only just over 18 months, I managed to get myself on four detachments down to the Med – to Malta, to Sardinia, and two to Gibraltar, and by ferry across to Tangier in Morocco. On the return from Gibraltar, the weather in Cornwall was atrocious for May. There was a very strong cross wind from the northeast –we were coming in on RW 31 and at about 300 feet while we were still in cloud on radar finals the port engine surged. Somehow, I reacted automatically, throttled back the port engine, selected take-off flap, kept the aircraft on the glide path, and eased the port engine up again; by the time we broke cloud all was normal. My boss Wind Commander Edmonds who had come along as navigator, on this leg of the journey had swapped his ejection seat for the 'Rumbold' seat beside me. It would have been impossible for him to bail out at such a low level, so having seen exactly what was going on, he must have been a very relieved man when the engine picked up again.

In August 1976 I learned that I had been posted to RAF Valley as a QFI on the Folland Gnat. This was going to be a real challenge.

RAF Valley, Anglesey

Our eldest son Andrew had just commenced boarding school in Truro when we left Cornwall for Wales. We left him behind – much to his dismay: for at half term and at the end of term as a 12-year-old he would be faced with a very long rail journey by himself from Truro to Crewe, where Babs would meet him off the train for the second half of the rail journey, followed by a similar journey in reverse at the end of his vacation. Meanwhile we arrived at our future RAF quarter a few hours ahead of the removal van. By now we also had two more dogs –both cross breeds. The first one, Trudy, a terrier/something combo, that Babs had acquired to keep her company while I was away on detachments. The second, Scamp, a sort of Sealyham terrier, we had inherited from Babs' brother's son Simon, whose upwardly mobile Mum did not permit dogs in her RAF Quarter. Then, just to complicate matters slightly with our move in, shortly after we arrived, Trudy gave birth to four pups in an empty RAF holdall kitbag in the bottom of a wardrobe in one of the bedrooms!

It was fortunate that we arrived with about 4 weeks to spare, for it gave me plenty of time to familiarise myself with the Gnat on the cockpit trainer in the Simulator Flight. This Cockpit Trainer Simulator was a basic familiarity trainer complete with ejection seat and harness, and fitted with a control column, throttle, switches, cockpit instrumentation, together with the correct electrical indications and sounds for engine start up and shut down checks; it was an essential piece of kit to get up to speed on cockpit drills. For those unfamiliar with this aircraft, the Folland Gnat was just about the smallest fastest aircraft in being. It had, I believe, been originally developed as a lead in trainer for the Lightning. Not only was it very small, but also it sat very close to the ground. If you stood alongside it you could easily look into the cockpit. It had a 45-degree sweepback wing form, and could cruise quite happily at height at about .92M, and attain supersonic flight in a dive. But it also had a very thirsty jet engine: most sorties were of the order of about 45 to 50 minutes. This was somewhat of a disadvantage as an instructional vehicle, in that the instructor could demonstrate a particular facet of the aircraft once, allow the student to attempt the same, then if that was unsuccessful, usually only one more cycle of demo and practice could be carried out before moving onto another exercise. This feature, however, generally sorted out the men from the boys. You could either fly the Gnat or you couldn't.

When I met the rest of the budding Gnat QFIs on the course I found that (just as on my course in Norway) I was by far the oldest member on it. Most RAF pilots seem to commence on fast jets and graduate to the bigger slower ones later in life; I appeared to have done the reverse; I was just approaching my 38th birthday. My few weeks personal familiarisation now paid off, and I managed to stay up to speed with my course. It was an exciting aircraft to fly. There were a few times just after I went solo, when I felt like a rider on a runaway horse, trying to catch up with the aircraft rather than control it.

The Gnat was also the first aircraft that I had flown where the ejection seats were arranged in tandem fashion, and on one particular mutual sortie – where two student instructors are crewed up to 'give back' the instructional patter for the exercise to each other, before doing the same to one of the staff – we almost came to grief. The usual procedure is for one pilot to say, *"You have control"* and the other pilot to reply *"I have control";* or if as instructor, you feel your student is about to do something dangerous, you say (with much more vigour and expression), ***"I have control"*** to which the chastened student would respond *"You have control."* On this particular sortie, quite early in the course, I was in the back cockpit and Byron Walters, an ex-Lightning pilot, occupied the front. We had taken off on R/W32 and turned right hand to depart from downwind to the east at 1000 feet. I can't remember who was flying the jet but whoever it was didn't get the correct response from the other pilot. The Gnat being almost inherently unstable would not fly straight and level unattended. In this case, it rolled smartly to the inverted, and adopted a distinctly nose down attitude. I thought to myself, *"This is punchy stuff at 1000', but no more than is to be expected from and ex-Lightning pilot."* Simultaneously Byron was thinking, *"This is punchy stuff at 1000' feet for an old Canberra pilot."* Fortunately, we both realised that neither of us had control, and again, we both chose to roll the same way out of the manoeuvre. Everyone in the ATC tower must have been looking out over the airfield, since no one commented about our Gnat's descent inverted down to about 500 feet before regaining circuit height.

I was now on my 5th instructional tour and had achieved a fair number of instructional hours. For this reason, although I did not have any experience on fast jets, my new squadron boss and flight commander felt that my relatively 'advanced age' and previous experience in contrast to the much younger much more 'gung ho' instructors on their first tour, would be suitable for those occasional students who, because of some innate lack of self-confidence were less able to maintain the 'monkey do as monkey see' pace required for every phase of the student course. In retrospect, I also believe that my bosses were aware that because I had not flown the latest and fastest jet the RAF had on offer, I could probably empathize more with a student's inability to immediately grasp and perform immaculately a required manoeuvre without resorting to sarcastic deprecation and verbal abuse of those who knew that they could fly any modern fast jet but who could not relate to someone who could not. I'd been on the end of that type of instructional technique, and I knew that it did not work. The downside of flying with such students on occasion demanded a high degree of concentration, especially in the early stage of my instructional career on the Gnat.

The Gnat, as I have mentioned, was a super little aircraft to fly, but it had one or two quirks particularly in its powered flying control system. The power control system on the Gnat normally moved the tail plane as a slab; using the hydraulic system. As an aircraft approaches supersonic speed, there is quite a large change in the centre of lift over the wings, and because of the Gnat's small size, the room for fore and aft movement of the control column in the cockpit was very limited, hence the power controls to the tail plane incorporated a complicated electro-mechanical linkage within the fuselage (the celebrated cam mechanism and Q gearing), that *"through a system of levers"* expanded and contracted to compensate for changing air speeds. Essentially this system adjusted the angle of the slab tail plane while keeping the control column in the middle of the cockpit to allow full movement. Similarly, the deployment of the undercarriage also caused a large change in trim and performance. Thus, flying in hydraulic 'Power,' *automatically* reset the slab tail plane at an attitude that was the optimum for the flight conditions. However, there were also elevators on the tail, which could be unlocked; now not only did the tail move but the elevators did as well –you were now flying 'Unlocked,' this resulted in a much more 'mushy feel' on the stick. Finally, as a last resort, if you lost hydraulic power to the control system, you could maintain flight by flying in 'Manual' –in essence you were back to WW2 metal rods and wires to move all the control surfaces. But as the only surfaces available to maintain level flight on the tail were two quite small elevators, it was essential to make sure that the tail plane and hence the aircraft was in trim at a certain speed before exhausting the remains of the hydraulic system, otherwise the aircraft was uncontrollable with insufficient elevator authority to hold the nose up or keep it down. All ex-Gnat pilots will be familiar with the mnemonic –STUPRECC, the drill to be carried out. In essence this drill decreed that you reduced the **Speed** below 400 knots/. 85M, **Trim** the tail plane to the ideal sector while there was still some hydraulic pressure and regained level flight, **Unlock** the elevators, select the hydraulic **Power** cock off, **Raise** the guard on the standby electrical trimmer, **Exhaust** the remaining pressure in the hydraulic accumulators by stirring the stick, **Check** that the aircraft was still controllable, and **Change** to the manual trim switches (the hydraulic trim switches being now useless. This drill *had to be done* in that particular order –in the *exact* reverse order to get back to power controls.

On one particular night flying sortie, whilst flying with a student who was not quite up to speed, we returned in 'Manual' to the airfield from a radar pattern, before carrying out an overshoot at the runway threshold, then climbing and turning out over Carnarvon Bay to 1500 feet to prepare to return to powered flight. Unfortunately, being unable to see my student, who was doing the drill from the front cockpit, he mistakenly selected the powered control system back on before he selected the undercarriage up. We were somewhere abeam Aberffraw - about 10 miles along the coast from

RAF Valley, when the aircraft reared up totally out of trim. I grabbed the stick and put her into a steeply banked turn. We were somewhere about 1500 –2000feet at about 180 knots, and it took all my strength to hold the stick forward. I knew if I let go, the aircraft would pitch up and stall, and in a deep stall the rate of descent was very high. Alternatively, the aircraft would probably have flicked and commenced to spin; and at 1500 feet-ish there was little likelihood of us getting out. The stick force was such that I wouldn't be able to hold it for long, so I called up Frankie Foster, the Duty Pilot in ATC, and dispensing with the formal call sign, said *"Frank, It's Dobz here,"* and explained my problem. Fortunately, he knew exactly what had happened, and just like René the French hotel keeper in the TV series 'Allo, 'Allo, he said, *"Listen carefully, I will say this only once; I know what you have done, you now need to make the same mistake in reverse to get back into manual and then do the proper drill to get back into power."* This we did and recovered and landed, oozing sweat somewhat inside our rubber immersion suits, had a meaningful post flight debrief, and then went for a meal and a beer or three.

There was plenty of flying – 30–40 hours per month, all short 45 to 50-minute sorties: general handling, close formation and tactical formation, and low level at high speed over most of the UK. In the Gnat, the instructor's seat was not stepped up, and thus most of the instructor's forward view was obscured by the top of the student's ejection seat in the front cockpit, which required the instructor to peer round one side or other to see where he was pointing. At night, especially, when carrying out flapless circuits, which necessitated a nose high attitude, there was precious little to see. In recognition of this, the powers that be had installed a sector air speed indicator in the rear cockpit just above the left coaming that enabled the QFI to monitor his approach speed without having to look inside at the main instrument panel. It was generally recognised that doing a flapless approach at night in a crosswind, which required the pilot to point the aircraft nose a bit into wind, such that you could actually see the runway was preferable to doing the same when the wind was right down the runway. However, on such occasions on late finals one could generally tell by the sharp increased intake of breath from the pilot in the front that you either weren't lined up with the tarmac or you were getting too low!

The Day Dawns

After our arrival on Anglesey from Cornwall, it didn't seem to make much sense to travel up to Scotland for "Dad's annual Survival Camp" holiday, when the sea was literally about a mile away. Instead, as Andrew's School summer term came to an end in the summer of 1977, Babs, Paul and I drove down to Cornwall to pick him up and having travelled down there, we felt that it would be a good idea to start our vacation at a holiday camp not far from Truro. The camp had lots of amenities and a large swimming pool that both the boys really enjoyed. The camp also had a large used paperback library; but there wasn't much of a selection –mainly romances and adventure stories. However, as I mentioned at the beginning of this odyssey, I have loved reading so I was compelled to pick from the few non-fiction books; one on the historical evidence and reality of Christ, and another on a theory that mankind was more likely to have been created by an extra-terrestrial source than evolve on earth.

Again, as I mentioned in my introduction, do we entirely control our destinies? For some months previously there had been a few small signs on the "way in which I was being directed," even before I crashed. Most mornings, well before I went to down for Met brief, I used to take both our dogs for a walk. Early in December (1976), on a very cold clear frosty morning, when there was not much light pollution, the stars appeared clear and brilliant. I could recognize most of the primary stars in the main constellations. As I stared into the predawn sky and my eyes became more used to the dark, I could see even further stars of a fainter magnitude, and it set me thinking about infinity. Beyond those stars were whole galaxies, and beyond those galaxies were others. To all intents and purposes, it went on forever. I almost fell over when I thought about something that never ended.

From this arose the second line of thought that stemmed from the book that I had read on man's creation mentioned above. At this time Von Danikin's books that mankind's arrival was caused by 'space gods' were very much in the vogue. I devoured these, before moving on to Worlds in Collision. In this book Immanuel Velikowsky hypothesises that the earth was in near collision with both Venus and Mars some 3500 years ago. The gravitational pull of these planets as they passed by the earth caused the earth's rotation to briefly cease, and great hailstones to rain down on the earth, evidence for which Velikowsky sited the Book of Joshua. My eldest son Andrew had been given a King James Bible by Bab's brother Brian some years previously. For the first time in many years I opened a Bible up and read **"The LORD cast down great stones from heaven upon them unto Azekah, and they died: they were more which died with hailstones than they whom the children of Israel slew with the sword. Then spake Joshua to the LORD in the day when the LORD delivered up the Amorites before the children of Israel, and he said in the sight of Israel. Sun stand thou still upon Gibeon; And thou moon, in the valley of Ajalon. And the sun stood still, and the moon stayed, until the people had avenged themselves upon their enemies. Is not this written in the Book of Jasher? So the sun stood still in the midst of heaven, and hasted not to go down about a whole day. And there was no day like that before it or after it, that the LORD hearkened unto the voice of a man, for the LORD fought for Israel" (Joshua 10:11-14).** Of the two authors Velikowsky appeared to me to be more authoritative than the somewhat lightweight Von Danikin. I had opened a Bible and had appeared to find a possible explanation for something that had happened almost 3500 years previously. Maybe there was something to this God thing after all?

Meanwhile my life as a pilot continued as normal. In late 1977, two of us, Roger North and I were detailed to rendezvous with a Vulcan loitering at about 40,000 feet somewhere over the west Midlands. We made the rendezvous with the Vulcan and attached ourselves in loose formation on either wing tip, while the Vulcan flew towards North East Scotland. The Vulcan was now imitating a Russian 'Bear' bomber, while the Gnats were posing as Soviet Kelt cruise missiles carried by this bomber, which would be used to attack ships at very low level. With some 100 miles to go, we were released in quick succession against a Royal Navy task force that was stationed some miles out to sea off Buchan Ness north of Aberdeen. We were launched as dusk fell, descending at high speed through 8/8th cloud, to low level over the sea. Although the Vulcan gave us headings and ranges to the task force, there was no radar control provided; neither was there any indication of how low the base of the cloud sheet was, so again it got a bit sweaty as I punched down through the cloud tops at around 4000' at a high rate of descent. I hoped that the altimeter was accurate and that I had set the correct regional pressure setting (Arrival at Nairobi all over again!). I got VMC at about 1500' over a somewhat dark and wave tossed sea. We had also been ordered to extinguish all our navigational and anti-collision lights to make it more difficult for any visual sighting by the RN. This was fine, but it also meant that neither Roger nor I had any idea where either of us was in relation to each other as we flew back and forth over the fleet and by now it was getting quite dark. (Just like night flying at RAF Manby all over again). However, having made a few passes over the ships –sensed as lighter shapes over a now black sea, we headed (individually) for RAF Kinloss, to be informed by their Air Traffic Control that they were open but it was snowing, the runway was slippery, and that they would be closing just as soon as we had landed, i.e., we would appreciate it if you got your skates on!

After putting the aircraft to bed, we discovered the reason for ATC asking us to expedite our recovery, for when we adjourned to the bar, we found some visiting Canadian aircrew on an anti-submarine warfare exercise were introducing their British counterparts to the pleasure of Moose milk. This was a concoction of whisky (?), something else alcoholic (?), milk, scoops of ice cream, sugar, ingeniously contained in a large zinc plated bathtub. Above the milky surface, the blocks of ice cream stood proud like icebergs, upon which someone had tastefully sprinkled grated nutmeg. When we arrived, the Canadians were ladling this mixture out to anyone who presented them with a pint glass. There are many varieties of Moose milk recipes, but this particular concoction seemed so innocuous: it was vaguely reminiscent of an ice cream sundae with a hint of something medicinal in the background; it seemed simultaneously to fulfil the advice to have something on your stomach before drinking while you drank!

First Prang – February 1978

By the spring of 1978 I was becoming quite au fait with my new life as a fast jet flying instructor; I still had hopes of making it onto the front line on the Buccaneer. However, my whole life was about to take a completely different turn from this point on. From my previous 'escapes and escapades' as related above, one could say that I had been very 'careless and lucky' on a number of occasions. However, in 1978, in my 40th year, my attitude to 'luck' changed, when in February and April, I had two major accidents.

On the first, I had gone along for the ride in the back seat while Dougie Mee, the unit air test pilot, carried out a check of the air fuel ratio control system at height. This system ensured that the engine did not introduce too much fuel into the engine during large rapid throttle movements. The system checked out OK at height –about 35000feet. On the recovery back to Valley I asked Dougie if I could carry out a Practice Forced Landing (PFL) into Mona airfield, our relief landing ground. The PFL was flown with the engine at idle, while the pilot guesstimated when to turn onto finals and when to lower the undercarriage, then lower the full flaps such that the aircraft would arrive safely on the runway and not in the undershoot. It was accepted that the latest touchdown point could in reality be about 1/3 way down the runway from the threshold. From this point in the real situation the aircraft could be brought to a halt within the remaining runway distance, while in practice, when the throttle was opened the aircraft could safely get airborne again. The procedure went well, we touched down at about 160 knots and I applied full power. Mona runway is only just over 5000feet long, and we now had only something of the order of 3500 feet remaining, quite sufficient to get airborne with a good engine, but as I opened the throttle, the RPM built up very slowly and stagnated about 80%. By now we didn't have much runway left and we were going much faster than on a normal touch and go landing, so when the engine failed to accelerate, we had no other options than to attempt an abort. Dougie took control and streamed the braking parachute – which failed to deploy, we ran out of runway, and encountered the jet barrier (a steel and nylon cable contraption) at some 100+ mph. The barrier should have brought the aircraft to a halt, but the retardation had no more force than jumping through a paper bag. The aircraft actually pulled the barrier out of its mountings. The fin caught the top steel cable, the aircraft briefly got airborne again and then after about 100yds slammed into an earth and stone bank, but fortunately the aircraft did not break up, burn, capsize, disintegrate, or explode. However, the nose undercarriage leg collapsed and was pushed up into the fuselage just under the rear ejection seat where I was sitting. This force tensioned my ejection seat handle firing cable to the point where it was like a hair trigger. When we had come to rest, I had made my seat safe (as I thought), as had Dougie, who also opened the canopy. I then rapidly unstrapped and stood on the seat – which if it had fired would have projected me about 100 feet into the air without a parachute. Even if I had still been attached to the parachute, it would have been fatal for me for this particular seat's limit was 90knots minimum airspeed at ground level. I heard of this second narrow 'lucky' escape a few hours later – while having a few beers to celebrate the first 'lucky' escape. It subsequently transpired that the Air Fuel Ratio Controller, which feeds graduated amounts of fuel into the engine as it accelerates, had failed.

Second Prang – April 1978

About three months later, on a flapless approach to the main runway R/W14 at RAF Valley, I felt that my student was getting a bit too low on the glide path (we were at about 250 feet and just over half a mile out). I told him to increase power, which he did – I saw my throttle lever in the back cockpit, which was mechanically linked to his in the front, move forward a bit. But the RPM continued to reduce very slowly. I thought, *"That's funny, this is very similar to the previous incident at Mona."* By now I had my attention fixed inside the cockpit on the relevant instruments and warning panels trying to figure out what was going on. There were no signs of any failure – the Jet Pipe Temperature, the Fuel Tank Pressure, Fuel contents, Oil Pressure, Fuel Pump Pressure were all normal. Only the engine RPM showed a slow decay. At this point I heard a still, quiet, but very authoritative voice, very clearly command me to *"GET OUT."* I grabbed the seat pan handle of the ejection seat, and yelled to the student *"Eject, Eject,"* and pulled my handle; we had about 150 feet altitude, but were in a slow descent.

The ejection seat had two handles – pulling the face blind handle above my head jettisoned the Perspex canopy *before* firing the seat, but– if you were in a real hurry, the handle located just between your legs on the seat (hence seat pan handle) was quicker as it sent the seat through the canopy. In the Gnat it was normal for the rear seat pilot to eject first if you went through the canopy, because the windblast caused Perspex fragments from the canopy to be blasted into the face of the pilot in the back cockpit if the front pilot went out first. I was in the chute about 10 seconds, and my student in his about the same. He said that as he left the aircraft, he saw the primary and secondary systems warning panels lit up like a Christmas tree, *and* he was close enough to the ground as he ejected to see individual blades of grass. He drifted out into the estuary and landed down on the beach. As I went out, I saw my student's seat clear the aircraft; while the aircraft with the loss of weight was now pitched up at about 20 degrees nose high. My parachute then deployed; I was violently swung round; I just had time to appreciate that I was very close to the ground, before I landed feet, knees, chest, face, in a gorse bush, like a sack of coal falling off the back of a truck. Just beyond the gorse bush was a 10 to15 foot slope of huge rocks running down to the beach. If I had landed in those, I would have been a paraplegic at best. (See previous photograph, which shows the parachute draped over the rocks).

Now here is an interesting fact. That morning, Babs, my wife, had had a premonition that something was going to happen to me, and she had prayed *"Lord, keep him safe."* Since then I have never ever dismissed female intuition; it's the good Lord's gift to the female of the species instead of logic! I am not joking. A man prides himself on reason and logic but you can spend hours unsuccessfully trying to figure out all the pros and cons to a problem, cause and effect etc., when your wife comes along and says, *"Why don't you try that Dear?"* You do, and behold it was so, and everything works perfectly first time. It's a way of keeping men humble, but it can be a real pain in the butt to the male ego! Secondly, as I was forced to admit, God had answered this quick prayer of faith by my wife! Moreover, on that same morning, Babs was in the Officers Mess at a wives' club coffee morning, when 'Boz' Robinson the station commander came rushing into the room. She knew right away that he would come over to her, which he did. All he said was, *"Dobz has ejected, but he's OK."* – Not entirely true, I had two compression fractures in the vertebrae of my lower back.

I know for a fact that *if* I had stayed with the aircraft for just a few seconds more trying to figure out if I could land the aircraft with the remaining power, both the student and myself would either have died, or been very seriously injured. The aircraft slammed down in the mud of the estuary some 100 yards short of the runway threshold, the damage was such that both of us would, at the very least, have lost our legs. The Accident Report commented, *"The captain's very prompt analysis of the situation saved both pilots' lives."* (See photograph below). The fault was traced to the disconnection (caused by the failure of a split pin) of the auxiliary drive shaft connected by a bevel gear to the engine, which resulted in the simultaneous failure of the fuel supply, electrics, hydraulics, and flying controls!

Now I'm vain enough to consider myself sharper than Homer Simpson, but I'm not sharp enough to analyse a fault that wasn't showing on the warning panels, and since there were no obvious signs of engine failure, you can't just abandon the aircraft because something just doesn't feel right. So, on this occasion I had not only got away from a crash landing, and a very low-level ejection, but I also escaped being mangled on the rocks. However, I never did see the official accident report. Was it because the RAF could not countenance my conviction that I had been *'commanded'* to get out?

Immediately after my crash I was taken by helicopter on a stretcher down to the RAF Hospital at Wroughton near Swindon and spent three weeks on my back in a bed while the compression fractures to my vertebrae healed. Shortly after arriving there, Wing Commander Dougie McGregor, who had been the Chief Flying Instructor at Valley, some months previously, somehow heard of my ejection and rang the hospital congratulating me on my escape. But by this time as he was the Air Attaché (I think?) in Washington; this had an unforeseen consequence. The nurses on the ward thought that I must be some VIP to get a phone call from the British Embassy in

America, so they wanted to put me in a private ward, but I said I preferred to be with all the other injured service personnel. I had plenty of visitors: Babs, my Mum, and Babs' Mum and Dad and her brother Brian and his family came down to see me. But by the end of the three weeks lying flat on my back in a bed I was amazed how weak my legs had become. A 22 Squadron Rescue chopper came down to Wroughton to take my back to Valley, and I was overjoyed to be back home again with my family. Shortly after I arrived, I heard on the grapevine that there was a dining in night on in the Mess that evening, so in a fit of bravado I got into my Mess kit and walked the 300 yards to the Mess. Fortunately, it was dark, for my progress must have looked like the last stages of Captain Scott's expedition in the Antarctic as I stumbled along. I stayed just long enough to have a beer or two before I decided that discretion was the better part of valour and that I had to get home before I ran out of strength completely.

Although I had been let loose from Wroughton hospital, I was still not fit enough to fly, so I spent about two hours every day in the gym under the tutelage of a PE instructor, but the squadron didn't waste my inability to fly. Every QFI had to do a two-and-a-half-hour spell as duty pilot up in Local Control in the Air Traffic Tower about once or twice a week, and since it was well known that I couldn't fly, I was used as a makeweight when any other instructor 'discovered' that he couldn't do tower duty for some reason. I was Duty Pilot when RAF Valley had the annual AOC'S Inspection. The Air Officer Commanding, Air Marshal Bairstow, who had a somewhat pugnacious manner and didn't suffer fools gladly, came up to look around the Local Control on his inspection of the ATC Tower. He glared at me, as I endeavoured to stand at attention, since my back still hurt a bit occasionally, and said *"Do you do this duty often?"* *"Every day Sir without fail"* I truly answered him. He looked intently at me to see if I was taking the Mickey out of him, harrumphed, and stalked off.

A few weeks later my next treat was a return trip down to the RAF Hospital to have a final clearance to fly cleared by the medics. As I previously mentioned, I had in fact received two cracked lumber vertebrae when I ejected. The trip by train was very similar to that I previously described when I went from St Mawgan in Cornwall to London. It took about 5 or 6 hours each way with three changes en-route. There was however transport waiting at Swindon station for me. I went in to see some Air Commodore Doctor. He looked at me and asked how I felt, I said fine. He asked if I could bend over and touch my toes. I promptly did so, and just as I touched my toes, he gave me what seemed to me to be a Karate chop with the edge of his hand in the part of my back that had been injured. It didn't hurt, but I shot back up to the vertical. *"Yes, you are fine,"* was all he said. And that was it. A twelve-hour journey for a two-minute medical 'check-up'; I was dismissed and sent on my way.

However, on the way down to Swindon I had an interesting experience. On one leg of the train journey, I can't remember how it came about, I felt that the Lord was telling me to witness to a man who was sitting at the far end of my carriage on the opposite side. I would think that he was aged about 30, well built, with very handsome chiselled features and smartly cut blond hair. In addition, he was wearing a zipped up black leather motorcyclist's jerkin and black leather trousers. With the addition of a Nazi armband he could have easily enrolled in the Waffen SS as the ideal Nordic man. I tried to ignore the prompting but it wouldn't go away. At the next station, where I had to change, he got off as well, and I thought that would be the last that I would see of him. Unfortunately, he settled down in a comfortable relaxed pose on one of the benches further down the platform; he too was waiting for another train. I had some Christian tracts with me, so screwing up what little courage I had, I walked up to this man and holding out the tract so that he could see the title, I said, *"The LORD wants me to give you this."* He flushed, stood up – all 6 feet plus of him, and unzipping his black leather jacket, he said in a loud harsh voice *"This* (indicating a large purple horned goat's head design stencilled on his white T shirt) *is whom I serve!"* I said, *"OK"*, and turned around and left him. I stood for the next ten minutes, on the platform waiting for my train. I had an uneasy thought that if this guy was really incensed against Christians, it would have been very easy for him to come up behind me and 'accidentally' push me into the path of the train as it arrived.

Initially my narrow escape did not appear to have had any affect upon my life style. Apart from being convinced that I had been 'ordered' to 'get out', I was still the same character that I had been previously, and yet even before I really understood that Christ was my Lord and Saviour, there were changes occurring within me, within my spirit and in my attitude to 'things religious,' that I wasn't aware of. Certainly, the other pilots and instructors were aware that something had changed; some dismissing me as having gone slightly odd; others, if they used the Lord's name blasphemously within my hearing would then apologise to me for doing so! This final part of my odyssey is an attempt to account for these changes. The latter end of this narrative may prove heavy going if you are not inclined to be fed many quotes from Scripture, and yet this is exactly how I was led from my fatalistic agnostic outlook to one that increased and continues to increase in love and trust in my Saviour Jesus Christ and seeking to walk in a true Christian way.

Return to Flying and Religion

Finally, 3 months after my crash, my back was healed. I returned to flying –now on the Hawk as the Gnat was just being phased out, and everything was returning to normal. Then one-day Babs informed me that we had been invited to a christening. Up until then, I had never inclined to any philosophy or creed that tried to explain what happens if and when you die. At that time, I was an agnostic fatalist. I believed that you could take all the necessary steps to ensure your survival, but if your time was up, your time was up. So apart from the odd wedding, christening, or funeral of someone who had crashed, I never went to church. And, even when I did go to church, I went without in any way being attentive or committed to anything that was being said. You know the sort of thing. You sit at the back and think about getting the car serviced, taking the dog to the vet, wonder if you have enough beer for Saturday's BBQ, and how long it was until you could go on leave. However, the inexplicable command *"Get out"* –clear as a bell, just prior to my ejection had me foxed. I went to *that* christening, which was in a C of E church in a large wooden hut by the married quarters. It was a friendly service of the *"happy-clappy"* kind with lots of modern Christian choruses; nobody spouted (long boring passages – for me) from the Bible and it was altogether non-theologically challenging. At the end of the service as we left, the vicar Niall Griffin beamed at us, and said that he hoped that we would come again. Babs had *also* been praying for me to do that, and I found myself saying, *"Yes we will!"*

At this point I became religious. I had left my *"May the Force be with you"* agnosticism behind. I'd been given a clear warning that had saved my life; I was going to church; I was trying to read the Bible; I was dipping into Christian books; I was hearing a Christian message, and I was trying to figure out where I fitted into a scheme that had God in it, but who was God? As I said above, you can go to church and never be involved, or you can go to church for years and years and be religious but without ever knowing the truth of the gospel – especially if the church that you attend doesn't actually tell you! So often the 'Christmas Message' broadcast on the radio or television is quite 'woolly' and vague. If through my circumstances I hadn't felt prompted to understand what import Christ meant to mankind, I doubt if I would have perceived it or have been inclined to pursue the matter further from such addresses. Within a few months, Mr Life-and-Soul-of-the-Party was Mr Indispensable-for-the-Sunday-Service: I was setting up the chairs for the service, issuing and collecting the hymnbooks, and taking round the offering plate. Mr Life-and-Soul-of-the-Party was now really trying to make up for lost time with God. Pretty soon, all the other instructors were saying, *"Dobz has got religion."*

They were correct. I was being religious. I had got religion. So, what is religion? Everyone at some time has sat an examination, usually at school, university, or even for progress in one's chosen career or occupation. I am certain that no one has ever sat any exam without knowing what the pass mark was. Well, all religions (bar one) are akin to sitting an exam without knowing the pass mark. It is a *"do-it-yourself attempt to obtain enough brownie points to impress God."* But there is a vast gulf between what we think of as being good and what God counts as righteousness. Trying to amass enough of our righteousness to satisfy God's requirements for righteousness is equivalent to trying to cross the Grand Canyon using lengths of six –foot planks and lots of ropes. *But people still try!* They: - 1. Attend church as regularly as clockwork, 2. Go on pilgrimages, 3. Wash themselves in rivers, 4. Give away all their money, 5. Do great works of charity, 6. Whip themselves with cords to atone for their sins, 7. Devote their life to a life of service, and a million other things all based on the belief that doing enough good work gains them salvation. They work on the assumption that God *will not or cannot* refuse them for trying their best. Well He can and He does. God in fact views our efforts to be self-righteous as foul; the Bible says, **"Our Good Works are like filthy rags" (Isaiah 64:6).** The Hebrew word used here means exactly that - used sanitary cloths! The Bible adds that it is, **"Not by works of righteousness which we have done, but according to His mercy He saved us" (Titus 3:5).**

And, **"For by grace are you saved through faith, and that not of yourselves: it is the gift of God. Not of works, lest any man should boast" (Ephesians 2:8-9).** In other words, our good deeds cut no ice with God if by these we attempt to earn our salvation. In this respect true Biblical Christianity is different from all other religions. However, at this point in my life, all I understood grace to mean was a few words spoken before you ate. I subsequently found out that grace is God's unmerited favour, which I didn't deserve.

Home Coming

Go forward to October of 1979. By now I had been flying the BAE Hawk for over a year. On this particular day I was flying No 2 in a close formation pair. Each aircraft had a student in the front seat with a flying instructor in the back seat. Part of the trip involved a tail chase. The leader would call *"Setting 95% power, for tail chase follow me, Go."* He would then break formation, and after a count of 3 you broke after him, slotted in behind him at about 150-200 yards distance and then call *"No2 in."* Think of a Grand Prix. If a car in front takes a corner correctly while the car behind goes wide, then the separation between the two cars will increase; ultimately if both cars do this consistently the lead car will lap the second car. In the air if the lead aircraft continues to turn more efficiently, he will get on your tail and 'shoot you down.' But in a three-dimensional environment there is another manoeuvre that can be used to put the second aircraft out of position. This can occur when the lead aircraft flies a large barrel roll – a corkscrew manoeuvre. Much of his forward energy is taken up in the roll. If the second aircraft flies a lesser diameter roll, his forward vector is greater, and this again puts him in front of the other aircraft and again in a potential shoot-down situation.

On this particular day, the lead pulled nose high almost into the vertical to execute this barrel roll manoeuvre. My student followed, but flew the manoeuvre incorrectly. This rapidly reduced the separation (usually about 150 yards) between us, and because we were climbing very steeply, the airspeed fell off quite quickly. My student also rolled further than the first aircraft, and we got into a belly-to-belly position such that we lost sight of the lead. I immediately took control, but by the time that I had regained visual on the lead he was sliding down ever so close to me just above my canopy, as both of us had run out of speed, so we drifted past each other. I was amazed at the number of the rivets, vents, drain holes, stencilled instructions, and oil smears on the underside of his aircraft. If he had collided with me, it would have been impossible to use the ejection seat. This was the 3rd occasion within about a year and a half that I been very close to death.

A few days later, certainly not much later, I was working down our farm road clearing scrub and musing, *"What would have happened if I had been killed on this last occasion, or if I have another accident subsequently?"* You would have thought that by this time, having gone regularly to church for a year and by now having been confirmed into the Church of England– (by the Bishop of Bangor no less!) I would have been quite relaxed and confident about any events of this nature. *But I realized at that point without a shadow of a doubt that despite* <u>*all my efforts*</u>*, I had no assurance; I would be lost eternally, and I would go to a literal hell, the outer darkness, the lake of fire!* This was not surprizing. From my previous history, in which I have tried to enumerate the things that I did, many of them prompted by foolishness, bravado, or lack of forethought, and the way that I have treated people, then it is apparent that I have not by any means led a blameless life. And like all of us, if the occasion warrants it, i.e. if it is something that we really, really want, and people or events get in our way, we can ignore them, or exploit them, or walk over them, or bend the rules to our advantage.

There is a poem – slightly modified by me, that neatly encapsulates the passage and shortness of human life. It's called, 'The Light Of Other Days' or 'Oft In The Stille Night' by Thomas Moore (a 19th century poet).

> *Oft in the stille night, ere slumber's chain has bound me,*
> *Fond memory brings the light of other days around me,*
> *The joys and tears of school days' years, the words of*
> *friends once spoken,*
> *The eyes that shone, now dimmed or gone, the sturdy*
> *frames now broken.*
> *Thus in the stille night, ere slumber's chain has bound me,*
> *Sad memory brings the light of other days around me.*
> *When I remember all the friends so once linked together,*
> *I've seen around me fall, like leaves in wintry weather,*
> *I feel like one who treads alone some banquet hall*

deserted,
The lights are fled, the garlands dead, and all but he departed
Thus in the stille night, ere slumber's chain has bound me,
Sad memory brings the light of other days around me.

If we are honest with ourselves, and look back over our lives, then '*Sad memory will bring back the light of other days around us,* and we become aware of our offences against those we have encountered on our journey through life. But now I was not only being confronted with my offences against people that I had met, I was now being made aware that there were my sins against God, whose existence, holiness, and perfect justice I had never considered and totally ignored. I knew that if I died there and then, I would appear, as the Bible says, at the final judgment, *and I would be found guilty.* The Bible puts this in black and white; **"It is given unto men once to die and then the judgment" (Hebrews 9:27).** As my situation began to sink in to me, I ceased my attempts to clear the scrub went back to the house, in tears, a very, very disturbed man. I had in a word discovered the truth of what the Bible says, **"There is none righteous no not one, for all have sinned and come short of the glory of God" (Romans 3:23).** I had been convicted of being a sinner.

Conversion

In the house I now had some Christian paperbacks in my book collection; one of which explained what was required of me. Firstly, **I had to admit to God that I was a sinner.** (Well that was no problem, as I have said, we can all relate to memories that can gnaw at our conscience in the stillness of the night. Things I had said and done; people I had offended, or who had offended me, and who I hadn't forgiven. I had definitely come to that conclusion). Secondly, **I had to get down on my knees,** repent of these things, and ask God's forgiveness for my past. This was harder, since like all of us; it's nice to think that we are in control of our own destiny. We can regard the stored experiences and memories in our minds as a series of rooms to which we have the key; some rooms we are happy to open up to the 'general public' as it were; others we keep firmly locked shut, a bit like Dorian Grey. I had to humble myself and admit that I couldn't fix everything for myself (In fact, since then, I have discovered that I can't fix anything for myself without the LORD'S help). Thirdly, **I had to believe that God by sending His Son Jesus Christ had paid the penalty for all my sins by His Crucifixion; and by His resurrection He had obtained for me eternal life.** Fourthly, **having recognized this I then had to ask Him to be my Lord and Saviour.** I was now beginning to appreciate that a gift is not yours until you personally receive it, but that depends how much you actually want it!

I didn't have too much of a problem on this score. Someone once said, the thought of approaching death concentrates the mind wonderfully. Having recently narrowly escaped death on three occasions, I accepted all these requirements. I went outside our house on a beautifully starry night –sometime in late October '79, and knelt down in our driveway, and prayed this prayer. *"Lord, I confess that I am a sinner. Please forgive me Lord Jesus Christ. Please come into my heart and be my Lord and Saviour. Amen."*

Nothing happened. The testimonies of some who have prayed this prayer seem to indicate that they heard Handel's Hallelujah Chorus, but in my case, nothing; no heavenly choirs, no angels, no singing, no bells, no lights, no celestial music etc. *"Maybe God hasn't heard me?"* so I prayed again. Again, there was nothing. I suppose that I felt a bit disappointed, but I knew that I had done what was right. I'd like to point out here that it is very important that you not only ask Him to be *your* Saviour but *also your* Lord. Quite a lot of so-called Christians desire salvation, but are very much less keen on making Christ the Lord of their lives in all that they do, say, and think!

About three days later, while at home by myself, I was suddenly aware that I *had* been forgiven. I fell down on my knees and this time I cried tears of joy. Just like John Bunyan's Pilgrim when he came to the Cross – I felt as if I had had a weight taken off my back, and my sins had been dealt with and were no more.

Now I'll be the first to admit – and my family will definitely confirm this, that I have been no plaster saint, and at times I have failed abysmally. But whatever we aspire to do in this world takes time, whether it's as babies learning to talk, as toddlers to walk and run, as children to cycle, as teenagers to drive a car, we usually start by falling over, falling off, or even occasionally crashing. For instance, if you borrowed your Dad's car after you learned to drive, and then dented it; I'm certain that he would not have let you continue to drive it if you denied that you had damaged it; however, if you had owned up, he would probably have let you have a piece of his mind, but have been more sympathetic and let you continue. Similarly, as long as we keep a short account with God and we are honest about our failures, we can continue in fellowship with Him, **"If we confess our sins, He is faithful and just to forgive us our sins, and to cleanse us from all unrighteousness" (1 John 1: 9),** and really know the LORD *is* our shepherd. To emphasise this very important point let's go back to the matter of receiving presents. Think about it. When you received a Christmas or Birthday present from your Mum, Dad, brother, sister, wife, children, or friends, they would have been hurt if you had declined to accept their gift. They would have been similarly insulted if you had offered to pay for it, or offered to wash and dry the car/dishes, or do some similar task for them for a year in order to earn it. A gift is a gift; they wanted to give it to you out of love, they didn't want you to work for it. As the Bible says, "For God so loved the world, that he gave his only begotten Son, that whosoever believeth in him should not perish, but have everlasting life." (John 3:16) Thus, as the Bible says, salvation is a gift from God: and you certainly can't earn the gift of salvation, which is only His to give; but like any gift, it's not yours *until* you personally accept it. *No one nor any minister in any church had ever told me this.*

There's a well-known picture – 'The Light of the World', by one of the Pre-Raphaelite artists – William Holman Hunt, showing Christ knocking on a door. Not only that; the door has no external handle – so it can only be opened from the inside, but the door is covered with briers, ivy and weeds – this door hasn't been opened for a very long time. This picture really depicts condition of the human heart. The text associated with this picture is **Revelation 3:20 "Behold I stand at the door and knock. If any man hear my voice and open the door, I will come in unto him and sup with him, and he with Me."**

There are various ways in which we can respond to a knock on the door. You can hear someone knocking, but choose to ignore it because you are snug and warm and comfortable. Or you might go to the door and shout, *"Who's there?"* Then in response to the caller's answer, you shout back, *"No thanks, not today –or ever"* and go back to whatever you were doing. You might open the door a few inches and talk to the caller, or even open the door fully wide and talk, while ensuring that the caller stays outside. It's only when *you invite the caller in* that you can truly say that you have fellowship with him. It is the same with our relationship with God: it only when you personally believe that Jesus Christ died for your sins and invite Him into your life/your heart and yield yourself to Him that you can say that you have a fellowship with Him and the Father. God's Gift is only yours when you accept Him. You may never ever have heard the Gospel explained like this. I certainly *never* had the Gospel clearly explained to me by anyone in any church in all the years that I had so irregularly attended; and there were numerous occasions when I should or could have been dead. These, and subsequent experiences that I have had, sincerely convinces me that the Bible is not just pie in the sky –it is the truth.

If this present life is all there is, as Professor Richard Dawkins and others would have us believe, then Shakespeare's Macbeth was right – *"Life is a tale told by an idiot – full of sound and fury signifying nothing; a poor player that struts and frets his hour upon the stage, and is heard of no more"*, and who of us can say how long is our personal full hour upon the stage! If there is no final reckoning, when we die, that's it. If this is so, then every evildoer from Hitler and Stalin right down to the least miscreant – everyone who has done any kind of evil – has escaped justice. Ultimately, if there is no final reckoning, then as Francis Albert Sinatra used to sing, *"I did it my way"* is the rule, do what you like, stay ahead of the sheriff's posse, and even if you die it doesn't matter. **Hebrews 9:27** quoted above speaks of judgment, but there are many more Scriptures that speak of salvation in Christ **"He that heareth My word, and believeth on Him that sent Me hath everlasting life, and shall not come into condemnation, but is passed from death unto life" (John 5:24).**

There are many who *will not believe* because in involves giving up some treasured possession, profession, standing with one's peers, or position attained in this life. Forgetting or ignoring the fact that the Bible informs us that **"it is given unto man once to die, and after death is the judgment" (Hebrews 9:27).**

Many will also say, *"Well you believe that if you will. I don't believe."* Blaise Pascal, the 17th century French mathematician and philosopher had a convincing argument against this line of attack. *"Suppose, said he, that you are right, and God does not exist. As I go through life, when I am faced with all the problems, troubles, and pains that can and do occur, then I pray, seek guidance, advice, mental and spiritual comfort from this non-existent God; and amazingly, although events do not always turn out the way that I want, yet by a series of amazing coincidences I am led, comforted and guided – which you of course attribute to sheer chance and some psychological conditioning. At the end of our days, if you are right, we will both die and that will be the end of it – I will die never knowing that I am wrong. On the other hand, if I am right and you are wrong and God does exist, then my life does not change – I am still led and guided and comforted; and when I die I go to be with this incredible Being who has given Himself for me, while you, having refused all your life to believe and accept His forgiveness and guidance, will now suffer eternal separation – a self-inflicted punishment for all those who had an invitation to be saved but through their own volition chose not to be."*

Now, all the conclusions and knowledge that I have written above, did not just come to me all boxed up neat and tidy within the space of a few days. Some things I understood immediately, others I had to learn the hard way, and I am learning much more even as I write. Life really is a pilgrimage, an Odyssey, with *"many dangers, toils, and snares"* as John Newton's well-known Hymn Amazing Grace describes it, but having received God's gift of salvation, He ensures that He will lead us home, **"The LORD will perfect that which concerneth me" (Psalm 138:8).**

Act Seven

A Six Year Extension

In August '78, concurrently with my growing spiritual awareness, and having regained my fitness to fly following my Gnat crash, I commenced a quick conversion and instructional course onto the BAE Systems Hawk. I enjoyed flying the Hawk – it was a bit more of a pussycat to fly than the Gnat, and quite a different feel to it, but it also had a much better endurance; so instructional sorties could be tailored for the slower pupil. Thus, instead of 45 or 50-minute trips, sorties of 1 hour 10 minutes were possible. The serviceability was very good, and with plenty of aircraft, 40 to 50 hours instructional time per month was not uncommon.

By the early summer of '79 when I had less than one year left of my three-year tour, I was asked what I would like to do for my next posting. I still had hopes of getting back onto an operational aircraft, so I requested a tour on Buccaneers. Eventually the word came back that as I was now in my 41st year, by the time that I had completed my present tour and completed the training and commenced my operational tour I would be in my 43rd year and the RAF would not get much of a return for its money.

Amortization was the official name for this policy. To train a pilot to fly a modern front-line aircraft cost an awful lot of money;

therefore, the RAF normally expected its pilots to remain for two tours and then return as a QFI on the same type. Moreover, it is not beyond the bounds of possibility that the powers that be had become acquainted with the Dobbie name in relation to aircraft write offs and the accrued cost to the UK Defence Budget. Prior to my two prangs my cousin Gordon who had flown for the Fleet Air Arm had also ejected from a Sea Hawk, and a DH110 Scimitar –at night! Therefore, the options I was offered were a return to instruct on the Canberra or the Jet Provost, or become a pilot on the Hercules, where, as an older pilot, I could continue to fly for much longer, and, where (presumably) life as a transport pilot was deemed less stressful than at the sharp end? As I didn't fancy returning to the Canberra or the Jet Provost, and flying the Herc didn't seem very exciting compared to what I was doing, I requested a tour extension at Valley. A few weeks went by before I was informed that this had been accepted and that I had been given a six-year extension –in effect two further tours as a fast jet QFI. A request for an extension like this was very much to the RAF's liking because the postings branch at the MOD found it very difficult to get personnel to volunteer for RAF Valley, being, as it was perceived by the young bloods, completely out in the sticks. This was true, for before the advent of the A55 expressway, it took a *long* time to reach Anglesey from the M5/M6 motorway, and many of the pilots were single and liked to pay frequent visits to the 'Big Smoke' (i.e. London) and other civilized places, so the thought of long car journeys each way to see their girlfriends or fiancés at weekends did not appeal to them at all. There was one young American, a USAF exchange officer from a up market part of New York who on his arrival at RAF Valley – on one of those rare Anglesey days when there's lots of wind, cloud and rain, when he saw Holyhead, he said *"Holyhead's not the end of the world, but you can sure see it from there!"* In many ways the relative isolation and rural character of North Wales reminded me of Scotland, and I was in no hurry to leave. When I finally retired from service at RAF Valley on my 65th birthday in November 2003, my three-year tour had lasted 27 years!

House Hunting

But by my return to flying in 1979, Babs and I had been married 15 years and in all that time, we had lived in 13 different addresses, almost all of them private hiring or RAF Married Quarters. The one exception was six months spent in our bungalow near Cambridge. I doubt many wives would have put up with our nomadic lifestyle complete with children and dogs and frequent separations on diversions, exercises, and detachments. At this point I realized just how very fortunate I was to have married a girl who had not only been acclimatised to frequent changes of address during her parents' time in the RAF, but also had a very tolerant nature. She also of necessity had had to change schools frequently with the result that she missed out on gaining any school qualifications. However, some years after we had moved into our new house, she did a correspondence course with the Open University and gained a BA (2-2) honours degree. I was immensely impressed with this, as I had only achieved a pass degree while attending university full time.

Now, with a total of about another 7 years on Anglesey, we were unlikely ever to move back down to Cambridge, so now seemed like a good time to invest in another house. Moreover, the Government had recently dispensed with capital gains tax, which meant we could now sell our bungalow without incurring a tax penalty. We searched round the local area but without success. However, Babs' brother Brian, who was now OC Admin Wing at Valley, had heard of an old farmhouse for sale quite close to the base. When we went to inspect it, we found that it had been empty for at least a year or more, and the hedges and garden were completely overgrown. It was a big solid two-storey house of sound construction built around the end of the 19th century. Attached to the main house was an older house, which comprised of a large entrance room that had been a kitchen, an attached annex, and stairs to a loft bathroom from which a further short flight of stairs gave access to the rear upstairs of the main house. In addition to this house there was a complete set of farm buildings, which included a very much older cottage dating from the mid-18th century, all in quite good condition, set in about 2/3 of an acre of ground –the original farmyard. All the buildings had been constructed with timbers that had been salvaged from various shipwrecks of which there were quite a few in the 19th century round the coasts of Anglesey. On our initial survey, the surveyor listed some quite rare foreign timbers.

House selling and buying, as most know, is a bit fraught. We were, as was usual with such cases at the time, at the end of a long line of buyers and sellers, and we ended up with a bridging loan shelling out lots of money to the bank for a few months until our bungalow was sold. I originally bought the bungalow for £3800 and eventually sold it for £23000, and bought Tai Hirion (Welsh for Long Houses) for £28500. We had taken out a £16000 mortgage, but by the time that we had paid off our bridging loan, the lawyer's fee, and various other expenses there wasn't an awful lot of money left over. I suppose that I should have taken out a much larger mortgage, but I was worried about the interest payments. Hence, when we finally moved into Tai Hirion we did not have a lot of ready cash to furnish it, but we managed to make it basically habitable by purchases from the local auctions and salerooms, although at one point, as the autumn chill set in, a basic central heating had been plumbed in, but we still did not have the central heating boiler connected up, the electrical wiring was in the process of being replaced, and our only cooking facility was a Calor gas two ring hotplate, which latter state existed for some months until we could acquire an electric cooker. Meanwhile, Babs having coped with the boys over the summer and the disruption of the move now took them by train on the first of many journeys to Crewe to see them off on their way back to college in Truro –which left just Babs and I to move into our new house with our two dogs. Babs was also doing a secretarial course, and both of us were attending the local C of E church on the camp. The autumn of 1979 was very busy.

Once we had moved in, there were lots of other minor things –and not so minor things that had to be done in the house –a dozen or more of the 187 windowpanes were cracked or broken, and some fairly large draughts coming in through window and door frames had to be excluded. All the rooms needed redecorating (painting and papering) and one or two needed many repairs to defects in the plaster. The house at some point had been used as a hunting lodge, and the walls of what became our main lounge had dozens of rusty nails, that had been used to hang game. All these had to be extracted, but because they were rusty, they pulled out chunks of plaster, so one of the first DIY skills I acquired was basic plastering. In another room there was a huge modern stone and brick fireplace that seemed quite out of place for the small size of the fire. I decided to remove two levels of bricks from the top. When I tried using a wrecker's bar to lever the top bricks away, the whole fireplace tilted outwards, I thus discovered that the fireplace had been designed to conceal what had been on old-fashioned Victorian fireplace some 6-foot square and 3 feet deep. The only recourse was to remove the whole brick fireplace, and seal off the chimney –which we did eventually and made it into a TV alcove. But for some months there was a pile of bricks, cement fragments, and lots of dust and soot spread over the concrete floor. Meanwhile all we did was keep the 'path' clear of dust as we went through this room from the kitchen to the main front stairway. The upstairs bathroom also required complete renovation. At one point there was no wall or door at the top of the back flight of stairs that led to the toilet, so anyone using it, usually sat 'enthroned' whistling loudly to indicate occupation! During the school holidays Babs, the two boys and I developed our DIY skills to a further level. On one occasion we discovered how to nail 8' by 4' plasterboards to ceiling rafters by hoisting each board up using brooms, and holding it there while we hammered in large headed galvanised nails. Our first winter there was very frosty. The plastic out-let pipe from the bath and washbasin exited the external wall and flowed straight into a rainwater drainpipe. In the extremely cold weather, this now froze solid, and we had to pour hot water over it from a kettle in an attempt to melt the ice sufficiently for the bath water to drain away. But there was one compensation, there was a great supply of wood – logs planks, old timber in the out buildings; this we chopped and sawed up and used for days on end in large open fire in the now electrically lighted sitting room. As we worked our way through all these problems, I can remember praying and saying, ***"Lord, we just*** *want this house to be warm and dry and comfortable,"* which was what indeed He granted!

Just a few years before we bought our house, the TV series 'The Good Life' commenced, and John Seymour wrote 'The Complete Book on Self Sufficiency.' Along with quite a few other flying instructors who had bought their own houses, Babs and I set about becoming self-sufficient! After we had cleared out all the young trees and bushes, I found that much of the soil was only about a foot deep, under which was a very hard layer of boulder clay. However, some of the ground was very good and deep, but the former occupants, before the advent of council rubbish collection, had buried lots of old Victorian rubbish – old tins, crockery and bottles; amongst this detritus we found a mariner's brass telescope, mariner's brass rule, and a brass bell! In another part as I was digging it over, I came across a large rock that I decided needed to come out. But after I had gone down about 2 feet, I discovered that this particular rock was still attached to mother earth. When I had finally cleared the garden of the rocks, accumulated rubbish, weeds, undergrowth and small trees in order to plant vegetables I was somewhat concerned about the number of small birds that seemed to inhabit the nearby hedges and their potential for feeding on my plants. I prayed a simple prayer, *"Lord they are Your birds, please don't let them eat my vegetables."* And that's exactly what happened; we lost some vegetables to other pests, but none to birds. In addition to this wild life, apart from the perennial pet dogs and cats, we owned our own animals – a nanny goat, Vietnamese potbellied pigs, a cockerel and hens, and Muscovy ducks.

During which time we became quite expert in many DIY skills: plaster boarding, replacing doors, windows, as well as window and door frames, adding electrical circuits, cementing, concreting, laying drains, roofing, laying slates, and some re-plumbing, this last skill courtesy of Andrew our eldest son. For while it took on the aspect of painting the Forth Bridge, there always seemed to be something else to do. However, it really was a lovely old house, and it was warm and dry and comfortable. I eventually sold it after some 37 years of occupation.

Once we had settled in to our new home I continued to cycle to work; a tradition that I had started at Cottesmore, and continued in Cyprus and Cornwall. The shortest route from Tai Hirion to the camp was down a single-track road that had tarmac last laid on it during the Second World War, but was now heavily potholed; this usually resulted in frequent punctures! The road crossed the main Holyhead London railway through two level crossing gates; however, the line was easily negotiable via two wicket gates. But at the next obstacle – the airfield crash gate, I had to lift the bike over it to get access to a taxiway on the camp. The whole journey was some two miles, but kept me fit, especially as the average wind at Valley – according to the Met Office was around 18knots/20mph, generally blowing head on or the beam going to and from work. But this route had the advantage of being a lot less expensive than going by car (5 miles each way); for contrary to popular belief we did not receive a fuel allowance for travel to work, and using the bike also left the car available for Babs to get out and shop.

Growth in the LORD

As I wrote previously, I had come to the LORD, but other than a very basic knowledge of salvation I did not attain or seek to attain much else in the way of Christian teaching and ethics, so I went through many trials, temptations, and tests. Stumbling frequently, getting things wrong, upsetting and hurting other people; my wife and children in particular. Up until then, Babs and I had rarely ever had arguments, but now we seemed to find misunderstandings arising out of nowhere. There is an old joke told from the First World War where a message as originally sent said *"Send reinforcements we're going to advance"* becomes on reception, *"Send three and four pence, we're going to a dance."* These misunderstandings seemed to beset us for some time. The saving grace was that we loved each other dearly, and so after every spat we tearfully made up, but it could not have been easy for our boys to witness their parents' discord. Subsequently, I learned from St Paul's letter to the Ephesians that Christians do not (or should not) wrestle **"against flesh and blood** (i.e. against each other)**, but against principalities, against powers, against the rulers of the darkness of this world, against spiritual wickedness in high places" (Ephesians 6:12)** Notice that this dark power and his minions *are* the rulers of *this world*, as Satan himself informs Christ **(Luke 4:6).** This statement may be a surprise to many who think that mankind controls its own fate. However true Christianity, as taught in the Bible tells us that we are to **"Be sober, be vigilant, because your adversary the devil, as a roaring lion, walketh about, seeking** whom he may devour: **Whom resist steadfast in the faith, knowing that the same afflictions are accomplished in your brethren that are in the world" (1 Peter 5:7-8).** Eventually, through many trials we slowly learnt the nature of the true enemy of mankind and as believers eventually learned to use the weapons assigned to us according to Scripture.

Matthew

By 1980 our two eldest boys were travelling to and from Truro by themselves, Andrew, being now almost 16 and Paul 13. When they returned home for the summer vacation in the autumn of 1980, I went to pick them up from Bangor station. I casually asked them, *"If you were to have a baby brother what do you think we should call him?"* Paul's face took on an expression of concentration, but all Andrew did was loudly exclaim *"Whaaaaaat!"* And so, in February 1981, after a gap of 13 years, our third son Matthew James, was born. It was almost like learning the art of parenthood anew!

With our new baby we continued to attend the church on the camp every Sunday for some time, until a new vicar came. He seemed OK, but our weekly Tuesday evening house group didn't have the same close fellowship, and not long after he had arrived, he announced that he was inviting some members of the Baha'i faith to a discussion. This may have been an attempt to engage them in an exchange of views as to what they believed. As I have said, I didn't know a lot about the Bible, but I knew enough to know that beliefs of this particular cult deviate greatly from the Bible, and I had no intention of having my yet very sketchy beliefs scrambled by someone who was probably adept at mental reservation and seeming plausibility. With this in mind, on the next Sunday we drove into Holyhead, heading for the large C of E church there. On the way, we drove past an Elim Pentecostal Church, outside of which was a chap I immediately recognized from the camp. He was a lovely little old Welshman called Robbie Roberts, who worked in the Central Flying School Squadron as the office cleaner. He regularly quoted Scriptures and witnessed to us when we met him while getting into our flying kit in the CFS building. When we arrived at the C of E church it was shut for some reason, so rather than have a completely wasted journey; we returned to the Elim church. The minister Neil Morgan was about to commence a sermon from the book of Jonah. In fact, if I remember rightly, he preached from the whole of the book of Jonah. Now this to me was unusual in itself. In almost every church that I had been to previously, the vicar's sermon had more often than not been much more light weight, usually including homilies along the lines of *"When I was passing the golf course this morning,"* but never a straight and extended exposition of Scripture. It was a great blessing to go to a church that actually believed the Bible to be the Word of God. Our association with the Pentecostal church lasted ten years, during which time both Babs and I got very involved, she in running the Sunday school, and I was elected as a deacon and then as an elder. The other point of interest was the number of QFIs during the 1980s at RAF Valley who were born again Christians; at one point almost one third of the 36 QFIs were believers, (or at least attended church regularly).

My other memories of my early days as a Christian were the answers we had to prayers. I was laying a 4-inch plastic waste pipe from a newly plumbed in kitchen sink; but the drain had to go under a very large broad stonewall. Fortunately, at the bottom of the wall was a rainwater gulley, but unfortunately right at the edge of the gulley was a large block of black basalt that protruded so far into the gulley that the pipe would not go through. The only tool that I had any chance of breaking the rock was a large felling axe. So, this time I prayed, *"Lord help me split the stone."* Standing with my back to the wall and my legs apart, I swung the blunt end of the head of the axe against the rounded end of the stone. Now if you have ever tried to split hard rocks in this way, you will normally feel a painful vibration travel back up your arms as you hit the rock, and the only result will be a slight chip flaking off. But on this occasion, I got a clean break. A large chunk came off, which was easily removed, and the pipe went through the gap with no difficulty! Sometime later, when Matthew was about three or four, I was carrying a large plastic bucket that was half full of water. Matt said, *"Let me help you Daddy."* I slid my hand down the handle closer to one side of the bucket while Matt held the other side of the handle. As I mused over the fact that although he had his hand on the handle and he thought that he was helping me, I was doing all the carrying; at that point I had the impression of a quiet voice within me say, *"That's how I am carrying you!"*

On another occasion, I returned to duty after a period of leave. Babs had driven me in to work because it was raining heavily. As I arrived at the squadron ops desk just before the main met brief at 8AM, I was informed that because the weather was going to be bad later in the day, I would be landing away that evening and night stopping at some airfield in Scotland. It was wintertime and all pilots were required to wear immersion suits, a one-piece rubberised suit worn over two or three layers of underwear and thick socks so that if you ejected over the sea, you would stand a chance of survival until you were rescued. I was incensed with rage. I complained bitterly to the other pilots who were going up to Scotland with me, **"I've been on leave. Couldn't someone have phoned me and told me to bring in my overnight kit"** for the thought of spending an evening in a hot Officers Mess bar in an immersion suit and very sweaty underclothes, with no washing or shaving kit, and then having to put on cold sweaty underclothes in the morning was ghastly in the extreme. Babs had just left; I couldn't get hold of her because she was going shopping – this was before the days of mobile phones. I went to the met briefing, found and briefed my first student. He was taking his Instrument Rating Test with me as his examiner, on a sortie at low level to the Isle of Man. Being extremely irritated is not good when one is about to assess the accuracy of a student's instrument flying. We went out to the aircraft and got airborne, already somewhat hot and sweaty in my immersion suit as we flew at low level over the Irish Sea, and all the while I was inwardly fuming over the thoughtlessness of my 'mates.' At some point during the sea crossing I remember praying **"Lord, take this anger** *from me"* –and He did –just like that. I found myself at peace, composed, with no thoughts of irritation against the programmers, and found myself in harmony and all sweetness and light to my student; a very definite illustration of **1 Peter 5:7 "Cast all your care upon Him, for He careth for you."**

To round off this section on the Lord's care for us, let me relate a journey we took down to Bristol to visit Niall and Jerry Griffin – (Niall had been the vicar in the church on the camp when I had first started to attend church). By this time, while spending quite a bit of money renovating the house, our finances were getting quite stretched, our VW had packed up and our only car was Babs Mum's very old Vauxhall estate that we had bought for £200, (Her Mum and Dad had settled a few miles away in the local village not long after Matthew was born). On our way back from Bristol, we wondered whether we should drive directly back up to Anglesey through the middle of Wales, or detour via the West Midlands to my Mother's house on the A5 north of Birmingham. This seemed right so we opted for the second choice. Coming down a hill on the main road into Stratford on Avon, with Babs and I in the front of the car and Matt in his carrycot on the rear seat, (but with no rear seat belts!), I pressed the brake pedal. It went all the way to the floor with no retardation at all! There were cars and traffic lights ahead and nowhere to stop on our side. There were also cars coming in the other direction, but there was one good space between two of these cars. I made a snap decision and steered across the road pulling sharply on the hand brake. This other side of the road had a high kerb, but in the gap between the two cars, just where I was aiming, the kerb dropped away where there was a wide grass verge and a large gap leading into a field. We managed to a halt on the grass verge in the gate way and stop the engine. Suddenly there we were, all alone, complete silence, no traffic at all – a very quiet still Sunday afternoon on the outskirts of Stratford upon Avon. We wondered what we should do now. Amazingly we had stopped right next to a telephone box. We tried contacting one of the motoring agencies, but somehow, we could get no response. I went down to the crossroads, some 50 yards away. In a shop window there was an advert for a breakdown service. I went back to the phone box, but being a Sunday afternoon, I didn't have much hope of getting an answer; but I did, and shortly afterwards a breakdown truck arrived and our car was towed away. We then walked a few hundred yards into Stratford and came to a small hotel. Having booked in and still feeling a bit stressed, we gratefully retired to our room, whereupon we found a Gideon's Bible by our bedside table, and felt that the Lord had been with us in all this. We mused what would have been the result if we had chosen to return through mid-Wales, and this had happened on the twisting winding hill roads somewhere between Brecon and Dolgellau.

Shortly after this my Mum sold her house in Wilnecote and came to stay with us. We had plenty of room, and so we made one of the downstairs rooms into a bed sitting room for her. She fitted in easily to our life style for her remaining few years. Then one night about 2 or 3 o'clock in the morning, on the last day of April 1987, I woke up in bed and had a sudden inclination to go downstairs to check whether my Mum was all right. She was fine; we had a few minutes chat before I went back to bed. Because I usually left for work quite early, we didn't disturb my Mum while we had breakfast. I had only been at work for about an hour when Babs called the camp. Fortunately, I wasn't on the flying programme, so I got her call in the coffee bar. She said, *"I've just been in to see your Mum. I'm sorry darling, but she must have passed away within the last hour."* I went home; she was lying in bed, apparently sleeping peacefully. I kissed her forehead as a goodbye. I was very grateful that the Lord had wakened me and allowed me to speak with her before He took her to Himself. I had also explained the Gospel to her some time before, and had the joy of hearing her recite the sinner's prayer.

After the cremation, Babs, Matt and I took her ashes up to Abernethy and had them interred in my Dad's grave. We visited a few friends and relations while we were there, and also Broadwell Cottage, where I had grown up – now suitably modernised.

DCGI

I was now in my 44th year, and had flown over 22 years continuously, and by April 1982 I had been instructing at Valley for some 5 years non-stop at what could at times be a fairly intensive occupation. At this point, my boss felt that I was becoming a bit tired and stale, and asked me if I would become the Deputy Chief Ground Instructor (DCGI). This suggestion was either because I had been too long in the groove, or that the 'wheels' were becoming alarmed by my radical change in lifestyle from one of the boys to a born-again Christian. But if I was truthful with myself, I *was* becoming a bit blasé. It became so normal sitting in the back cockpit while the student taxied down to the take-off point for R/W32 while listening to his checks, that I could find my thoughts drifting off. I would look across some acres of rough grazing land and see the gable end of my house about a mile away, and immediately my mind would flick onto whatever project I was involved in. On occasion we would arrive at the take-off point, and I would suddenly realise that I hadn't zeroed the altimeter onto the take-off pressure setting (QFE), and so I would ask the student what he had set, because my altimeter looked a bit out! So, one way or another, I agreed that a break would be a good idea.

The DCGI's job was quite interesting. It involved giving lectures on aerodynamics, weather, aircraft systems, and the history of NATO, and setting and monitoring exams. But for me the main topic was combat survival and resistance to interrogation. Each course of students that came through RAF Valley had a few weeks in the Ground School before commencing the flying phase. And each course had to complete a three-day survival camp in the Snowdonia National Park. To be able to teach this effectively it was necessary to have attended and passed the Combat Survival Officers Course at RAF Mountbatten in Plymouth, which I had volunteered for in 1978. It was also required that I attend the Resistance to Interrogation (RTI) Course at an Army base at Ashford in Kent just prior to commencing my tour as DCGI.

At this point, I would like to note in passing, that an Army

Officers Mess is subtly different from that of the RAF. There is an old joke that says the Army are gentlemen trying to be officers, the Royal Navy are officers trying to be gentlemen, and the RAF is neither trying to be both! The Officers Mess at Ashford really exuded a feeling of an upper-class gentleman's club. Every officer at Ashford appeared to own a Labrador, English Setter, Irish wolfhound, or some other upper-class canine. They could be found everywhere; it was almost impossible to go through the Mess without tripping over them. They were, I must admit, incredibly well trained, for they sat, lay, or posed imperiously in their appointed position, ignored all other dogs, and did not move, whine, or bark.

I also heard a story while I was there about an Australian Army exchange officer who went for breakfast early one Sunday morning. There was only one other occupant of the dining room. He was sitting reading the Times (what else), and wearing his officer's hat. The Aussie sat at the same table, said *"Good morning"* but received no answer. The mess waiter arrived, the Aussie ordered his meal, and it was delivered to him, he looked at the other occupant at the table and said, *"Pass the salt please."* Again, there was no reaction, his silent companion continued to read his paper. The Aussie tried again. Clearing his throat slightly this time, he said in a slightly louder voice, *"Excuse me, could you pass the salt please."* Still no reaction! By now the Aussie was getting quite frustrated. This time he rapped on the table with his knuckles, and said somewhat peremptorily, *"Would you pass the salt please."* At this the other officer looked up in a somewhat irritable way and said somewhat haughtily, *"When an officer of the Queen's Third Royal Hussars wears his hat at breakfast, it means that he does not wish to speak, neither does he wish to be spoken to."* The Aussie, so the story goes, who by now had become quite annoyed with this snooty Pommie and his quaint custom, then stood up, stepped up on to the chair he was sitting on, strode across the table, and put his foot in the other man's plate of scrambled eggs, glared down at his adversary, and said, *"When an officer of Her Majesty's Royal Australian Army walks across the table and stands in your scrambled egg and says pass the salt, it means pass the b****y salt."*

Exercise Hawkeye
The student survival course (Exercise Hawkeye) at RAF Valley occurred every three weeks, commencing very early on a

Wednesday morning. We got up about 3:15AM, Babs with young Matthew now strapped up in the back of the car drove me to the Officers Mess left me and went home – and back to bed. We, the Directing Staff and students, having dined on the mandatory massive cholesterol laden breakfast of egg, bacon, sausages, beans, fried bread, black pudding, and tomatoes (optional mushrooms), washed down by lots of hot sweet tea followed by marmalade and toast, left the Officers Mess and departed in two Land Rovers and a three-ton truck. By the time that we reached the Ogwen Valley in Snowdonia it was either quite light (summertime), or quite dark (wintertime). Every few hundred yards we dropped off a pair of students from the three-ton truck, kitted out with their survival gear, and left them to navigate their way across the hills and bogs to the campsite in the Crafnant Valley. The staff team coordinating the exercise was comprised of: the Chief Ground Instructor (CGI) Squadron Leader Roger Ouston, the Station Navigational Officer Ian Muir, myself, and two sergeants - John and Ron, as well as another couple of QFIs, who had opted to come along and help out. We assembled two large heavy-duty tents, joined them together, set up our camp beds, the portable mess kitchen, and got a large fire going outside. Then one of us would walk about ½ mile up to the RV and pick up (hopefully) all the students and lead them to their campsite – about three hundred yards away from us. Here they were given an ample supply of pine poles and left to make whichever type of survival shelter with them and their parachutes that they felt best able to do from the examples shown to them in the Ground School. The only food they *officially* had was an RAF survival ration pack between two of them. There were a few who brought along contraband in the form of chocolate bars, but since the idea was to find out how well you could survive on what a downed pilot would have in reality, most guys stuck to the rules – and after the huge breakfast they could probably have existed on that alone.

Meanwhile our two sergeants kept us from hunger with large supplies of bacon butties, cooked on a Calor gas stove, so that we didn't starve before lunch. The Staff ate extremely well at all times. In the afternoon of the first day and the morning and afternoon of the second day there were practical demonstrations of various survival techniques –making use of ground cover, camouflaged hides, catching game and fish, signals to attract rescue aircraft, and a staff critique of each survival shelter. Additionally, during the first day, two large live rabbits were delivered, and – for those with a nervous disposition, they may want to look away now – I clubbed, killed, skinned and gutted the first rabbit – well out of sight and hearing of the other rabbit. Then the second bunny was offered up to whichever student had enough bottle to do the same – or the one who looked absolutely horrified by the whole procedure!

On the evening of the first night, the staff led all the students up to a disused mine, (there were not a few old lead mines in the Crafnant Valley). Here the students were made to sit at one side of the tunnel on very rough-hewn pine benches, with their feet in water that ran through the mine, while on the other side of the tunnel, on a shelf of gravel, well out of the water (naturally), seated on camp chairs at two trestle tables were the CGI, the DCGI, and an 'interrogator,' with the whole scene lit up by kerosene pressure lamps; attempting to re-create an atmosphere that the Spanish Inquisition/Gestapo/KBG would have approved of. The aim of this part of the course was to give the students a very basic introduction to the types of interrogation that they could expect to encounter, if they were captured. We selected a student, who stood in the running water and started off with the normal routine of 'hard cop' and 'good cop', which they had all probably seen on films. But we then introduced some other variations. When they initially arrived in the Ground School, they were each given an A4 sheet of paper, which had bone fide questions with spaces for answers on the top half of the sheet but left the bottom half blank except for the student's name in block capitals at the bottom. Then having written down their answers, they signed their name above the signature block. Subsequently, having collected in the forms, I would type in all sorts of spurious admissions of guilt on the blank part of the piece of paper and detach the questionnaire. During their questioning, the 'interrogator' would accuse his victim of something, which he would deny ever having done. At which point he would be presented with his 'signed statement – the bottom half of the A4 sheet, with 'his confession' and his signature.

I can remember one part of the RTI instruction that I had received at RAF Oakington during training, was a feature film of American servicemen held as prisoners in a North Korean POW Camp, showing the techniques used against prisoners, and how to resist brain washing. One POW was pressurised over a long period with the same question again and again, *"Who started the war?"* until he gave in to the brain washing and responded with the answer, *"The United States started the war."* Not long after this, six of us went to see some film in Cambridge in which one actor actually uttered this line, *"Who started the war?"* To a man, we instantly all spoke out aloud, *"The United States started the war,"* much to the mystification of the rest of the audience, but it convinced us of the technique!

Another trap that we set for the students was to ask the senior students, once they had completed their survival course, if they knew any members of the next course. This occasionally delivered some gems. One lad related how he had been standing next to a telephone box that had all the glass punched out in Doncaster railway station, while his mate rang his fiancé. This observant young man had remembered much of the conversation and some quite choice titbits of familiarity between his mate and his fiancé. When I called this unfortunate lad forward for interrogation, I gently led him into a recollection of his telephone call to his fiancé, calling her by her name, and reminded him of much of what he had said to her. He was completely non-plussed, not to say embarrassed at my revelations. The students had been firmly briefed not to react to such slurs on their character or supposed treason, but one young man became visibly agitated and took my accusations of disloyalty completely seriously, and started shouting back at me that he was not a traitor. Eventually we had to stop and reassure him that this was not for real. But the students really appreciated the above examples as it showed how easy it was to get under someone's skin with a little bit of information.

This questioning was quite gentle compared to two other examples that I heard from other sources. In the first, an army officer was being questioned about his unit and the name of his CO. As the questioning began, the interrogator commanded his prisoner to empty his pockets and pass over his wedding ring, which he put in one trouser pocket. The questioning continued, but the officer under interrogation remained silent. The questioner then unobtrusively pulled another ring out of his other pocket and said, looking straight into eyes of his victim, *"Since you will not reveal the name of your CO, I am going to destroy this ring,"* at which point he took a large club hammer and flattened 'the ring.' The victim now jumped up and shouted, *"This is beyond a joke, I am going to report you to Colonel X."* *"Thank you"* said his tormentor, *"that's all I wanted to know"* and pulled the real wedding ring and handed it back to his victim.

On the other exercise 'the prisoner' having had his hands tied behind him, also had a hessian bag smelling strongly of petrol put over his head. He was led into the interrogation room, the bag was removed, and questions asked. He maintained his silence. At which point, someone produced a red painted container with the word 'PETROL' prominently stencilled in white on the side of it, and sloshed it over the prisoner. The 'petrol' was actually water, but with the smell of real petrol fumes still in his nose, and the mental association of 'PETROL' being poured over him, it would take a lot of mental determination to remember that this was an exercise.

As previously mentioned, during my time as DCGI I gave instruction to the students in the various ways of resisting interrogation. Unfortunately, by the 1980s, nearly all the potential enemies that future RAF combatants would face paid scant regard to the rights of prisoners of war under the Geneva Convention. However, by this time I had acquired a small library of books written by diverse persons who had survived interrogations and hardships inflicted by the Gestapo, KGB and other organisations by various stratagems. Some of these prisoners had been Christians, and so I had an opportunity to broach the subject to my students from the point of view of those prisoners who had successfully called upon the Lord to deliver them. As is usual in such circumstances, there was some mocking laughter, and disbelief, but some considered the proposition seriously. One lad walked out of the lecture – I didn't rebuke him, if he felt that it was beyond the remit of resistance to interrogation, then he was free to do so – otherwise he could have accused me of brainwashing him! However, I hope that the words that I spoke may have stuck and become a source of comfort in a time of stress, as subsequently the RAF was engaged in a number of minor wars in South Eastern Europe, the Middle East, and Afghanistan. As had been remarked, there are no atheists in a foxhole!

The terrain in the Snowdonia National Park over which the escape and evasion exercise took place was quite rugged. Essentially there were three parallel valleys, each with a reservoir and a small river. These valleys all pointed northeast and ran down into the valley of the River Conwy. On the map each valley was only separated from its neighbour by about 2 miles, but in reality, crossing such terrain on foot was much further. The students were briefed that they had been shot down in an eastern European country called Slobovia, and the aim was to cross the border into Freedonia. There would be 'armed' enemy border patrols deployed against them. In good weather and during the long half-light of a summer's night, the trek across the moors presented no problem. The students would be released at intervals in the first valley to make their way to a safe rendezvous in the third valley. The staff would then deploy in the two Land Rovers and set up guards at known choke points along the minor road in the middle valley. The students had been warned against following tracks and roads, so if they stuck to the rules, other than having to make a bit more of an effort through some bogs and streams, they could make the RV without too much of a problem, from where they would be driven back to base camp. However, in the cold dark rainy and at times icy weather of the autumn and winter, it was a much harder proposition for the escapees. Those of us on the staff were armed with powerful torches, parachute flares and trip wire flares –which went off with a loud bang and lit up the countryside for miles around. The whole area had at various times been used by mining companies leaving behind spoil heaps and mine workings. There were also aqueducts either in the form of large metal pipe lines or concrete channels, and Forestry Commission plantations of dense small conifers, crisscrossed by paths and tracks, and some minor roads, which were only suitable for four-wheel drive vehicles. Stepping out suddenly from under the trees with a torch and shouting in pidgin Russian/German at a couple of escapers could be a really frightening experience –I'd been on the receiving end of that.

There was one particular track that climbed up to the brow of the hill above Trefriw that I remember distinctly. I had crammed about ten students into a long wheel-based Land Rover and manoeuvred the heavily laden vehicle in gathering gloom, to their drop off point. To complicate things further, it was in late autumn, and patches of sheet ice had formed where the rainwater ran across the bedrock, but with the help of the students who hopped out of the Land Rover, they pushed me back onto the track and clear of the ice. Having seen them all safely on their way at intervals as night fell, I now drove back down this track in the dark, which had a very steep gradient, with a number of hairpin bends and dropped about 600' in the space of a mile. The surface, mainly glacial drift and gravel, was in places deeply scoured by rainwater gullies and liberally sprinkled with rocks brought down by heavy rain. Coming down this track using the foot brake to keep the speed down, and driving in first or second gear would normally have been no great problem, but this particular Rover's brakes were somewhat spongy, and it also tended to jump out of gear unless the gear lever was held in. Holding the steering wheel with my right hand, flooring the brake foot pedal with my right foot, holding the Rover in gear with my left hand, and occasionally pushing in the clutch pedal with my left foot and changing gear, before swapping my left hand to the hand brake, I managed to manoeuvre the beast round the sharp downhill U bends without running off the road, or skidding off the road on the icy patches. This was no mean feat as the turning circle on a long wheel-based Land Rover is akin to the Titanic trying to avoid the iceberg. It really was the scariest drive I have ever done! I can't remember praying anything specifically, but I know that I prayed. If the Rover had come off the road it would probably have continued to roll to the bottom of the hill. However, having arrived safely back at the campsite, the staff now all piled into both Rovers and we disappeared down to the very comfortable and warm pub in Trefriw for an hour and a pint or two before driving back up another valley to intercept the students. The hour in the pub was also 'de rigueur' for the staff so that we could fortify ourselves against the elements.

Despite the rugged nature of the moors, and the mainly unmarked mine workings, generally we had no injuries apart from one or two poor unfortunates who had slipped on icy rocks and become soaked in swollen mountain streams. These guys were removed to the Land Rover and given some dry clothing before moving on. One lad I encountered was so cold that he would have sold his grannie for a cup of tea.

However, on one memorable winter exercise, when we had released the students from the far valley, on the final descent into the Crafnant valley where the main campsite was, two students either became 'temporarily unsure of their position' or decided to evade the 'border guards' by going around the far end of the exercise area. I was with Ian Muir, (who as Station Navigator, provided expect assistance to pilots on the intricacies and finer points of navigation) in a Land Rover when we saw red distress flares being fired off. This was the signal for a real emergency. We drove off at high speed along the shore road on the eastern side of the Crafnant reservoir. We almost came to grief ourselves when the track we were following suddenly dropped about two feet into a new unmarked water gulley. When we finally got to the area where we thought the flares had come from, we found one student stumbling around in a very dazed fashion, and unable to talk. By now it was also starting to snow.

We delegated the recovery of the rest of the students to the other staff members, while we drove the injured student to the main hospital in Bangor. At the hospital a nurse took the student into a warm room with a chair and cut off his soaking wet, muddy flying clothes. He was still very dazed, and only speaking in a very slurred fashion, but apart from a slight amount of blood on his forehead, he did not seem to be injured. When we asked the nurse if he was badly hurt, she took a pair of medical pincers and, walking round behind him, carefully clamped them on a lock of hair at the back of the student's head, and lifted up a great flap of his scalp, under which we could see his skull bone! She said he would be kept in for some time. The next day, we went back to look at the scene of the accident. The student and his companion had partially descended a steep slope covered in fir trees, when the lead student had slipped and fallen head first over a fifteen-foot drop onto another slope covered in leaf mould, earth under which was a large rock, which had been the cause of his head wound. At this point his mate, who was now clinging to a tree for dear life, had alerted us with his distress flare. On the OS map that we were using, there was an indication of steep ground, but no indication of vertical drops. Moreover, just about 50 yards to the right of where the student had fallen, there was a cliff about 70 to 80 feet high! Happily, although the student was concussed, he recovered and completed his flying training on a later course.

At the end of every escape and evasion exercise, we gathered all our wet, cold, and muddy students round a huge great bonfire at our tent site, and fed them on a combination of steaming hot soup, stew, corned beef and slabs of bread, together with the odd beer.

Eventually having clocked up 100 Hawkeye exercises in my three years in Ground School, in March 1985 I returned for what was to prove to be my final flying tour. This was very much as before, but I could feel my body groaning a bit more after a sortie that involved teaching a student max rate turns (all at 6'G' i.e. six times the normal force of gravity) followed by an aerobatics session, that required similar forces. Although I had intended to continue to fly as long as possible, I knew that it would come to a halt sooner rather than later.

Diminuendo

I have written previously that mishaps in the air are most usually caused by bad weather, aircraft unserviceability, pilot error, or a combination of these. Well this next event took place on a beautifully clear day, with light winds and almost unlimited visibility. Maybe this was why I relaxed. Quite frequently low-level navigational exercises (nav exes) were carried out in sometimes quite marginal conditions; but today I thought, *"Hey this is going to be fun."* My student was tasked with planning and flying a low-level route up to RAF Kinloss in Morayshire, transiting at 2000feet from RAF Valley over the Irish Sea, via the Isle of Man, before letting down to 250feet low level at Burrow Head in southern Scotland. After clearing the Southern Uplands, the route then threaded between the Civilian Air Traffic Control Zones and Areas of Glasgow and Edinburgh airports –following a route roughly abeam Lanark, Bathgate, and Linlithgow, before re-entering the relative freedom of the Highlands. My student gave me a resume of the significant features on the route, and passed me a set of maps – which were a duplicate copy of his.

The technique for Low Level navigation at 420 knots was to use a six-minute fix. Thus from the start point and at each turning point, we endeavoured to stay on track and on time by accurately flying the correct airspeed and heading (with any wind effects on heading and the Indicated Airspeed factored in), keep a good lookout – (vital at 7 miles a minute with the possibility of encountering other aircraft military, light civilian aircraft, hang gliders, large birds, power pylons, and obstacles such as TV Masts), and then when within 30 seconds of the turning point, check the new heading and speed for the next leg. Then having identified the turning point, accurately turn onto the new heading, checking the stopwatch, and the IAS.

Now on this particular sortie, the start point was over Burrow Head, just south of Whithorn, in Galloway, Southern Scotland. The student had marked the start point and each turning point on the route by drawing a small pencil circle (about the size of a 1p coin) centred on it, followed by a pencilled line showing the new track with the heading and time marks for the leg boldly marked in pencil in a neat little box alongside the track. However, here we come to one of those little things that could probably account for the disappearance of Amelia Earhart over the Pacific. All the maps that we used had dashed magnetic variation lines running almost vertically down the chart that showed the amount by which the magnetic heading varied from true north, and right through the middle of the first start point turning circle that my student had drawn on the map was a dotted blue line showing the magnetic variation over that part of Scotland. The nav ex track was 012 degrees, but the student had mistakenly used the magnetic variation line (about 008 degrees) and marked this down as his track. Thus, we had a four-degree built in error to port from his original route. His duplicate set of maps that he had made up for me looked good – so off we went!

We descended on the Solway coast, and commenced the nav ex. The first fifty miles were over the rolling fairly featureless Southern Uplands. We crossed a few valleys each with a road, scattered small villages, and forestry plantations –this all agreed with the route on the map. I then noticed about a mile off to starboard a smallish metal mast on a hill, and I began to have a suspicion that this mast should have appeared about the same distance off on our port side. Shortly after that we came over the last of the Southern Upland hills, and there in the not too far distance was Glasgow, Glasgow Airport, and

Glasgow Air Traffic Control Zone approaching us at 7 miles a minute. *"I have control"* as I pulled the aircraft into a tight high G turn to starboard, and headed roughly east until I felt that we were now back on our approximate correct track. Shortly afterwards we regained our correct route and continued to Kinloss. When we landed, I looked at the position we had been in when I had spotted the mast and estimated that we must have flown through the edge of the Prestwick ATCZ – a civilian controlled area that commenced from ground level. I decided to give Prestwick a call by phone. When I made contact with the controller, I said *"Did you notice any aircraft infringe the eastern boundary of your Control Zone at about 1130 hours this morning?"* There was a pause, and then a voice said, *"No, we have nothing recorded."* Then after another short pause, the voice continued, *"Who's calling?"* I said, *"It doesn't matter"* and hung up. The bliss of old-fashioned untraceable telephone calls!

The second event was somewhat more complex, and I didn't escape justice this time. I arrived on the squadron at about 7.45 one morning and was told that as the weather in North Wales was unsuitable, I was to lead a close formation of three aircraft up to Lossiemouth in Morayshire, and complete the training sorties up there. I collected all the formation briefing slides and wrote down in felt tip pen all the details –frequencies, call signs, diversions, emergency procedures, etc., before I went to the main met brief. But at the end of the met brief the station commander stood up and said that all officers who had been in charge of detachments on the recent Taceval Exercise were to stay behind for a debrief. As that applied to me, I had no option but to stay. I finally left the briefing room at 8:30. Our original take-off time had been 9 o' clock, but this looked a bit tight now. I went to the coffee bar and collected the two other instructors with their students. I was solo in the lead ship; the two-student wingmen were under instruction as they had somehow fallen behind in their formation training. However, when we went to the formation briefing room it was upside down; everything was covered in large sheets and a couple of painters were decorating the walls. Obviously, we could not use the overhead projector or the screen on the wall in these circumstances, so I rescued the briefing slides from under one of the sheets and we retired to another room and I quickly briefed the QFIs and the students while I held up each briefing slide against the light from a window, and tried to ensure that every one had noted down all the relevant information regarding loss of contact in bad weather, radio failures etc. Formation land away sorties also required an authorising officer –the Squadron CO or Flight Commander would do, but all the 'wheels' had apparently vanished until I finally tracked one down also carrying out his own briefing in another office. I persuaded him to come along to put his signature on the authorisation sheet. As we walked out to the aircraft it was 8.55.

After start up as we taxied out, my number three reported that he had some unserviceability and he was returning to dispersal. Normally we would have scrubbed the trip, but the weather at Valley was going to stay poor all day and this formation sortie was quite critical, even if it was only for one student. I and my number two got airborne and turned north, contacted London Mil Radar and got clearance through Airway Blue One. At this point I noticed that not only was my TACAN unserviceable but that I now had a nagging toothache. The TACAN –i.e. Tactical Air Navigation was essentially an instrument that indicated one's range and bearing from a selected airfield. I notified London Mil that I would like Radar assistance to get me to somewhere about Loch Tay. As we levelled at high level and set cruising power, I heard my number three come up on the VHF channel and say that he was now serviceable and that he was taxiing out and if we held over a designated point, he would catch up with us. I gave him the OK and nominated a position and level where he could expect to find us. The weather cleared when we got north of the Scottish Border, I could now do a vis-ident on the ground, and I knew where I was for as a teenager I had hiked and biked, and subsequently flown in a Chipmunk over the area. We were now in a clear area for the free airspace over the Scottish Highlands never changed! After flying some formation for some twenty minutes, eventually my number three joined us and we were altogether again. But by now we had to crack on and complete all the breaks and joins, echelon, line astern, and tail chase before we ran short of fuel. But this time when I landed, and checked in at Ops I was asked if I had been flying formation in the Western Perthshire area, I said that I had. I was told that a civilian aircraft had filed a flight violation against me because he reckoned that we had infringed the mandatory minimum horizontal and vertical separation from civilian air traffic.

I now found time to look at my high-level transit map; and there it was – a *new* airway. I should have studied the airways map to make note of all civilian airspace restrictions before I got airborne, but in the mix up in getting airborne I had missed checking this, and since I was very familiar (as I thought) with the airspace above the Scottish Highlands, I hadn't bothered to update my knowledge. The result of this mishap was a rebuke from the Station Commander, and told to sharpen up.

My last error also took place in southern Scotland. It was the middle of winter, the ground was snow covered, and the visibility wasn't very good, and some of the time it was dreadful. My student had been tasked with a low level nav ex, with IP-Target runs. This last item required the student pilot to navigate to a fairly obvious feature (the Initial Point) on the ground. Then, having found the IP, hit the stopwatch as he passed over the IP on the heading for the target, which could be a very small hard to identify object (a telephone box for instance). If the IP run was flown accurately, the target should appear pretty much on the nose at the calculated time for a simulated weapons release. We carried out a couple of IP target runs reasonably well considering the weather, but on the final run heading east the visibility was so bad that we failed to spot the target at all. I told the student that we had enough fuel for one more try, so I took control and turned right onto a reciprocal heading to keep clear of the high ground to the north. As I rolled out on west, I noticed through the fog and low cloud that we were intermittently just out over the sea. That gave us sufficient info to return to the IP and successfully complete another run. This time when I returned to base, I got another rocket. Apparently, on the westerly leg over the coast, I had infringed a Royal Navy gunnery range: they were just in the process of firing off some ordnance when we virtually flew through their sights. Although *"Guilty as charged My Lord,"* was all I could plea, I also felt that the events of the last year and a half indicated that I was losing my edge. Although the flying instruction wasn't difficult, it was all the peripheral things that went with it that could become tense making. There were days when it was pure joy. At other times, the changes in the programme, the pressure to get the sortie planned, briefed and to get airborne on time, with the occasional rapid change of aircraft if the first one went u/s. This together with days when the sorties consisted of max rate 6g turns and aerobatics as I mentioned previously, were quite possible to take in your stride when you were young and fit, but now if I was honest, I could feel quite happy if the sortie was scrubbed and I could just take it easy for the next hour or so. I had hoped that I could have continued to fly regularly until I was 50, but as I approached my 49th birthday, I decided that I was going to call it quits on full time flying.

However, there were some bright moments in 1987. Phil Askew another Christian QFI and I landed at, as it then was, RAF Aldergrove in Northern Ireland. Phil and I had been tasked with giving a presentation about the joys of being an RAF pilot to the students of Queens University Air Squadron. The 'troubles' were still going strong, and security was tight. Being serving officers, we were given a car and an official 'driver' who could have doubled for a heavy in a James Bond film any day. As he drove us round Belfast, he gave us a running commentary, delivered in an incredibly strong 'Norn Iron' accent. However, what he told us was very illuminating. *"That's where Wully Cannaly was knee capped, puir sowl."* *"That was a nice wee shap*[shop] *before it got burnt doon."* Then driving slowly past the Falls Road, he said, *"I wouldna go down that road if you paid me. In fact I don't think even President Reagan would go down there,"* and much more of the same.

It was also about this time, while I'm on the subject of "Norn Iron", to relate another story that I heard from Ron Hepburn when I met him many years after the parting of our ways during training. By then Ron had been in civil aviation for some time, and he related the following interesting experience. Just prior to departing Aldergrove (Belfast Airport) en-route to Heathrow he was approached by an official photographer who wished to take some publicity photographs of a take-off for the Northern Ireland Tourist Board. The aircraft that he was flying at the time was a Boeing 757. As he taxied out for one end of the runway, the photographer was driven off in a Land Rover in the other direction to the other end. Now Aldergrove has quite a long runway (some 2700 metres), and Ron knew by the time that he reached the end of the runway, he would be some 1500 feet in the air. The photographer had also come to the same conclusion. Both Ron and the photographer simultaneously chose to solve the problem but were unable to communicate this fact to each other.

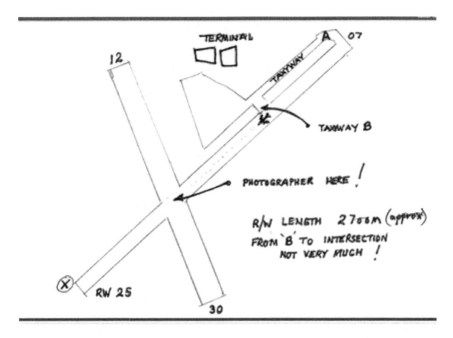

Aldergrove runway has access tracks from the taxiway onto the runway at specific intervals. Ron's aircraft was not heavily laden so that he knew that he would be able to get airborne using less than the full length of the runway, so he requested access onto the runway for take-off point **'B'** that was some hundreds of feet down the runway from the threshold. Meanwhile, as already noted, the photographer had also realised that the aircraft would be well airborne by the time it reached him if he took up a position at the far end of the runway (**'X'**). He also obtained clearance to set up his Hasselblad camera and tripod mount at the runway intersection some hundreds of feet short of the end.

You may now anticipate what was about to happen – I saw the photographs sent to Ron by the cameraman. As Ron entered the duty runway, ATC asked them to expedite their departure, as there was another aircraft on finals. Fortunately, he was able to select full emergency power rating from the engines, which reduced the take-off run. Even so, there are a series of shots of Ron's aircraft getting closer and closer to the cameraman with the wheels still firmly on the runway. The ultimate photograph shows Ron and his co-pilot peering saucer eyed over the edge of the cockpit, while the last one is a blur of some part of the aircraft just before the photographer fled for his life.

The weekend of 15th - 18th of October 1987, proved to be my last full-time sortie. The squadron were very kind to me and I was let loose with two aircraft from RAF Valley, to route via RAF Chivenor in Devon, for Sintra, a Portuguese Airbase about 20 miles from Lisbon. But as we flew down to Chivenor, not only was the sky overcast, it also had a distinctly 'heavy weather in the offing' look to it. Next morning when I awoke – quite early, everywhere seemed unnaturally quiet; it reminded me of the opening pages of John Wyndham's science fiction classic The Day of the Triffids. I switched on my bedside light. It came on – but shone with a very feeble light. I looked out into the corridor – the only lights that were on were one emergency light at each end of the corridor. I began to wonder if there had been some sort of nuclear exchange during the night and Chivenor had only just survived. I wasn't far wrong, for having washed and dressed, I made my way to the TV Room, to join a few other mystified pilots. The only channel functioning, was BBC1, but the presentation was not as slick as one might expect. The newsreader appeared to be sitting at a table in a very hastily prepared back room with none of the usual paraphernalia around him, informing the nation that the country had been struck with a very severe storm overnight. After listening to the details, I found a public call box by the Mess entrance hall and tried to put a call through to Babs, but I couldn't make the connection. I and the other pilots tried a few more times to contact Valley before take-off, but again to no avail.

Consequently, we headed off for Portugal not knowing whether our families were part of the casualty list or not. En-route to Portugal there was an incredibly strong jet stream on the nose at our initial level of 37000 feet, but we managed to get clearance to climb above it and transited at Flight Level 450, easily overhauling the civilian jets still battling with the jet stream some 10000feet beneath us. We had a splendid few days in Lisbon and the surrounding area, and on our return, we were relieved to find that although Valley had had communication problems, all our families were safe and well.

The Simulator Flight

At some point before ending my days as a flying instructor I had decided that I would join the simulator flight. This was effectively an elephants' graveyard for old pilots with no career prospects, but was bread and butter for all who wanted to stay connected with flying. I felt quite sad when I realized that my flying career was over. However, my boss Chris Taylor put it succinctly to me, *"Dobz, if you can put your hand into a bucket of water and leave a hand shaped impression in it when you take your hand out, then you know that you are irreplaceable!*

The original Hawk simulator, having been designed in the mid-1970s before the advent of the modern electronics, had an analogue computer. It had its limitations, but considering how old it was, it was very effective. But by 1999, the serviceability of this venerable old machine was now being maintained with difficulty by the ground crew, who had to search far and wide for spare parts; one particular item, I remember, was obtained from Dublin! It was almost reminiscent of Scrapyard Challenge –the TV Show, which features teams of dedicated technicians cannibalising items from a variety of sources to make one complete machine. Happily, by this stage, a new Hawk simulator, courtesy of BAE Systems, had just been completed next door.

I was also fortunate in that my youngest son Matthew was now being taught how to use a computer at school. Always being of the opinion, that a father should be able to competently demonstrate anything to his offspring, I went out and bought a second hand 386 computer, while both Babs and I did a basic computing course in the local town, so that using a computer in the simulator did not come as too much of a shock. However, along with my 386-computer came some software, one of which was a flight game called F15. The graphics were very basic, but it ran quite well on the 386. There were three different scenarios, if I remember, Central Europe, the Middle East, and Vietnam. In each case you were a pilot of an F 15 fighter, armed with 1000 rounds of ammunition, and various air-to-air missiles. If after the sortie you landed safely you would be promoted, rearmed, refuelled, and continue your career with promotion. Each pilot had three lives, thus after being shot down three times or after three crashes, you were definitely dead, and you had to restart all over again. Having flown for many years I didn't think that it would be very difficult to fly this game. However, young Matthew, now about 11 years old progressed from 2nd Lieutenant to Major General and amassed something like 100000 points, while I never made it past Major. History repeating itself!

Being a simulator instructor was significantly different from being a flying instructor. (Photo above shows Jock Byrne and myself in typical relaxed mode awaiting our next student). On a simulator sortie, the student, having been briefed, strapped himself into a complete Hawk cockpit that was fitted with an opaque Perspex canopy so that the student flew every sortie in IMC (cloud) conditions. Meanwhile, the instructor sitting in front of two TV screens whose visuals consisted of only words and figures set up the sortie profile from his consol. This included all the requisite 'weather' i.e. wind, turbulence, altimeter settings, runway in use, followed by a selection of emergencies for that particular sortie. When the student checked in on the R/T, the instructor now doubled as Air Traffic Control, progressively being the voices of the Local, Approach, London Military Area Radar, and finally Valley Radar Director, and Talk Down controllers; simultaneously advising and instructing his pupil as a flying Instructor; and at the appropriate moment feeding in various emergencies for the student to cope with, while making a mental note whether the student used the correct drill, made the correct R/T calls, flew the aircraft safely while making the right decisions. In addition to all of the above, the instructor had to write down his comments and give graded marks in boxes in the student's simulator folder. It was a bit like trying to fill in an Income Tax return, while watching a complex plot on one TV, and Match of the Day on the other, while simultaneously carrying on a conversation with someone else in another room; mentally I found it quite stimulating. But there were also drawbacks. The sortie was of strictly one-hour duration. Hence, if the student was slow to get strapped in and complete his cockpit checks (10 minutes was the norm from strapping in to getting airborne), then consequently the remainder of the sortie had to be accomplished in lesser time. You could not over-run, for although the 'turn-round' servicing for each sortie was minimal, any over-run meant that the next instructor would be hovering at your back, pressurising you to finish.

Apart from training the students, all instructors were required once a month to carry out an SCT (Staff Continuation Sortie) trip in the simulator, and practice the drill for any emergency that they might experience in the air. The simulator flight also differed from the squadron in that there was much less chance to employ banter. Such good natured – at times bitingly accurate – humour was usually directed against any pilot who, when he started to line shoot about his prowess in the air, was reminded of previous clangers that he had dropped. As there were not a few ex -Lightening pilots on the staff, (who took every opportunity to impress us lesser mortals of their tales of derring-do with WIWOL tales, i.e., "When I was on Lightenings"); there was no shortage of targets. On one particular occasion, a senior officer – an air commodore no less, and ex – Lightening pilot, arrived for his SCT sortie, and was regaling us with what an incredibly short time it had taken him to fly from Scampton to Valley. But some months previous he had flown a Hawk and had overstressed the airframe when he had greatly exceeded the maximum speed with the flaps down. I had done this myself, so I thought that he was fair game, so as he said this, I asked him, "Was that with flaps up or down, Sir?" It's amazing what you can get away with if you add 'Sir' at the end of such questions! The Air Commodore stopped in mid flow; there was a short series of incoherent sentences, "What, I, I, I,...well I," before he regained his composure. That was bad enough, but just as I asked the question, Jock Byrne who had been taking a large gulp from his coffee mug, exploded in a vain attempt to stifle a laugh *and* retain the coffee in his mouth, and the Air Commodore narrowly escaped being engulfed in a cloud of aerosol coffee particles as well!

However, even as a simulator instructor, I was increasingly aware that although I was very fit, I did not possess quite the same energy levels to do this job and fly even on an occasional basis. Therefore, a few years later, I decided that it was unlikely that I was ever going to fly again, and in May 1990 I finally retired from the RAF.

Retirement

A few years previously in 1986, Paul, our second eldest son, had spent a year out in Amman in Jordan as part of a team of young people who were helping in a home for handicapped children run by a Swedish Charity, during which time he had visited Israel. And so shortly after I had retired in May 1990, Babs and I decided that we would go for a two-week holiday to Israel, but Paul and Matt persuaded us that it would be vital for them to accompany us. Andy our eldest son would probably also liked to have come, but he had just got married! Moreover, since Babs and I had originally budgeted for only two, the financial arrangements already had to be stretched quite comprehensively. After landing at Lod Airport very late at night, we took a taxi to Joppa and stayed in a Christian guesthouse. Thereafter we stayed mainly in youth hostels, moving from Joppa up to the Christian Centre on Mount Carmel, then to a hostel in Acco where we visited the extensive Crusader Castle remains there; then on to Tiberius, visiting many of the villages mentioned in the New Testament, and having a cruise on the Sea of Galilee; thence to Jerusalem to a hostel called "Mr A's," which was down a side street, just left of the Jaffa Gate. Most of the hostels were quite basic but clean and the charge for bed and breakfast was effectively £1 a head per night, which meant that we had ample funds to tour, which included the Golan Heights, Israel's northern border, Masada, bathing in the Jordan, the Sea of Galilee, and the Dead Sea, and negotiating Hezekiah's tunnel. We travelled everywhere courtesy of the Israeli Egged Bus Company. It was quite strange to sit in a crowded bus with many of the passengers being Israeli soldiers, complete with weapons. There was no direct link from Acco to Tiberius, so we had to get off to make another connection. The crossroads where we waited for the next bus were on a hillside looking down over the Sea of Galilee. I was amazed at just how small the area was that encompassed most of the action depicted in the Gospels. But Paul was now studying Arabic at Leeds University as part of his course in September was about to spend a year in Cairo and didn't want his passport stamped with an Israeli stamp as he wanted to visit Sudan and Libya. As it turned out it didn't matter for on returning to the UK on the 2nd of August we found that Saddam Hussein's army had just invaded Kuwait, and the whole of the Middle East was now somewhat tense. As there seemed that it was very likely that there would be a war in the Middle East very shortly, Babs and I were quite worried about this. On the morning of Paul's departure, we got up very early in time to take him to catch the train from Holyhead. As we loaded the car Babs looked up into the night sky, and saw the crescent moon with the planet Venus occupying a position close to it. I felt the Lord say to me, *"If I can arrange for the night sky to show the symbol of Islam when your son is about to leave for an Islamic land, then fear not."* Amazingly, when he returned a year later, the moon and Jupiter were in a similar position. **"The heavens declare the glory of God" (Psalm 19:1); "For with God nothing shall be impossible" (Luke 1:37).**

Another interesting visit came about when the church in Holyhead organised an aid visit to Christians living in the Eastern Bloc, and now as a civilian I was able to accompany a small group who went to Prague in what was then Czechoslovakia just a few weeks after the fall of communism. This was my first extended visit to an ex-Communist country. The milieu was everything that I had expected; the still over-officious officials, basic transport, a feeling of life returning to a country that had been under tyranny for a very long time, to a country that was many years behind in modern amenities in what the West now took for granted. This was particularly evident when we walked around the city itself.

Virtually all the buildings appeared to be in a bad state of repair – boarded up windows, peeling paint, crumbling brickwork, and scaffolding holding up walls that were obviously about to fall. It would be safe to say that much of the city had not had any renovation since the Munich crisis of 1938.

During the remainder of the summer of 1990, I caught up with many jobs that I had had to put on hold for lack of time. Initially after my retirement I had thought of applying to become a pilot with Mission Aviation Fellowship – a Christian organisation that flies single and twin civilian aircraft in various tropical parts of the world, delivering medicines and carrying out casualty evacuation of sick and injured people from dirt strips in many remote areas. However, I was politely informed that, at my age, I would only be considered as an operations officer located somewhere in Kent. Meanwhile, quite frequently I got a telephone call from Jock Byrne – an ex A1 instructor and ex- Lightening pilot who had also retired from the RAF to the simulator flight, saying that I should return as a civilian instructor. He was quite persistent in this, for which I am eternally grateful to him, and so in October 1990, I returned to the simulator flight, as a civilian, and as such joined the Civil Service, who, for some strange financial reason were tasked with making up the total number of instructors from civilian sources should there be insufficient RAF pilots available.

However, being a simulator instructor did have its advantages. The task was normally two or three one-hour sorties per day, with an additional 15-minute brief and debrief before and after the sortie. The rest of the time was your own. Consequently, I managed to become quite adept at The Daily Telegraph crossword, and I also managed to teach myself New Testament Greek; at least to a level that enabled me to read the original from a Greek New Testament. I also made a start at Hebrew, but I found this to be much more difficult, although I eventually managed to make sense of the words sufficiently to be able to look them up in a Hebrew concordance. This was very useful as subsequently I found myself constrained to write a book entitled A Revised Chronology of The Bible. The essence of this book is to demonstrate that the present received chronology of the Bible has been adapted to conform to the received secular accuracy of the Middle Eastern History. This in turn produces some very large anomalies in the history of Israel, and the interpretation of much prophecy, which is also very dependent upon the accuracy of secular dating of the Fall of Babylon. This subsequently affects the date of the Crucifixion, and also leads on into a future interpretation of the end days.

In 1999, we transferred to the new BAE simulator. This was an amazing piece of equipment that gave a full 360-degree visual picture. The pilot sat in a cockpit that was in the middle of a dome on which various projectors displayed a continuous picture of wherever the aircraft was and whatever it was doing. The instructor's consul also had visual screens that duplicated what the student saw, and could even show the aircraft from many different perspectives. It was quite fun to fly this simulator, but if while doing aerobatics, one of the ground crew came up and stood alongside the cockpit it could be quite disorientating.

Reunions

Coincidently with the change of venue to the new BAE SYSTEMS Simulator in 1999, I also elected to go part time. When I went part time, I could not understand how I had been able to work full time and do all the jobs around the house and garden. Subsequently when I retired completely in 2003, I couldn't understand how I had been able to work half time and get any jobs done at all! When I finally said goodbye to the RAF in 2003, including my time with the RAFVR, I had spent some 45 years – my entire adult working life as a student pilot, pilot, flying instructor and simulator instructor. During this time, I had amassed some 6500 hours – not very great by airline standards, but quite a lot of sorties, when they averaged about an hour each; together with about 8500 simulator hours. I had no regrets, I would do it all again, but I felt that I had given all that I could and I was now ready to move in a different direction.

Just before we moved across to the new BAE SYSTEMS Simulator, a new instructor arrived – Dick Davis. One day the telephone rang in the office and I answered it, giving my name. There was a pause before a woman –with a Scottish accent answered, *"Is that the Tony Dobbie that used to be at Perth Academy?"* I said, *"Yes,"* and she explained that she had been the year above at the Academy, that her name was Liz and that she was married to Dick Davis. She also told me that in 1997, there had been a School Reunion. From this I gained the telephone numbers of a few old school friends, and in March 2001 Babs and I drove up to Perth for the 50th anniversary of our arrival at the school.

It was a difficult few days. About 100 miles from home, the exhaust of our Volvo blew off just aft of the manifold. There was no diminution of power, but the noise inside, accompanied by a violent high frequency vibration, was incredible. En-route we encountered extremely heavy rain in a thunderstorm. We lost one wiper blade and took a lightning strike, that didn't do the radio much good. Secondly when we got there, both of us fell down with very bad sore throats and headaches (car fumes?), but I had a very pleasant time reminiscing, and trying to guess who I was speaking to! Generally, it was either the voice or the eyes that triggered remembrance. I suppose that we all keep an image in our minds eye of what we want to see when we look in a mirror, *"Mirror, mirror on the wall,"* and that we will be instantly recognizable. That we are not was forcibly brought home to me when we first gathered together in the foyer of the Salutation Hotel in Perth. Two girls from my year, who were part of the organisers of the reunion, and who had also been on the committee of the Moncrieffe Club with me, came up to me, and one of whom I had gone out with a number of times, peered closely at me, and said, with great question marks in their voices, *"Tony Dobbie??"* But I did have a chance to witness to some of my old school friends, especially one who was dying of emphysema. We went back in September 2007, and in October 2010, we also travelled to Glasgow for the 50th anniversary of our departure from Glasgow UAS.

Final Words

For those of my readers who have followed the story so far, this is the end of my wanderings. I have tried to faithfully indicate how I travelled from being a rebellious youth to a much older and (hopefully wiser) man, who, through God's good grace had escaped certain death and found salvation in Christ.

Looking back over my life and time as a pilot and flying instructor; during that time I thought that I had been fortunate or lucky, in that the scrapes that I got into did not leave me permanently paralysed, incapacitated, or seriously ill, particularly since the close shaves that I have described in the above pages were only the major ones; for in addition, there were quite a few others in the air, which potentially had just as much danger; as well as other escapes during my childhood and youth. When I recall those times it is easy to see where I could have been seriously injured, but was not! But after my miraculous escape in 1978 I progressively began to realise that the LORD in His grace had preserved me all along, and long enough to be able to hear the Gospel, and relate my experiences. Had I refused to accept His forgiveness, then I have no doubt that I would have gone the way of all unbelievers.

This book, I hope has been a warning to those who assume that they are in total control of their destiny, and that their existence ceases with death, and secondly, I hope that it has been an encouragement for those who are seeking the LORD for answers to prayer. There are probably many other aspects of prayer that I have not mentioned, but if you are in earnest and ask the LORD for wisdom and guidance for your own particular needs, then you will receive it.

This book, will serve as a warning to those who do not know the Lord and assume that they are in total control of their destiny and that their existence ceases with death, for as Hebrews 9:27 tells us **"it is appointed unto men once to die, but after this the judgment."** May the Lord bless you with a greater knowledge of His infinite love to fallen mankind. Secondly, I hope that it has been an encouragement for those who know the Lord and are seeking the LORD for answers to prayer. There are probably many other aspects of prayer that I have not mentioned, but if you are in earnest and ask the LORD for wisdom and guidance for your own particular needs, then you will receive it.

May the LORD bless this work, and may it be to His glory.

Short Index of Service Terms, Abbreviations, and Other Trivia

SECO Huts - 'Seco' was a name derived from Selection Engineering Co Ltd. The huts were constructed from pre-fabricated components made of timber, concrete, asbestos and wood wool.

Operational Conversion Unit (OCU) - Always known as 'OCU' where pilots and crews (where applicable) were instructed in the aircraft systems, trained to fly, and carry out the type of tasks that they would be required to do when they joined a frontline squadron.

Quick Reaction Alert (QRA) - QRA duty on bomber/ strike squadrons lasted 24 hours. A practice call-out usually occurred about twice a week at any time of the day or night. The crew – who could be eating, sleeping or carrying out target study, had to pile into the QRA car (A Standard Vanguard estate – 0 to 60 in 60 seconds), drive out to the aircraft (which was on a dispersal on the airfield close to the take-off point), strap in, get the engines started, and be ready to taxi within the statutory 15 minutes (normal) readiness state. In order to fulfil this requirement, each crew travelled everywhere together, ate together, and generally had five adjacent rooms to sleep in. In the V Force in the UK, these rooms were often in SECO huts; the standard of which varied between basic 1950s Butlin's chalets and upmarket Stalag Luft 3 huts. In 2 ATAC in Germany, the accommodation was much more modern and much closer to the aircraft. The Two-minute alert described in this book tested this system to the limits!

1 Group & 3 Group - There was a certain amount of competition between No 1 Group and No. 3 Group. No. 1 Group, equipped with Vulcans operated from the more northerly airfields, such as Waddington, Scampton, Lindholme, and Finningley in Lincolnshire and Yorkshire; while 3 Group airfields, in the balmier southern climes of Rutland, Huntingdon and Peterborough, and Norfolk were at Cottesmore, Wittering, Marham, and Honington. Being equipped with the mighty Vulcan, 1 Group expressed this superiority in football league terms as being "1st Division North" as compared to us who were "3rd Division South!"

Landing Aids In Bad Weather - There were a number of runway approach aids used by the RAF. When recovering to an airfield in bad weather, ATC would direct the aircraft to descend to 2000 feet above the airfield, carry out the pre-landing checks, and then turn the aircraft onto the extended centreline to the runway in use at about 10 miles. At 8 miles ATC would begin the final approach to the runway using one of the following methods.

- **GCA (Ground Controlled Approach)** - The aircraft would commence the final descent, while maintaining a 3-degree glide path, following instructions from a controller who would instruct the pilot to increase of decrease the rate of descent, and turn right or left by a few degrees. This system enabled the aircraft to arrive at a point about ½ mile from the runway threshold at 200 feet altitude (the Decision Height), at which point the pilot looked up from the instruments and landed – if he could see the runway, or overshoot and go around for a further radar or divert.

- **SRA (Search Radar Approach)** - On this approach, because the radar equipment only indicated the range to touchdown, the pilot was passed advisory information of the height that he should be at various ranges, e.g. "Three miles, you should be passing 900 feet."
- **ILS (Instrument Landing System)** - A receiver in the aircraft picked up signals from a transmitter on the airfield. This information was displayed on an instrument in the cockpit, which had a vertical and a horizontal needle – which if the pilot kept them crossed in the middle of the display would also bring him out at the ½ mile, 200-foot point.

Instrument Rating Test (IRT) - Once a year, every qualified pilot in the RAF employed in active flying duties, was required to undergo an IRT, while being tested by an Instrument Rating Examiner (IRE), to ensure that he was capable of flying accurately and safely when lacking any visual horizon, due to cloud, rain, snow, dust storm etc, when the horizontal and vertical visibility was below certain limits. Each test normally required the pilot to take off, climb to height, level off, fly to another airfield, make an approach (GCA, ILS) overshoot at Decision Height, climb back up to height, fly certain manoeuvres using the full instrument panel, and a limited instrument panel - by covering up the main artificial horizon, altimeter, and compass, before returning to base and making a further approach on limited instruments. The pass was assessed (according to the accuracy of the pilot's ability), as White, Green, or Master Green.

List of Photographs
Unless otherwise stated, all photographs were taken by the author.

Act 1
1. My father – Andrew Dobbie (Photographer unknown)
2. My mother – Winifred Dobbie (Photographer unknown)
3. Ayton House, Perth (Photographer unknown)
4. SS Tuscania (Photographer unknown)
5. Winifred Dobbie in Laurel Canyon, Hollywood (Photographer unknown)
6. Grand automobile (Photographer unknown)
7. Winifred Dobbie on the West Coast of France (Photographer unknown)
8. Broadwell Cottage, Aberargie (Andrew Dobbie)
9. Andrew Dobbie in his postman's uniform (Winifred Dobbie)
10. Glen App Castle (Photographer unknown)
11. German soldier overlooking the town of Coblenz just after the Rhineland was re-occupied. (Photographer unknown)
12. Traction-engine and threshing machine (Photographer unknown)
13. Combined Cadet Force (Photographer unknown)
14. Cultebraggan Camp, Perthshire (Photographer unknown)
15. The Moncrieffe Club organizers. Yours truly in sports jacket
16. The author (assuming his best Marlon Brandon pose) (Photographer unknown)
17. Chipmunk training aircraft at the Glasgow University Air Squadron (GUAS) airfield at Scone, near Perth.
18. Ariel 350 motorbike ready for the ride to Costa Brava
19. The author in Spain (Peter Cameron)

Act 2
1. Ron Hepburn polishing his shoes
2. Basic training at South Cerney in Gloucester
3. BAC Jet Provost 3
4. De Havilland Vampire
5. Ford Anglia 100E
6. Babs "Bubbles" Dobbie
7. The Blue Lion pub in Hardwick near Cambridge
8. Handley Page Victor 1 (MoD)
9. Shivering next to a Victor at RAF Cottesmore. Left to Right: Dick Gommo, John Wiliamson, Self, Steve Stevenson, Jim Bowman (Captain) (Photographer unknown)

10. Boeing B29 Superfortress and Convair B-36 Peacemaker in Offutt air force base in Omaha
11. Babs Dobbie on the beach in Biaritz, 1963
12. Gan Atoll in the Maldives (MoD)
13. Tropical rainstorm Butterworth Malaya
14. The author and Babs on their wedding day, March 1964
15. Handley-Page Victor dropping bombs (MoD)
16. The author with a very large puppy, A.K.A. - Suki!
17. Fylingdales BMEWS (Ballistic Missile Early Warning Site), Yorkshire (MoD)

Act 3

1. Canberra BI8 (MoD)
2. Heinkel He-111 over the East-end of London on 7 September 1940 (courtesy of the Luftwaffe)
3. Suki hurdling a fence
4. Winter Survival Course in RAF Bad Kohlgrub, Bavaria, 196. Back row – Geoff Wilkinson, Tony Stephens, ?,?,?, Front Row -Pete Evans, Self, Pete Jones; Karl Wilhelm Instructor (Photographer unknown)
5. Out for a spin with the Red Arrows, 1967
6. On the coach with 16 Squadron on our way to the Amstel Brewery, Amsterdam, 1967
7. Amsterdam, 1967
8. Happy Hour at Laarbruch (Photographer unknown)
9. The author on the East-German border, Helmstadt (Photographer unknown)
10. The author and his re-built MG-TC
11. Babs and Andrew, our first son, Germany
12. Firing a cartridge to start the engines on a Canberra BI8 (John Adams)

Act 4

1. Tathwell Cottage, Lincolnshire
2. BAC Jet Provost 4
3. Ailsa Craig (Photographer unknown)
4. The family, 1973 (Annie Thomas)
5. Canberra T4 from No 231 OCU (Photographer unknown)
6. Suki

Act 5

7. Lockheed C-130 Hercules (MoD)

8. English Electric Lightning F.6 over Cyprus (MoD)
9. Wg Cdr Martin Bee, in the cockpit of an English Electric Lightning with No 56 Sqn geared up after the Turkish invasion, July 1974.
Left to Right on Wing: ?, Steve Horridge, Stu Wilson, Keith Hartley, Mike Hall the Nav, Tom Hewlett, Wg Cdr Martin Bee, Bob Cann, Rod Brown, Dave Wooldridge, Mike Hall the pilot, ?, ?. Left to Right on Ground: Self, Ian Hartley, Dave Hemmings, Sqn Ldr Clive Mitchel, ?, Sqn Ldr Gracie, Cliff Spink, Sqn Ldr Maurice Williams, ?, Sqn Ldr Henry Ploszek
(Photographer unknown)
10. Mont Blanc
11. HMS Hampshire off the coast of Cyprus
12. The last Canberra out of Cyprus (Photographer unknown)

Act 6
1. Canberra T.T. 18 (TT = Target towing) (Photographer unknown)
2. Canberra with Rushton target deployed (Photographer unknown)
3. Folland Gnat in vertical climb (BAE Systems)
4. Avro Vulcan flanked by two Folland Gnats (Matt Dobbie)
5. First prang, engine failure on take-off at RAF Mona (MoD)
6. First prang, stopped after nose wheel collapsed going through a field boundary (MoD)
7. Second prang – ejection landing site just short of the main runway R/W14 at RAF Valley. I landed in a gorse bush otherwise my chute would have taken me into the rocks on the sea shore (MoD)
8. Second prang – what was left of XR544 (MoD)

Act 7
1. BAE Systems Hawk trainer with Snowdon in the background
2. Tai Hirion
3. Babs and Matthew
4. Me and Matt outside Broadwell Cottage
5. Escape and evasion survivors in the hills above the Conwy Valley
6. Yours truly (Photographer unknown)
7. Diagram of Ron Hepburn's take-off from Belfast Aerodrome
8. A close call (Photographer unknown)
9. BAE Systems Hawk trainers en-route to Portugal
10. Me and Jock Burns relaxing in "sims" (Photographer unknown)
11. Mike Pritchard (a friend from church) in Prague just after the fall of Communism.

12. Me in Prague (Mike Pritchard)

A Few Final Photographs

The author with the Handley Page Victor K.2 (XH673) at RAF Marham in Norfolk, East Anglia. (2020)

The author outside the Blue Lion pub, in the village of Hardwick some 5 miles west of Cambridge. (2020)

Printed in Great Britain
by Amazon

78842851R00169